W9-AJM-060

ODo

Rosie O'Donnell

Rosie O'Donnell

Her True Story

George Mair and Anna Green

A Birch Lane Press Book

Published by Carol Publishing Group

A Birch Lane Press Book
Published by Carol Publishing Group
Birch Lane Press is a registered trademark of Carol Communications, Inc.

Editorial, sales and distribution, rights and permissions inquiries should be addressed to Carol Publishing Group, 120 Enterprise Avenue, Secaucus, NJ 07094.

In Canada: Canadian Manda Group, One Atlantic Avenue, Suite 105, Toronto, Ontario, M6K 3E7.

Carol Publishing Group books may be purchased in bulk at special discounts for sales promotion, fund-raising, or educational purposes. Special editions can be created to specifications. For details, contact Special Sales Department, Carol Publishing Group, 120 Enterprise Avenue, Secaucus, NJ 07094.

Manufactured in the United States of America
10 9 8 7 6 5 4 3 2 1

Library of Congress Cataloging-in-Publication Data
Mair, George, 1929–
    Rosie O'Donnell : her true story / George Mair and Anna Green.
      p.   cm.
    "A Birch Lane Press book."
    ISBN 1-55972-416-1 (hc)
    1. O'Donnell, Rosie. 2. Comedians—United States—Biography.
  3. Motion picture actors and actresses—United States—Biography. I. Green,
Anna. II. Title.
PN2287.027M35   1997
792.7′028′092—dc21
[B]   97-178
                                                 CIP

Contents

Rosie O'Donnell

1

Rosie's First Fan

Rosie O'Donnell met the world on a day full of promise, the first day of spring. She was born on March 21, 1962, to Roseann and Edward O'Donnell and welcomed into a lively household as their third child and first daughter. A good Irish Catholic family, it grew to include five children: Eddie, Danny, Rosie, Maureen, and Timmy. The first four were perfect stair steps, just a year apart; Timmy, however, is three years younger than Maureen. One little known fact is that as a young child, Rosie's nickname was Dolly. "My little brother couldn't say 'Roseann,' so he called me Dolly. Until I was twelve, my whole family called me Dolly."

There is some mystery surrounding Rosie's father and his job. He worked for Fairchild Corporation as an electrical engineer who designed cameras for spy satellites during the cold war. Rosie remembers him telling her that because of their advanced technology, people in Russia could read their license plates. "I said, 'Thanks, Dad. That's a comforting thought.' I'm in the bathroom thinking, 'They can probably see this in Russia.'" She also recalls that her father "was very depressed when the Berlin Wall came down." Whatever it was he did, Edward O'Donnell, who emigrated from Belfast, Ireland, provided a decent brick two-story home for his family at 17 Rhonda Lane in the suburban New York community of Commack, Long Island.

Though the family had their basic needs met, seven mouths to feed is still a big financial burden, and Rosie remembers the family making lots of small sacrifices, such as buying generic rather than brand-name products.

3

"We didn't really have many luxuries when we were children. We didn't have matching socks. Or top sheets for the bed, just the bottom sheet. We didn't have a blow dryer; we used an Electrolux vacuum cleaner with the hose on the turn-around side."

There were no family vacations to Disney World, like her childhood pal Jackie Ellard got to take. The O'Donnell family trips sound like a National Lampoon Vacation movie without the laughs. "My mom and dad would pile all of us kids in the station wagon and drive up to Niagara Falls—oh, that was fun," Rosie recalls sarcastically. "Twelve hours of driving with five little kids and two irate parents." Living on the fringes of the middle class did, however, provide Rosie with a well-grounded sense of economic reality that is still visible in her comedy today. She hasn't forgotten the struggle to make your month match your money.

Commack is a commuter neighborhood, exit fifty-two off the Long Island Expressway—that's how natives describe it. And though that same highway lured the young Rosie into nearby Manhattan to nurture her fantasy life and later took the teenage Rosie on her way to perform in forty-nine states, exit fifty-two remains the geographic heart and soul of Rosie O'Donnell. A touchstone she uses to keep herself grounded in reality.

"Our town had a lot of Catholics and Plymouth Volare station wagons," Rosie recalls. Later, in her stand-up act, she would say of the town: "It's suburban hell. Tract row houses one after another, exactly the same. Different-colored shutters were the only way you could tell them apart...home of the Commack Motor Inn, featuring gel beds and in-room Hollywood movies."

To be fair, the block where Rosie grew up is not as grim as she paints it. The street is lined with oaks and maples and rather quaint street lamps. The houses sit well back of generous front lawns and ample side yards—far more space than the ever-shrinking suburban lots of today. Rosie's childhood home has a pleasant partial brick front and a two-car garage and is *not* just like the house next door. There are sidewalks for strolling and a wide street for bike riding.

Rosie and her friends also enjoyed a wonderful park nearby called Hoyt Farm. About one hundred acres, it even had farm animals in addition to the playground equipment. Every Sunday evening in the summer there were live bands and people gathered for picnic suppers.

A former classmate remembers it as a good place to grow up. "We all used to leave our doors unlocked, and we walked to the buses by ourselves. It was the kind of town with extended families, where the grandparents lived with their families." Thus the first nine or so years of Rosie's life were spent in relative normality, cocooned in the innocence of the *Flying Nun* and *Partridge Family* era.

In addition, Rosie had a genuine, stay-at-home mom to greet her with snacks when she came scurrying home from Rolling Hills Elementary School. A conscientious mom who served as president of the PTA, Roseann O'Donnell, a blue-eyed, black-haired beauty, looked a bit like a movie star— at least her three sons thought she looked like Liz Taylor. But little Roseann's special bond with her was a shared sense of humor. "My mother was very funny—she did the equivalent of stand-up at PTA meetings—she made all the teachers laugh."

Rosie recognized an attractive trait that she chose to emulate. "When she came to visit the school and walked down the halls, all the teachers would come out of their classrooms to talk to her. So I knew she had this thing people wanted—that people would go to her, because of this comedy thing."

Roseann O'Donnell's sense of humor must have helped her to tolerate her daughter's impishness. One ritual Rosie recalls was the obligatory trip to the Christ the King Catholic Church every Sunday. "I used to try and hide at Jackie Ellard's house and be in the pool when my mom screamed, 'It's time for church.' But before I left for church I'd grab all the stuff from the junk drawer—like paper clips and buttons and rubber bands, so that I'd have something to do in church." Irreverent from a young age, Rosie found ways to dissolve into uncontrollable laughter in church. "My mother [would get] so mad at me."

Much of Rosie's childhood was shaped by her neighborhood, which was chock-full of other big Irish Catholic as well as Italian families. There were always plenty of kids around to play all sorts of games, starting with the Rockwellian basketball hoop over the O'Donnell garage. Rosie readily admits the influence of her brothers: "I was a tomboy—is that a shock to anyone? I didn't do ballet."

But she sure did sports. "I played softball, volleyball, kickball, tennis, and basketball; a regular tomboy jock girl and proud of it." Nor did she just play with the girls. "I was always the first girl picked for the neighborhood teams," she recalls with ill-concealed pride. "I got picked ahead of my three brothers, which I think still affects them. I always had time for a good game."

Rosie also managed to acquire a load of popular toys from the era—all of which she seems to still have. Rosie even swears she sent away for hordes of green plastic army men. She also played with her share of dolls, though many of them (Cher, Laurie Partridge, and the like) were collected more for their show business connections. Still, there was a bit of the nurturer lurking behind her tomboy exterior.

Commack in those years was a safe place for children to run riot on that best of all kid holidays—Halloween. And the O'Donnell kids had a trick of their own. Rosie and her siblings each took three masks when they went out, so that when they found a particularly noteworthy home—say one that dispensed full-size Hershey bars—they would run around the house, switch masks and voices, and return for second and third helpings. For Rosie, it was an early taste of theatrics, as well as an experience of chocolate abundance.

To any careful observer of the O'Donnell clan, it was clear that little Roseann was a ham waiting for a banquet. Her sister Maureen remembers her as a stand-up comedian almost before she could stand up. "Rosie was always telling jokes and doing imitations." One thing that made it easy for Rosie to develop a mimic's ear was her father's faint Irish brogue. Years later, she put that skill to good use, telling joke after joke at his expense, often exaggerating his accent.

Her stage debut came in the third-grade production of *The Wizard of Oz*. Around the O'Donnell home, acting out scenes from this classic tale was a happy pastime, except that Maureen always got to be Dorothy, and Rosie was assigned the role of the Mayor of Oz—no doubt due to her excellent ability to capture his distinctive voice. So in her own class, without her sister to compete with, Rosie desperately wanted to win the part of Dorothy. Instead she was cast as Glinda, the Good Witch, undoubtedly foiled again by her own talent. "Jan Brenner got to be Dorothy, and I never got over it. I remember it like it was yesterday," she said twenty-six years after the event. Years later, she wrote and performed her own parody of Oz in her stand-up act.

As the middle child of five, Rosie grabbed attention through her humor and her antics and quickly evolved into the classic class clown. She got away with lots of childhood pranks simply because she could fast-talk and jolly her way out of any situation. Gifted with a natural ability to entertain, little Roseann quickly became an ardent observer of the professionals.

While not all that interested in her studies at school, Rosie would have earned straight A's as a student of the performing arts. Television was ever present in her home, and as she recalls, "My whole family knew the entire fall schedule before it even went on the air. We had the *Newsday* supplement and we'd memorize what was on. We were a huge, huge, huge TV family."

Rosie grew up enchanted by such froth as *Gilligan's Island, I Dream of Jeannie*, and *Bewitched*. She was inspired by Marlo Thomas in the first feminist sitcom featuring a single career woman, *That Girl*, and later by her all-time favorite TV program, *The Mary Tyler Moore Show*.

Rosie's devotion to Mary knew no bounds. She dutifully kept a notebook about the show, and admitted years later that she might have been a tad compulsive: "I used to take notes all during the show, then copy them *over* into my MTM book. Can you say *therapy?*" Later she would review them again and again, as if for some cosmic pop quiz.

Though she learned early on that there was life beyond Commack, Rosie still drew inspiration from these shows about the possibilities that lay ahead for a girl on her own in the world. It was also the heyday of the prime-time variety shows hosted by the likes of Ed Sullivan, Red Skelton, and Jackie Gleason. Watching them, Rosie was exposed to every manner of entertainer from puppets to poodles, from the Beatles to Nat King Cole. But the variety performer Rosie most admired was Carol Burnett. She could dance, she could sing, she could act, she was funny—and she wasn't any typical Hollywood beauty. And Rosie wanted to grow up to be just like her.

One of Rosie's incentives to hurry home from school was an important ritual she shared with her mother—watching the cozy afternoon talk-variety shows put on by Mike Douglas and Merv Griffin. These easygoing guys presented the top talent of their day, from veterans to newcomers. Their shows served up true family fare—a long time before Sally or Jenny vied to book left-handed dentists who marry midgets. Mike Douglas even show-cased their beloved Barbra Streisand for an entire week as his cohost. Rosie soaked it all up, every last detail, and stored it all away for another day.

Nor was young Roseann limited to daytime or early prime-time shows for her inspiration. She quickly became adept at overcoming her mother's best intentions. "My parents would make me go to bed, and I would sneak down and watch Johnny Carson from the stairs." And then she would tiptoe back upstairs and act out the role of talk show guest to her bathroom mirror. "I would say, as if I was thirty, 'You know, Johnny, when I was twelve, I used to sit in my bathroom and talk to you.'"

And though the O'Donnells were not a showbiz family, Roseann O'Donnell instilled in her daughter her own passion for entertainment of all kinds. "She was into musical theater," Rosie says of her mother, "and really nurtured that part of my life." One of the first Broadway cast albums Rosie memorized was *South Pacific*. Her favorite song from the show? "Happy Talk." Those are vivid memories for Rosie, the good memories she wants to keep alive. "I'd listen to *Oklahoma* over and over, and I'd wait every year for *The Sound of Music* and *Mary Poppins* to come on television." Rosie was the kind of youngster who sang show tunes for Show and Tell. "Other kids are bringing in Barbie dolls, and I'm singing *Oklahoma!*" she recalls.

There was no contest when it came to picking their favorite Broadway performer—Barbra Streisand won that honor by unanimous vote. In fact, Roseann O'Donnell arranged her family's schedule around events such as a Streisand TV special or the release of a new album or movie. Rosie sees 1968 as a turning point in her life, because that's when the movie *Funny Girl* was released. Even at the age of six, Rosie knew that when she saw Barbra up on that screen, it reflected exactly what she wanted to do with her own life. It was almost as if the family had their own set of holidays and observances dictated not by the Holy Roman See, but by Hollywood. And great mimic that she was, young Roseann could soon do every Streisand song she heard, all in Barbra's distinctive Brooklynese.

"I'd go into the kitchen singing 'Second Hand Rose' with Barbra's accent, and my mother would laugh and laugh," Rosie remembers. "It was a great way to get attention, so I kept it up." And so her mother became her first, and forever favorite, fan. Soon her mom was calling in the neighbors to enjoy her talented daughter, giving her an even bigger audience.

Even though their finances were sometimes strained, the O'Donnells exposed their budding star to as much entertainment as the budget would allow. Rosie remembers seeing her first musical when she was just six years old—a production of *George M* at the Westbury Music Fair in Long Island. These firsts were important to her, as they seemed to imprint her with another aspect of her vision for herself. At the same venue, Rosie also attended her first concert, performed by the Carpenters. Karen Carpenter was unique. In addition to singing, she did double duty as the group's drummer. She inspired Rosie to take up drumming in the family garage. To this day Rosie still plays a fast set of traps. She remembers the concert well, especially the part afterward when she stood around waiting for an up-close glimpse of her new role model. Suddenly Karen Carpenter passed by her— and "I reached through the fence and touched her sweater. It was like a big thing for me."

Looking at Rosie's fifth-grade class picture there is no portent of the tragedy to come. It shows a totally normal little dark-haired girl, captured in happy innocence. Yet all that was about to change forever.

Rosie's fondest childhood memory is sharing lemon drops with her mother in the third balcony of Radio City Music Hall. This is a gigantic theater, full of gilded splendor, one where a little girl could easily fall in love with the glamorous stage production that preceded the film. The Rockettes, in all their high-kicking, leggy perfection. A hall that resounded with live music from the spectacular pipe organ must have inspired young Roseann with more reverence than any church could ever have. This was her cathedral. A place to confess her deepest yearnings. A place with a movie screen so large she could lose herself completely to the story. To the illusions. To the magic. In the darkened theater, sitting safely next to her mother who understood such things, any dream seemed attainable to the starstruck young girl.

It is New Year's Eve 1995, some twenty years later. Rosie is standing in the absolute center of that magnificent stage. In the spotlight. Performing her comedy act to a sold-out house of 6,000 fans at Radio City Music Hall is Rosie O'Donnell, star of stage, screen, and television. Star of her own fantasy life come true. Actress Madeline Kahn was in the audience that night and came away extremely impressed, as she later told Rosie: "When I saw you onstage I was awestruck—you were a real goddess. You reminded me of Birgit Nelson and a little bit of Jane Russell, too—kind of a hybrid. You were a diva." The only person missing from the audience that night was the one person who would know best what this meant to Rosie. And what Madeline didn't notice was that Rosie seemed to toss a few extra jokes up to the third balcony, and beyond.

⟶ 2

A Death in the Family

In December 1972, at the age of thirty-six, Roseann O'Donnell was diagnosed with pancreatic and liver cancer. Her descent was swift and confusing to her five children. "They told us at first she had hepatitis," Rosie recalls. "They thought that was a big word and kids wouldn't know. But I went to the library and looked it up, and it said it was a disease that you got from dirty needles. I thought to myself it was from sewing. That's the kind of household it was—you had to draw your own conclusions, because you weren't really allowed to ask."

Rosie remembers trying to visit her mother in the hospital. "At the time, you weren't allowed to go in if you were under twelve, so the nurses would sneak us up in the Emergency Room elevator."

Irish to the end, Roseann O'Donnell died four months later, on St. Patrick's Day. Four days before Rosie's eleventh birthday. And that was excuse enough for Edward O'Donnell of Belfast to drink himself into years of denial. "My father told me, 'Your mother passed away,' and I didn't know what that meant. And that was the end of the discussion." Their father never spoke of his grief with his family, and the children were discouraged from even talking about their mother. They were not even allowed to attend her funeral.

"I don't really have a clear memory of her, since my father did this Let's-pretend-it-didn't-happen, Irish Catholic, repressed denial thing," Rosie said. She added, that in his own misguided coping process, her father removed everything of her mother's from their home, "in some kind of tragically wrong 1970s version of grieving that my father partook in. There was nothing left. I only have two pictures of her and none of her things." Her mother was just obliterated. Her father even sold her mother's blue station wagon without warning, soon after she died. The car had provided a safe place for Rosie to grieve. "It still smelled like my mom," she said, recalling how she used to climb into the backseat to sit and think. Rosie did manage to salvage a ring of her mother's, which she used to wear all the time, but "it was stolen when I was skiing, so I got a new one instead." That is the ring she now wears every day on her right hand.

Because no one talked about her mother's death, and because she didn't have the sense of closure that a funeral brings, Rosie indulged in fantasies that her mother was still alive. When playing basketball, she pretended her mother was in the stands cheering. Sometimes she just figured her mom had escaped to California to flee from the responsibilities of their large family. According to Rosie her life at the time was "the denial buffet. For a long time I didn't believe it. Patty Hearst had just been kidnapped, so I came up with a fantasy that that was what had happened to my mom, too, and nobody was telling us."

Her sister Maureen, only nine at the time, says, "Rosie has always protected me. She is the one I always call when I have a tough day." One way Rosie coped was to read a lot. "I read books about tragic situations, people who had to overcome insurmountable odds. I read a lot of things about the Holocaust and mass murderers and people who had tragic accidents—just so that I could face my fear."

Somehow Rosie forged strength and inner fortitude from her pain and resolved to succeed, the sooner the better. "I remember thinking that my mom died in her thirties, and I had to succeed before that age, so that if I died I would have left something tangible." Rosie also felt that her mother had not gotten to live enough of her own life. "I made a conscious decision that I was going to do all that I wanted to do as soon as I could—in case that was my fate as well." It is common for people who lose a parent when they are young to fear that they will not live past the age their parent was at death.

Eventually, her mother's death became a reality when Rosie first visited the cemetery and saw the name she shared with her mother on her gravestone. "To see a tombstone with your name on it is very startling," she said.

Edward O'Donnell just disappeared from his family emotionally. He was often absent physically, as well, and the children were left to fend for themselves. Her father did make one gesture to introduce his children to other members of their family. "After my mom died, my dad took us to Ireland for a while," Rosie recalls.

Rosie admits that without any parental guidance or boundaries, the kids were all "pretty wild, with little respect for authority." Without a functional parent around the house, the youngsters miraculously did it all for themselves. "After my mother died, the five children fused together and became one functioning parent-children unit. We took turns being those roles for each other," Rosie remembers.

They all needed a Mary Poppins. Alas, "There was no Julie Andrews coming in. We sort of took care of ourselves and raised each other." Their mother had prepared them to some extent, and each child knew how to cook exactly one meal. "There were no specific role models assigned to the genders," Rosie recalls. "The boys had to cook and clean, and if there was a flat on the bike, somebody just had to fix it."

Somehow they sorted it out for themselves, with eldest brother Eddie, who was twelve, doing most of the cooking and cleaning. Tough-kid Rosie handed out the chore assignments, mediated the squabbles, and got into fights at school defending her siblings. Rosie, the elder daughter, remembers it all too well: "Most mothers just don't die when you're ten years old. I was the mother at that young age."

The O'Donnell kids discovered another method of coping—humor. "In my family being funny was a way you could communicate the truth without getting in trouble. You couldn't say, 'I'm in a lot of pain and we don't talk about mom's death and we don't have the right clothes,' but you could make a joke. Like: 'Oh, this is a classy dinner. What are we having, Ode to Pea Pods again?'"

Their neighbors did help out as best they could, Rosie was the best at getting herself "parented out" as she calls it. Her best friend, Jackie Ellard, lived nearby and her family often took Rosie in for a bit of mothering. Rosie also found help at school. "Teachers had a profound influence on my life," she said, looking back as an adult. "I get all emotional—when my mom died I had all these great teachers who really helped me."

Later on, her eighth-grade math teacher, Pat Maravel, became a real mentor. "She became a surrogate mom to me, she helped me stay focused and feel loved, and I think she had the biggest effect on me," Rosie recalled. "She took me under her wing and helped me through all those adolescent girl things." Rosie often says that if she hadn't become an entertainer, she would have become a teacher.

Even though there were some caring adults on the periphery to give her support, ultimately Rosie had to go through the grieving process alone and in her own way. When the pain became unbearable, she could escape into the familiar homes of her television fantasy families, where all problems were resolved in an hour or less. "In my house, television took the place of parenting," Rosie said years later. If she wanted to wallow in the down-home comfort of an intact family, *The Waltons* were available. If she wanted a family she could really relate to, there was *The Brady Bunch*, which was made up of a widow and a widower, each with three kids, who then marry. The show was the ultimate fantasy trip for any kid in that difficult situation.

It was a very short leap for Rosie to identify with those characters, and easy to see why at her young age she really thought her broken family could be fixed, and the O'Donnells could once again live happily ever after. "I could sort of see my family shown on television, in a more healthy rendition." Except that no new mother figure moved in to fill the void. "I lived all my emotional reality through theater, movies, and books," Rosie said of her later childhood years. "I come from a family that suffered a tragedy where emotions weren't dealt with on any kind of real level."

Another source of comfort for Rosie was to continue some of the rituals she had established with her mother, like watching the afternoon talk-variety shows. "No other family in my neighborhood was as obsessed with TV as mine was. We were allowed to watch TV twenty-four hours a day. And we did."

The movies that she was attracted to also offered solace: *Mary Poppins, The Sound of Music, Chitty Chitty Bang Bang*. Of those films Rosie said: "Those were the ones I was drawn to; they had the families I wished I had." It's no surprise that her all-time favorite movie is *The Sound of Music*. This is the musical classic about a large family where the mother dies and Julie Andrews, playing the role of a former nun is hired to be the governess, who becomes their beloved stepmother. Eventually, Rosie desperately wanted her father to remarry. By the time she was in high school, the family drama, *Eight Is Enough* appeared on television. Another motherless brood in search of renewal. Rosie has said that she "wanted [her] dad to marry Betty Buckley," the actress who did marry the dad on the show.

So desperate was Rosie to be part of a complete family unit, her fantasies turned to imagining herself in the lives of the single female performers she admired. "I had my fantasy parents, and also people that I wanted to be like or be around—people like Bette Midler or Barbra Streisand—I used to want to be part of their families, in some kind of distorted yet comforting way." As for Barbra, who was twenty years her senior, Rosie had an ultimate fantasy: "In my mind, I thought she'd marry my father and be my mom."

Twenty-three years later, Rosie meets Florence Henderson for the first time, the Queen Mother of TV moms, Carol Brady herself, and welcomes her on to *The Rosie O'Donnell Show*.

ROSIE (emotional): "You're our dream mom!"

FLORENCE (takes her hand): "Ever since I first saw you I wanted to hug you and be your mother, 'cause I thought you needed me—" (She leans over and kisses Rosie).

ROSIE (sincerely): "Yes I did, I always did. I looked to shows like yours, I really did. You were the inspirational role model, the kind of mom you wish you had. You did so much good for people, emotionally. It did nurture me."

FLORENCE (swaggers a bit, speaks to audience): "Rosie talks tough, but you're really a sweet, gentle, soft soul."

The interview ends with a touching duet, a parody of "You Are Sixteen, I Am Seventeen" from, what else, *The Sound of Music*. They sing about being fans of each other and how nervous Rosie was to meet Mrs. Brady. As Rosie has learned, it's never too late to adopt a new mom.

The loss of her mother has continued to profoundly affect Rosie in many ways. It becomes one of the things that defines her. As an adult, Mother's Day always presents a tough emotional hurdle to leap. It is a poignant reminder of her painful childhood that she is now a godparent to Pat Maravel's two children. "Bernice Ellard and Pat Maravel are given Mother's Day cards by me, because they were the mom I didn't have."

Speaking about the loss in 1996, Rosie said, "Typically, culturally, Irish people don't deal well with emotions, so I didn't really deal with my mother's death until I was twenty." In 1993 Rosie was asked what her current favorite TV show was, and she replied: "*Rescue 911*, because it always has happy endings. My therapist would have a field day with my attraction to that show, but I love it."

It took "many, many years of therapy" for Rosie to feel close to being healed. "I see all my memories through shattered glass," she said. In 1997 she spoke again about it, saying, "My whole life revolves around my mother's death. It changed who I was as a person. I don't know who I would be if my mother had lived, but I would trade it all in to see."

Hollywood has certainly exploited the theme of the motherless child in a long list of films, in everything from *Bambi* to *Cinderella* to *Free Willy* and *The Little Princess*. One movie came out in 1996 and so moved Rosie that she saw it twice: *Manny and Lo*. It's about two young girls who find an original way to cope with the death of their mother. They kidnap Mary Kay Place to be their new mom. Rosie said of the film: "So many children today go and find surrogate families—it's so touching the way the girls in the film miss their mom and how they find ways to remember her."

Again, speaking of her mother's death in 1996, Rosie said, "When my mother died of cancer, I remember thinking that if Barbra Streisand had gone on the *Tonight Show* and asked everyone to donate ten dollars to find a cure for the disease, there would be one. Everyone loved her so much, they'd get millions of dollars. I knew there was power involved in fame. And I knew I wanted it."

← 3

Little Tough Girl

As the O'Donnell kids began to create some order in their daily life, the family settled into patterns of behavior, some healthier than others. Rosie remembers Christmases as especially difficult for the children and their father. "We were up at dawn, the five of us, then he'd stumble down about ten a.m. and make us sit in order around the tree. Then he'd hand out the gifts one at a time...then we had to respond appropriately. He'd put a little Baileys in the coffee, then take a little nap, then he'd be the little-hung-over-Christmas-afternoon Dad."

Her father's love of the bottle did, however, enable Rosie's secret plans. She always knew when her father "had a few too many Michelobs." Her dad was a big fan of "Lonely Looking Sky" by Neil Diamond, and the morning after, the record would be stuck in its groove, "and we'd wake up and go, 'Oh, Dad's at it again.'" With her father passed out in the living room, the teenaged Rosie could safely pick his pocket. She took enough money to hop the Long Island Railroad into Manhattan, where she would buy a standing-room ticket for a Wednesday matinee performance of a Broadway show. No surprise, one of those adventures took her to see *The Wiz*, which must have been especially thrilling for her. Another fave was the hit show, *Dreamgirls*. "I'll never forget seeing Jennifer Holliday....I still get chills thinking about it," Rosie said recently.

Her room at home became a shrine to her passions, a safe place where she could sing her heart out to her bedroom mirror, holding a wooden kitchen spoon for her microphone. "My wall was covered with Bette Midler and Barbra Streisand—the entire room—and those were the two women I wanted to be. I would think of them on a daily basis," Rosie remembers. Even when she was at school and supposedly studying geometry, she was thinking: "I wonder where Barbra Streisand is right now? I wonder what Bette Midler is doing?" Those exercises provided Rosie with something to anchor her dreams to. "I was kind of an unhappy kid...looking for dreams to give me solace...and my dreams of them and performing and what I perceived their lives to be gave me such comfort."

Besides cutting classes to dash into Manhattan, Rosie also sneaked home early to catch her favorite soap opera, *Ryan's Hope*. She had no difficulty whatsoever identifying with the characters in this saga of an Irish Catholic family. Teenager Mary Ryan was her idol. There was undoubtedly a lot of vicarious living going on there at the O'Donnell home. Another favorite TV show was the huge hit *Laverne and Shirley*, and Rosie could relate to the working-class humor and the title characters' strong determination to get ahead. In her own mind, Rosie was certain *she* could play Laverne. And about twenty years later, she would get the chance.

As she began to explore the boundaries of her world, Rosie ventured out to more and more concerts and other events on her own and with friends. She was obsessed by movies, often going alone on the weekends, catching as many as she could in one day. She didn't care if that made her late for a party, but she recalls having a hard time finding anyone who shared her interest. "I remember when I saw *The Deer Hunter* and was really excited about it, but [my friends] were like, 'It's only a movie, who cares.'"

Rosie cared, deeply. And most important, she kept exhaustive scrapbooks on all her exploits. One star she idolized was not much older than she was. Rosie inundated Lucie Arnaz (daughter of an even bigger idol, Lucille Ball) with fan letters, and miraculously, "She wrote me back. I still have them." She seems to have saved every ticket stub and program from every show she has ever attended. Fan magazines. Autographs. Newspaper ads. Anything she could turn over in her hands to make her own fantasies more tangible.

In 1975 a groundbreaking, exciting new show debuted on NBC, *Saturday Night Live*. Rosie became an instant fan and a quick study of the distinctive characters created by the incredible cast those early years. When she was in seventh grade she got a perm for her long dark hair, and with the name Roseann, "everyone called me Roseanne Rosannadana—and that's how I started doing comedy. I'd do Gilda Radner impressions." That was undoubtedly made easier by Radner's portrayal of adolescent characters, notably Judy Miller, star of "The Judy Miller Show."

One wild and crazy sport among the teens of Commack was stalking singer and fellow Long Islander Billy Joel, whose first record had just been released. When Rosie got her driver's license, she and her buddy Jackie would take the O'Donnell station wagon and track Joel to clubs in Huntington, Long Island. Once they spotted him they would call all their friends, and soon the entire class had descended on him.

"We used to go to all these bars...and we used to like hunt him down," Rosie recalled. "He'd be there trying to hide."

Seeing Billy Joel in person meant that Rosie could say she had seen a rising young star in the flesh, making her feel somehow connected to the world of show business she so desperately wanted to enter.

As one result of growing up without much supervision, Rosie didn't have much respect for authority and "never did what anyone told me." But as she points out, she wasn't wild in the usual sense. "I never rebelled in traditional ways—I didn't smoke or have sex. I was rebellious in that I was always the boss. My father was not really around, so I did what I wanted."

When asked later on if anyone had worried about her antics, had worried about her cutting classes, Rosie replied, "They definitely worried." In fact, her father didn't understand what she was doing with all her late nights away from home. He would wait by the front door and when she finally arrived he would shout: "You're taking pot, aren't ya'!"

Her father also had his moments of concern for her future and didn't encourage Rosie to rely on her show business aspirations. That, of course, did not prove a deterrent. Like most teenagers, she believed she was one step ahead of the adults in her life. "I always felt I knew more than them. I got away with that attitude because I was funny. I was lucky I wasn't prone to getting into trouble. I was a kid prone to succeed." Childhood friend Jeanne Davis says, "she knew that she was gonna be a star, even if nobody else believed her. *She* knew." Jeanne also remembers that Rosie "gave her autograph [to my cousin] when she was eight years old...and said, 'Hold on to it—I'm going to be famous someday.'"

At Commack High School South, Rosie *ruled*, becoming, as she put it, "Little Miss Overachiever." Considering how busy she was with activities that mattered to her, it is somewhat surprising that Rosie earned decent grades. "I had a B average—I didn't study, but I have a great memory." One class she did well in was photography. A former classmate recalls that "even her pictures were funny. I remember one she took of her grandmother....I think she won an award for it." Rosie was also a member of the student council, was elected senior class president, and "played every sport." Including shortstop on the baseball team—and even that would prove to be a great career move! "I either wanted to be Joe Namath or Barbra Streisand," is how she summed up her hopes.

Rosie's terrific sense of humor, readiness for adventure and innate ability to energize any given situation made her popular. A former classmate remembers, "Rosie had a lot of friends. And she has not changed one bit since high school. I watch her show when I can, and that's her, that's the Rosie I remember."

A pretty young girl, with an athletic body, she was blessed with wholesome Irish beauty. Rosie was even chosen for the ultimate social honor when she was voted both homecoming queen and prom queen. With that kind of peer support, she was the quintessential life of every party.

Another classmate remembers her vividly: "Rosie O'Donnell's a pisser! She used to come to our house all the time. It was fun having her around. You could hear Rosie's mouth when you walked in the door. She was cracking jokes, just a very funny, happy, warm person."

Even though Rosie attended a public school, her close friends were all Catholic. "I never saw a Protestant person until I went to college," she claims. Their local hangout was Tiffany's Wine and Cheese, located in a corner of the local shopping mall. "We'd go with fake IDs and drink sangria and play Yahtzee. Then on our way out, we'd look across the street to see if there were any cars at the Commack Motor Inn of kids we knew from high school." The "CMI" as it was known, was the local den of iniquity with mirrored ceilings, no less. "That's where everyone in high school went to have their first sexual experience. Except for me," she is quick to add.

Sex was not the important rite of passage for young Rosie O'Donnell. Getting onstage, acting in a real play, hearing a whole theater resound with applause, feeling the vibrations in her toes—and in her soul. That was the ultimate experience of her teenage years. "My career really started in school, because I did all the school plays and talent shows. It was there I learned I wanted to be a performer." Her school chums loved her for it and voted her Most School Spirited, Class Clown, and Personality Plus. Many of them also believed in her dreams. "Everybody knew what I was going to do," she said years later. "On the yearbook they'd write: 'Say hello to Johnny Carson when you're a big star.'"

One honor that did elude Rosie in high school was getting cast as a lead in a school musical. To be fair, her choral teacher, Fran Roberts, also overlooked the talents of Ruth Ann Swenson, who went on to become a diva at New York's Metropolitan Opera. They both got their revenge on a special episode of *The Rosie O'Donnell Show* in February 1997. Billed as a Commack reunion show, it was a big hometown party, featuring members of the marching band, football heroes, and alums from Rosie's high school who made it big in the entertainment field. Sportscaster Bob Costas revealed that he had once been a bellhop at the infamous Commack Motor Inn.

Many of Rosie's former classmates and teachers showed up to celebrate her success. Rosie had a ball interviewing many old friends she hadn't seen in years. Sitting rather sheepishly in the front row was Fran Roberts. After Rosie and Ruth Swenson smugly told on the teacher who did *not* appreciate their early talents, they both autographed copies of their CDs and presented them with a flourish to their former choral teacher.

Rosie's inauspicious debut as a comedian took place at age sixteen, when she downed a few beers and accepted a dare to try her luck on open-mike night in the bar area of the local Ground Round restaurant. Though eighteen was the legal drinking age, a classmate recalls it was a snap to get served: "We never had to deal with strict drinking regulations like they do now." Rosie described the place as "a McDonalds, only with waiters." With more courage than material, she took the microphone.

"I had no act at all," she remembers with some embarrassment. "When you're sixteen you haven't lived enough to have any observations. So I hid behind a pair of goofy glasses, pointed at guys in the audience, and said things like, 'Hey Buddy, where'd you get that shirt—K-Mart blue light special?'" The thrill of performing—even badly—was intoxicating. "When you're sixteen you're so cocky, even when I bombed it was exciting."

Her looks helped her get away with it. "I was sixteen and I looked twelve, with this cute little haircut and big sweatshirt and sweatpants, and I was this little tough girl. The audience—grown-ups my father's age—were like, 'Look at this little kid with chutzpah.'" The nerve that she summoned back then amazes her now, but at the time she didn't know any better. "I was fearless."

In her last year of high school, Rosie did her dead-on impression of Gilda Radner in the Senior Follies. And just like it happens in the movies, a man from the audience invited her to perform at his comedy club. This would be a step up from the open-mike nights she had tried. She would be performing in front of an audience who paid to see professional comedy. So Rosie did the only thing she could think of to prepare. She hurried home from school the next day to watch *The Mike Douglas Show*, and as luck would have it, there was a funny new comic on his show that Rosie could study.

That night she tried her wings for the first time in a real comedy club. And she was an instant smash hit. They loved her—what a heady rush for a seventeen-year-old girl. "I killed! Everybody was screaming, 'That girl is so funny.'" But she fell to earth with a resounding thud the instant she left the stage and was surrounded by a mob of angry comics. "You can't do that! Where'd you get those jokes?" they demanded. "And I said, 'Jerry Sein-man or something. And I was so mad, because I thought, why do I have to write the jokes *and* do them? It's so unfair."

It was a huge letdown. "I thought once a guy told his jokes on TV you were allowed to use them. I thought a joke was a joke, like Bazooka Joe— you open it up and there's a joke. It never occurred to me that I was stealing." Well, at least she had the good luck to steal from one of the best, the budding young talent, Jerry Seinfeld. As Rosie had demonstrated, she was already a good mimic, so she not only lifted Jerry's jokes, she stole his cadence, his timing—everything!

Her first reaction was simple anger, and she immediately lost interest in becoming a comic. "I'm not doing this," she said at the time. "When you're an actress, they don't ask you to write the movie. I was so mad, and I thought they were ridiculous."

Utterly despondent, Rosie snagged a ride home from the club and rethought her options. "When I realized I had to write my own material I was so depressed. I thought, 'I'm never gonna be able to do this.'" At that time, Rosie didn't see herself as a writer, as someone who could just make up jokes out of thin air. Still, the thrill of generating real laughter and heartfelt applause was addicting from the start. So she decided to try another route and became an emcee at the many casual comedy venues sprouting all over Long Island. "It was pretty good for a kid. If you emceed you got fifteen dollars a night."

This move provided Rosie with a paid internship of sorts, where she could observe more experienced comics—onstage and off—without the pressure of performing too much herself. In fact, she still hadn't figured out how to write comedy. Instead, she returned to the Don Rickles approach, heckling the audience with not-so-clever quips like: "Nice haircut— Supercuts? That was my whole act," she admits now. "Really adorable."

Rosie is thankful that her self-delusions protected her from feeling as bad as she should have. "When you start at sixteen you have such a huge ego that you think you are the best thing in the world. That narcissistic immaturity served me very well, because when they didn't laugh—and they shouldn't have laughed, because I wasn't funny—I thought to myself, 'Well this audience stinks!' I had that huge, impenetrable self-confidence that only a child can have." She went on to say that years later, after a decade on the comedy circuit, she still marveled that she'd been able to go onstage with no material. "In hindsight, it's frightening to me. At the time, it wasn't frightening. It was empowering."

4

Hitting the Comedy Clubs

Before long Rosie learned how to develop observational comedy. "I watched every comedian and saw what they did. They'd take an experience from their life that was relatable. They put humor into it and presented it to the audience, who would go, 'Oh yeah, I've done that.'" So she started paying her comedy dues, zigzagging all over Long Island for a chance to pick up a Mr. Microphone and not much else.

After high school Rosie made a stab at college, though it didn't take much to put an end to it. Her father felt it was important to get an education and hounded her about learning something to fall back on. But Rosie felt that "if I had something to fall back on, then I'd fall back." She spent her freshman year on scholarship at Dickinson College in Carlisle, Pennsylvania, where she worked in the school post office as her work-study assignment. Not surprisingly, she didn't fit in. "It was a school for people much smarter than me," she said years later. The following fall she transferred to the theater department at Boston University where she got a work-study job in a video store. About six months later, her college career ended when a drama professor criticized her in class: "He told me the part of Rhoda Morgenstern had already been cast and that I would never make it as an actress." He had used as an example a character from her all-time favorite sitcom, *The Mary Tyler Moore Show*.

What that insensitive teacher didn't know was that while his harsh words would cause Rosie to drop out of college, they would also strengthen her resolve to succeed. At the time, Boston was a boomtown for comedy, and it was there that she got her first paid gig as a professional comic in 1982. It was a genuine trial by fire.

Paul Barkley, one of the owners of Boston's Comedy Connection, tells the story of how she talked her way around the door charge by telling the doorman she was a New York comic. That worked fine, except that one of the comedians booked at their other club was a no-show. So the manager found Rosie and told her they needed her. Paul Barkley recalled, "There was a car leaving right then, so without seeing her act, they put her in a car with Denis Leary and Steven Wright and sent them off on an hour and a half drive to a club called Plums in Worcester. She didn't fare too well, but they paid her anyway. There were no hard feelings. The manager from Plums called and said, 'Oh, my God—nice girl, but she definitely didn't have it.' She was panicky, but why not? That's why she signed the picture in the club 'Thanks for my first sixty bucks.'"

Barkley went on to say that it was especially ironic because several years later Rosie and Denis Leary won comedy awards in Las Vegas for best female and male comic. "They laughed, knowing that the last time they had seen each other was at Plums in Worcester."

After hanging around the comedy scene there for a few months, Rosie headed home to Long Island, where she held her only day job—working in the catalog department at Sears. By night, she emceed around the area, slowly began creating an act for herself. One place she frequented was the Eastside Comedy Club in Huntington, Long Island, where she worked hard to hone her skills. Rosie even joined an improv group called the Laughter Company, which performed around Long Island. The group quickly became very popular and attracted a loyal following. They performed sketch comedy that they had rehearsed as well as improvisations based on ideas tossed to them from the audience. It was fly-by-the-seat-of-your-pants comedy and terrific training for a performer. Karl Hosch, who is now a producer, was just a fan with a video camera in the early 1980s, and he taped the group "for posterity."

The tape showcases three guys and two young women doing reasonably funny stuff, though some of it is dated. Rosie appeared to be the youngest member and was very cute in a boyish sort of way, lively and trim, with a shag haircut and plenty of nerve. Of that time in her life Rosie has said she looked like a young British lad yearning to start a band. Their fast-paced show featured a variety of comedic formats in addition to the prepared sketches. They tended to go for a few good laughs, then cut the lights; hot recorded jazz played during the brief blackouts between scenes. In one of the sketches, Rosie and Bob played police officers masquerading as a bickering couple in order to talk a suicidal man off a ledge. (The guy decided his life wasn't so bad after getting a taste of theirs, and he happily stepped back inside.)

In another prepared sketch, Rosie adopted an Irish accent to play Sister Roseann, a prim nun teaching sex education to a class of teens. The humor was predictably sophomoric but went over well with the crowd:

ROSIE: "In this classroom there will be no exams, there will be no papers, but there will be an oral report, and if you don't come you fail."

BOY: "Is it going to be a hard test?"

GIRL: "I hope it won't be too long."

GIRL: "Do a man and a woman have to be in love to have sex?"

ROSIE: "No, not as long as they're married."

Not any worse than lots of humor that aired on *Saturday Night Live* over the years.

The group used another gimmick, which they called "dubbing." First they would ask the audience to call out a situation. Then, for example, Janie and Vinny remained onstage, acting the parts of a gay man and a lesbian at Fire Island, while offstage Rosie and Bob improvised their lines into microphones. The effect is a foreign film badly dubbed into English—and fairly amusing.

At least half their act was improvised, with mixed results. On one occasion, Dave played a priest hearing Rosie's confession, except she was a multiple personality and argued with herself over whether or not she had sinned—very funny. In another, Rosie and Vinny played a honeymoon couple with differing ideas on what would transpire. Here's some of the scene:

ROSIE: "I don't want to—you know—in there—I don't want to." [Stalling and whining] "I thought I wanted to, but now it's getting closer, I don't really want to."

VINNY: "Just relax, I'll call for some champagne...put you in the mood, then I'm sure you'll want to—you'd *better* want to!"

ROSIE: "My mother said you wouldn't make me..."

BOB [*arriving with bottle*]: "Château Neuf de Pape, 1925, 1936, 1927, marked down from 1995."

Finally, the troupe presented a rather complicated series of quick vignettes with a technique they called "freezes." This required very quick thinking and great stamina. First, two actors started an interaction of their own devising, for instance, two men in a foxhole shooting rifles. They spoke improvised lines, but all the props were mimed. Then, once they had gotten a laugh, and especially when the people onstage were in some interesting physical positions, the next member of the group who was "up" yelled out "freeze."

The actors held their pose for ten seconds or so, while the next person went onstage. Rosie then had the option of replacing either of them in the sketch, and she tapped the shoulder of the actor she wanted to replace. She would create an all-new scenario that fit the odd pose the remaining actor was still frozen in. She let him know what to do next by what she said and did. In this example, Rosie leaned over the remaining guy and pretended to supervise him decorating a cake. The rifle that he held in the previous scene became a pastry bag. Then he was "unfrozen" and continued to improvise in that storyline until the next performer yelled "freeze." The routine was fresh and entertaining and fantastic training for Rosie. After doing that several times a week off and on for a few years, she was ready for anything!

Hosch recalled that the group ended their improvs with fake sword fights (complete with sound effects made by the other players offstage). "They would yell 'freeze,' and then they would stab one of the guys. Bob would stab Vinny, then finally Rosie would look down at Vinny, who wouldn't move, and they'd go, 'Something's wrong, call an ambulance...what are we going to do?' Then the lights would go down, and Dave would say: 'You have just been victims of the Laughter Company.'"

Hosch also helped Rosie edit some of those tapes into an audition tape. He remembers her sitting in his living room discussing all the comics from Long Island. "She said to me, 'You can take it to the bank that I'm going to make it.' And she said it with such determination that you almost didn't doubt it. You knew that if she didn't make it, she was going to die trying."

It is a testament to her personality that Rosie did not forget the people who gave her the early breaks. Even after she had made it big on the comedy circuit, she still returned to the small clubs that helped her get started and worked for far less than she could earn elsewhere. She is a great networker and keeps in touch with her comedy contacts. She was undoubtedly paying attention every time she watched *A Star Is Born*, and realizes that performers often meet the same people on the way down that they meet on the way up.

Very early on she realized she needed to alter her name. After an emcee introduced her by her full name, Roseann O'Donnell, which sounded a lot like "Roseanne Rosannadana," Gilda Radner's popular character from *Saturday Night Live*, the audience became confused and booed her, thinking she was trying to rip off the popular Radner. So the quick-thinking emcee dubbed her "Rosie," and now it's hard to imagine her as anyone else.

Those first few years were the roughest, and she received little support from family and friends. "Time and time again, people told me to quit—that I was too tough, I was too New York, I was too heavy," she recalls. "But I didn't listen to them. I thought *You're all idiots!*" So with not much to sustain her but her own grit and determination, she finally improved to the point where she could get booked in small clubs. "I started on Long Island at the Ground Round, which was a hamburger joint where you could throw peanuts on the floor, and that was the main draw that got the people in there." Soon she was off touring the country, working for much less than her male counterparts at clubs and colleges. (A few years later, after she would become a headliner, Rosie became friendly with the woman who kept the books for a club where she appeared. As Rosie tells it, "The woman said, 'There must be a mistake here. It says you're only getting seven hundred dollars to headline. It must be seventeen hundred, right?' I was getting less than half of what the men would get.")

Despite the disparity in pay, as it turned out, her timing was perfect—though Rosie had nothing to do with it. What she couldn't have known back in high school when she first tried her comedy wings, was that the 1980s would become the golden decade of stand-up comedy, when nearly every small city had at least one Yuk Yuks or Laff Riot or some other comedy club with a corny name. At the peak of the craze, there were over 1,500 nightclubs that presented comedy. That's a lot of nights to book, and at first there weren't enough comics to meet the growing demand. Perfect for a young ambitious comic just starting out.

At the smaller clubs, especially, the economical method of housing itinerant comics was to stuff several of them into what became known as a "comedy condo." These apartments were kept for the sole use of traveling comics, almost always men who didn't feel obliged to pick up after themselves. Nor did the clubs spend much on housekeeping.

Rosie describes those early experiences in graphic detail: "You'd arrive in town and they'd have a kid come pick you up in a used Vega with a door that didn't close. You'd have to get in on the driver's side and climb over his lunch from Hardee's. All of us would be scrunched in the backseat, and he'd take us to this filthy condo where we would all live for days...with rotten leftover takeout food in the fridge and shower curtains with mold. Very disgusting."

But as she points out, she was in her early twenties and getting paid, and there was a certain excitement to being out on the road alone. But also fear. "The other comics were much older. They'd pick up women at the bars, bring them home, and have sex in the rooms next to mine. I was like twenty and totally freaked out from hearing these noises through the wall. I put the dresser up against the door. Everybody was doing drugs and drinking, and I was just this little girl on the road, scared in her room." With cocaine the drug of choice back then, it was not uncommon for a comic to stop by the club office after a gig to collect their pay and be asked if they wanted to be paid in "green or white."

It was, indeed, a strange other world that Rosie inhabited back then, but she did manage to find some humor along the way. "When I was just getting into comedy, I would stay in hotels in New York, where one [TV] station used to run three *Mary Tyler Moore* reruns in a row. I used to sit there laughing out loud, thinking, 'They're going to hear me laughing in this room all alone, and they're going to come in and get me.'"

Life on the road ruined many a relationship for comics on the circuit. Performers were away from their homes for long stretches and then touched base only briefly before heading out to the next gig. Most comedians sacrificed any kind of stable personal life in order to maintain their schedules. Besides, at the height of it, the guys were treated like rock stars, with groupies in every port. One veteran comic from that era said, "Not only could we get laughs, we could get laid." Rick Haas of Zanies in Chicago has seen most of the great ones in his many years in the business. "It's really hard. Jay Leno was really lucky. [He married young.] But most of the guys are still single. Very few of them have wives. And the ones that have families, usually they have kids after they've become successful."

Rick Newman, owner of the legendary New York club Catch a Rising Star, remembers what it was like for young comics. "They all came in rusty. When they were all beginning they didn't have their confidence or presence. Some of them were more comfortable than others, because they were more comfortable in their own skins. The gratification of discovering and nurturing new talent that evolves into great talent is the most exciting part of the process."

When asked if you can teach someone to be funny, he replied, "That's like teaching someone to be taller. You can't. You either have it or you don't. You can develop and get better at what you do if you work hard. It's called paying your dues."

So Rosie tirelessly crisscrossed the country dishing out laughs until eventually she had performed in forty-nine states. Perhaps her tab for dues was a bit shorter than some of the men she started out with, because at the time female comics were still a rarity. As Newman recalls, "It was certainly a boys' club back then, and even today, it still is. And I'm not just talking about the comics. I'm talking about the managers, producers, agents, network people."

Wende Curtis of the Comedy Works in Denver believes it was harder for women to break into comedy because it has always been so male dominated. "I feel like it's the audience perception, or something that we all buy into. You'll hear people say 'She's the funniest woman I've seen.' Well, why isn't she the funniest *comic* you've seen? I'm sure that when Rosie was clearing the way for other women, it was tough."

Rosie was quick to acknowledge other women who came before her. "Roseanne [Barr] really paved the way for all of us. I think she is a wonderfully funny woman. She bravely and courageously uses her own life to help other people, and I have nothing but respect for that, but I would never do that."

Being a woman was an asset when she started out, Rosie believes. "It was such a rarity to have a female comic performing at all in a comedy club that it helped me to get noticed. There were about six women working the circuit when I started, and there are probably six hundred now," she said at the Aspen Comedy Festival in 1996. She also remembers the competition between them. "Some women comics when I started were jealous of other women. They thought, 'If she gets the *Tonight Show*, I can't.' My philosophy always was, 'If she did, we can, too.' Success breeds success."

That outlook undoubtedly has a lot to do with why she's now at the top of her profession.

Being such an oddity, however, also created its own problems. Rosie remembers that at one club the owner threatened her: "You're the third woman we've had, and the first two sucked. If you stink, we're not hiring any more." Rosie recalled, "That's a lot of pressure, isn't it? The responsibility of my entire gender ever performing there again? It was horrible." Other times she was told, "Most women comics suck, but you were all right." What separated Rosie from so many others was that she seldom shrank from a tough challenge. She just wanted the prize more badly. She kept telling herself, she was at least *in show business*, and sooner or later, her break would come. She had to believe in herself to keep going.

Rick Haas of Zanies has his own theory about why there aren't more women in comedy. "It isn't that they're not funny onstage—it's what goes on offstage. It's hard enough for a man to do this...here's an example. A guy gets a booking at an out-of-town club. He drives by himself, maybe at night, to this club and parks in the dark parking lot, walks into a strange club, and does his show. That's hard enough for a guy. For a woman, that is a life-threatening situation. No wonder they don't do it more often."

He does go on to say that once a female comic has decided to hell with the risks, they can have an advantage, because they stand out from the herd more. "It takes drive. What sets Rosie O'Donnell apart? She's got that drive. Why is Rosie now the happeningest thing going, and Paula Poundstone is nowhere to be found? Drive," he said.

Another perspective is provided by Kathy Madigan, winner of the 1996 Comedian of the Year Award and a fellow client of Rosie's longtime manager, Bernie Young. She explained why she thinks there aren't more women in comedy. "The whole job is based on control. When you're out there for half an hour, you have to be in complete control of that room." She believes that comedians are the ones who have in effect, "raised their hands" and said they want to be in charge of any given situation. "I think men tend to leap at that opportunity more than women. They like being in charge and all that crap. Most women just don't seem to like it. It appeals to them in a way, but getting over that actual hump between thinking it and doing it, there seems to be a block there."

She also defined the difference for a performer between acting and doing stand-up. "When you're acting you're not being yourself. If you're in a movie that's bad, it's not necessarily your fault. But when you're onstage, those are your thoughts, and you're faced with immediate acceptance or rejection. And there's nobody else to blame."

Kathy also had some views on comedians in general. "In my opinion, ninety-nine percent of comedians are nuts. So they're gonna behave in nutty ways. I have no earthly idea why most get onstage, but most are type A, that's a given."

Haas also pointed out that the successful comics must also be incredibly good businesspeople and just plain smart. He refers to the comedy club circuit as the minor leagues, where comics learn how to bunt. "That means you not only learn your act but how to talk to people on- and offstage. Where you learn how to treat people, where you learn how to behave professionally. And where you just learn the business." This seems to be where Rosie excelled early on. Maybe it was her Catholic girlhood or good manners instilled by her mother. Whatever the source, Rosie behaved herself on the road and made a great impression on club personnel.

Paul Barkley of the Comedy Connection in Boston, where Rosie made those first few bucks, remembers very well how she behaved after she returned to the club as a more seasoned professional. "It wouldn't be uncommon for her to sit for two hours after a show by the door at a table and sign every autograph for every customer that was leaving. And that would be five hundred people lined up. And she would talk to them for a minute or so each and kiss and hug everybody on the way out—and this was for every single show. We actually had the problem where her shows were backing into each other! This 'Queen of Nice' is really true."

When asked if he's ever seen Rosie bomb, Barkley replied, "No, because people like her so much. When comics are well liked, they don't bomb. If something doesn't go over well, they usually look at the audience and go, 'Screw it—I tried something different.'"

Rich Newman of Catch a Rising Star describes Rosie this way: "She's like a thoroughbred. She's sincere, she's talented, she's funny, she's caring. She really is all those things, and the public sees that and knows it's the truth. No one has anything bad to say about her except for Howard Stern, and he looks like an idiot for saying those things."

Another perspective was offered by Jeff Penn of Garvins Comedy Club in Washington, D.C. He believes it takes a special kind of tough woman to survive the comedy circuit. "I noticed a large portion of the female comics were gay.... When you're gay, you have to overcome the biggest odds in the world. And in the eighties it was a tough time to be gay, and people were just starting to come out. Also, being a comic is not something that's viewed as typically female. It's hard to keep relationships, things like that."

One impetus to the comedy boom was the late-night debut in 1982 of a talk show hosted by veteran comic David Letterman. Although Johnny Carson frequently featured established comics—guys who played Vegas a lot—he rarely showcased new talent. As Rosie remembers it, "Carson was putting on only four new comics a year, and none of them were women." On the other hand, Dave's show became the place where hip, cutting-edge new comics could work out and get some exposure (at least to whoever was up watching TV at 1:00 A.M.).

Another factor that fueled the comedy explosion was the advent of cable television and its need for cheap programming. And what could be cheaper than putting a few comics in a club in front of an audience? So before long there were more comedy shows on TV than you could shake a martini at. And the advantage to cable, as far as the comics were concerned, was you didn't have to rewrite your material to comply with the censors. That was also the appeal to many viewers who were thrilled to receive adult programming flaming out of their very own tube.

Rosie, however, rarely worked particularly "blue." Her early comedy was filled with references to her Irish Catholic upbringing and her large family. She was—and still is— especially good at mimicking her Dad's brogue and his challenges with newfangled things, such as answering machines. Which is probably an exaggeration, since he must have been some sort of techno-whiz, given his occupation as an electrical engineer. Allowing for some comic license, Rosie admitted back in 1988 that her father "is not stupid. The jokes are done with love, and he kind of likes it. He'll tell me, 'Mr. Ryan at work saw you on TV and thought you was very funny, luv.'" Talking about her comic style back then she said, "Your comedy is just your life, and I try to be as real as I can. Everything in my act, if it didn't happen to me, happened to my sister."

Other popular bits from those days include her classic exercise class routine (delivered while exercising), in which she tells her aerobics instructor just what she thinks of the skinny young thing—while never missing a thrust or stretch: "I hate this class, I hate your skinny little ass." Though Rosie's challenges with her fluctuating weight have at times become fodder for her act and helped many women identify with her, she didn't fall into the Hollywood Body Trap. She explained, "People who try to change their essence to fit what they think Hollywood wants end up losing in the end."

Club owner Rick Newman assessed her appeal: "Rosie is someone both men and women can look at and go, 'She's one of us.' She's not one of those plastic people on television. And I think she's beautiful, but she's not what you look at in *Vogue*. Her beauty comes from so many different places. She has no hang-ups about herself, not just physically, but in every way. She's so compelling—she's just a star."

Another mainstay of her act is her encyclopedic recall of pop-culture trivia. Rosie had realized that show business had to be her life, and she intuitively knew that becoming steeped in knowledge about all aspects of it would somehow magically help her reach her goals. While she was on the road doing her act, Rosie carried a small notebook wherever she went to record her observations. She took it to shopping malls and video arcades, to McDonald's and the multiplex—and her observations reflected mainstream America back to itself in an amusing yet loving way, because that's her life, too. "I'm much more middle America than anybody ever realized," she said recently.

Rosie also made her mark in comedy by taking the high road at a time when guys like Andrew Dice Clay were selling out Madison Square Garden badmouthing women, gays, and minorities. She has never found it necessary or appealing to put other people down in order to elevate herself. "You don't have to be mean to be funny," Rosie has said. "It's weird to me."

Wende Curtis, of the Comedy Works, admires Rosie for that. "It says a lot about her character that she doesn't do that. She knows what it's all about and refuses to perpetuate it." Curtis also spoke about the challenges of booking female comics. "For instance, Margaret Smith may not have done well in my Tampa, Florida, room, which was more the hooting and hollering, show-us-your-tits sort of an atmosphere. I just couldn't put smart women comics in there because the audience was too stupid."

In 1988, Rosie summed up her comedy this way: "I make fun of what I know best. Growing up in a big family, learning not to hate your stepmother, dieting, listening to a four-year-old try to tell a joke—that kind of stuff." One critic aptly described her generation of comedians as being "raised by television, the almighty wet nurse."

One of the clubs where Rosie made a big early impression was the Indianapolis Comedy Connection. Chick Perrin remembers her well and understands her appeal. "She really stayed away from the PMS jokes. Audiences would get tired of women comedians doing male-bashing material, but Rosie never did any male bashing. She just told about her life, and it was funny." Perrin said that when she first came to his club he knew she had the aura of a star. "She just stood out. Tim Allen started here, too. Tim Allen, Jeff Foxworthy, Drew Carey—we've had all those people come through here. And Rosie had that same type of quality—just really killer shows, every show. You just knew it was a matter of time, and her time would come."

And her time did come very quickly. Rosie got her proverbial big break just like it happened in all those old movies she loves so much—in a talent contest. Ed McMahon's daughter, Claudia, spotted Rosie working at a club and offered to get her on her dad's brand-new show, *Star Search*. The ease with which Rosie made it on the show can be appreciated when you consider that during that first season in 1984, 20,000 wannabes auditioned for the show—on videotape and at open casting calls in forty cities. Nine casting agents withstood countless renditions of "Memories" and winnowed the group down to about 160 acts.

Jeff Penn remembers booking Rosie at that point in her career. "She was young and energetic, which was super. She had a real childlike charm onstage. She always had this glint in her eye, and the audiences always loved her. I don't remember her ever having a bad set. Rosie didn't rely on female issues; her stuff was very unisex. She was a lot of fun to be around."

Penn remembers sitting around with her one night when she was pondering whether to do *Star Search* or not. "A lot of comics didn't know if it was a good thing. It was an amateur show, but competition was tough. You only had ninety seconds—it was like shotgun comedy. You had to win the audience over and make them laugh in ninety seconds. I told Rosie, 'You should do it. It'll be great.'"

At twenty-two, Rosie O'Donnell took the big stage by storm and dethroned the reigning champ (an unknown who never made it big) in McMahon's *Star Search*. Comedian Craig Shoemaker, a buddy at the time, recalls her predicament. "I remember she said 'I won—and I have no more material!'" (Perhaps the material did thin out a bit—on one show, she even did an Elvis impression.) Looking and sounding like the suburban Long

Islander that she still was, Rosie sported the big, curly long hair popular at that time. "My Nancy McKeon phase," as she called it. Years later when asked about the experience she said, "I enjoyed it back then. I saw a rerun—how about that horrible hair...hello—and the pumps. Oh, a fashion felony." Felon or not, Rosie went on to defend her championship status four times. Though she didn't win the big $100,000 prize, she did wind up with $20,000. Considering that she had been living in a cheap Hollywood hotel and dining on hot dogs for the duration, that was no small sum. She remembers that the prize was "a huge amount of money for me."

Rosie wisely spent her money moving out to L.A., expecting to parlay her winnings into bigger and better things. The reality check soon came: "I thought that after I did *Star Search*, Speilberg would be at home going, 'She's the next girl in *E.T. 2.*'" In a town where a huge star like Robin Williams routinely appeared at the Improv to work on his act, being a semifinalist on some new talent show wasn't all that impressive. She ran into Williams at that time, and he had seen her on the show and recognized her. Rosie remembers she was her usual gushing self: "I was like, 'Oh, my God, Robin Williams said hello to me!'" Ironically, in 1995, Ed McMahon was asked who was the most successful person ever to appear on his show, and he replied: "I would have to guess Rosie O'Donnell, because of the variety of successes in cable, movies, etc."

A career as a stand-up comic was never Rosie's ultimate goal, but rather a means to an end—acting roles. Preferably in movies. Recalling the period right after *Star Search*, Rosie said, "I thought that was it. Now casting people would see me. But no. I couldn't even get on at the Improv." So, a bit disheartened, she returned to the comedy circuit. Her increased visibility did mean she could headline at some clubs.

One of those clubs was the Comedy Castle in Detroit, home base of another young comic and local boy, Tim Allen. Although Rosie was the headliner, booked for several days of shows and slated to go on last, Tim was the one the crowds had come to see. During his set, he got the audience all riled up with his now famous tool-guy-grunt shtick. So when Rosie came onstage the reception was tepid. The crowd had little interest in her stories and heckled her with chants of "Tim, Tim." This was a sobering experience for her first gig as a headliner.

Years later she still recalls it vividly. "Tim goes on and gets a standing ovation every night—I tanked. When I say tanked, I was horrible. They wouldn't laugh at one thing." Her solution was to beg Tim to go on last so she wouldn't have to follow him, and she could have a better shot at pleasing the crowd. He agreed.

When Tim Allen, now the star of TV's megahit, *Home Improvement*, appeared on *The Rosie O'Donnell Show* in 1996, Rosie finally had a forum to thank Tim publicly for what he'd done for her twelve years earlier. "You never asked me for the difference in the money, and you never told any other comics, 'cause it could have hurt my career back then, and it was very nice of you," she told him very sincerely. Tim shot back with: "But you owe me eleven hundred dollars now."

Mark Ridley, owner of the Comedy Castle in Detroit, has been in the business for eighteen years and has seen it all. He remembers that particular week as well, and also remembers that Rosie got better every time he saw her perform. "You could tell Rosie worked hard. You can tell when they really listen to the audience, and that was apparent with Rosie. She is in that upper few percent of people that really work hard on improving their act. She's got an incredible work ethic." He recalled what it was like when Rosie was starting out. "When a good female comic comes along, it's like a breath of fresh air."

For the next two years Rosie traveled around the country, gradually gaining recognition while continuing to polish her act. She also appeared as the opening act for some well-known stars. Her first big-time comedy gig was opening for illusionist David Copperfield at Caesars Palace in Las Vegas. It was a nerve-racking experience, to say the least. "I had to do twenty minutes on the button," Rosie recalled. The first show I did twenty-three. I was told by a rather scary guy that I had just cost Caesars Palace ninety-six thousand dollars."

Rosie was also told that if she wanted to do a longer set, then she would have to pay the difference in lost gambling revenues. Not surprisingly, at the next show she was so afraid to run over that she stopped mid-joke just to be on the safe side.

But there were other gigs that were a lot more laid back. She said, "One of the first big people I opened for was Dolly Parton. It was the greatest. I went to a lot of cities." Years later, Dolly recalled that her fans loved Rosie, even though she was a city girl, because "she was so real and so down-home and they understood her comedy. We made a good team." Rosie remembers the crew made fun of her reaction to one of Dolly's songs. "I would listen to the concert every night, and whenever she sang 'Little Andy,' I was hysterical crying." Understandable, for this was a sad song about a little kid without parents.

Slowly but surely, Rosie made her mark on the comedy scene, always alert for the next big break—since it looked like she was going to need more than one. The next opportunity came in 1986 while she was performing at Igby's Comedy Club in Los Angeles. The owner of the club, Jan Maxwell Smith, remembers Rosie very well. "She's a fighter. She will fight through a set. And she will fight for what she feels is right or important to her, whether it's about performing or a contract, or whatever." He went on to say she was "very New York. *Brassy* might be a good word....There's a hard edge to Rosie. Sometimes people will take it the wrong way." When asked what people like about her, he replied, "Her realness. She's not pretentious, and I think that, more than anything, endears her to a lot of people."

Another young comic, Dana Carvey, was also performing that night at Igby's, and an entourage, including NBC president Brandon Tartikoff and Lorne Michaels of *Saturday Night Live*, were due to observe his act. Rosie's manager asked if they would please, please stay and also watch her. So they did. And they hit the jackpot.

At that time, one of Rosie's best bits involved acting the role of a little child. "Have you ever had a four year old try to tell you a joke? Takes about two hours, has no semblance of order, wanders aimlessly—*you* have to know when it's over." Rosie then became the little kid, gestures and all, and she nailed it perfectly. Then she segued into female experience jokes. "Kids are fun, but not fun to have physically. And I hate it when women lie to women without children about that. 'Cause I'm scared of this birth thing...." Then she continued in a thick Long Island accent: "It's nothing—they put a little Vaseline on your thighs—the baby flies right out." In her own voice she continued: "The thing I hate most is when women say, 'Yeah, it's painful, but it's the kind of pain you forget.' I don't think so. I think if I passed a watermelon through my nostril, I'd remember the day."

The Oprah Winfrey Show was a new phenomenon at the time, and Rosie was quick to lampoon it. By today's politically correct standards, the joke could seem a bit racist, and Rosie would probably not do that bit today—particularly given their new peer-competitor relationship. The bit went like this: "Oprah's my favorite talk show now, but I think she's way too white on camera." She then pretended to be Oprah, speaking as she really does on her show, interviewing a black madam from a legal Nevada brothel. "Oprah" was upset that the woman wouldn't give her the juicy details she wanted. Then at the "commercial break" Rosie did Oprah as she suspected she really was—a sassy, jive talkin' broad from the 'hood who told her guests "what for." Her impersonation was hysterical, if in questionable taste.

Rosie shamelessly worked into her act that night at Igby's a plea to the startled Tartikoff to put her in a series. Impressed with her chutzpah as well as her talent, Tartikoff gave her a break. Club owner Smith remembers the evening: "From that night, Rosie was asked to come in for a meeting and she got signed to appear on *Gimme a Break,* and Dana was signed to do *Saturday Night Live*. So it was a great night for us and a great night for them. That really got her recognized in television, and then she went on to other things. She would still come back here and perform, though not as often, because as you get higher up the ladder, the demands increase— concerts, benefits, guest appearances. You almost never have downtime. And that's the sort of whirlwind that started to take over both Rosie and Dana."

5

"Maybe I'm Lebanese"

A whirlwind of a different sort spins around Rosie O'Donnell today, as the walls she has built to keep her private life secret began to tumble. As a nation we now demand to know every detail of the no-longer-private lives of our politicians. And increasingly, we want to know everybody's business. Hollywood stars are certainly not exempt. This hysteria reached its peak in October 1996 after Madonna had her child. Dozens of reporters armed with high-powered video cameras with extralong telephoto lenses camped outside her home hoping to be the first to capture mother and daughter on film—and the big money that would accompany such photos. They even rented nearby homes so they could peer in her bedroom windows.

At that time, other high-profile stars were becoming tired of constant video scrutiny. Finally, actor George Clooney (*ER* and *Batman*) did something about it. He started a boycott of the major Hollywood TV showcase, *Entertainment Tonight*. Since Paramount owns both the prime TV tabloid offender, *Hard Copy*, as well as *ET*, Clooney reasoned that if the biggest stars refused to give interviews to either show, they might be able to get them to back off. It didn't take long for the idea to catch on in Hollywood. The list of supporters included Madonna, Whoopi Goldberg, Steven Spielberg, and Rosie O'Donnell. Rosie had heard all the horror stories from Madonna and was eager to lend her support.

"It gets to be ridiculous, all the stalking with video cameras," Rosie said on her show. "I myself canceled an interview I had scheduled with ET."

After a few weeks, Paramount backed down and vowed to stop taping stars in personal moments. Rosie joyously noted the victory, saying, "I feel a little bit like Norma Rae!" On AOL she was even more direct: "We won, we won, we won. And good for them for owning up to their crap."

Under the old studio system a star's private life was as carefully orchestrated as her on-screen roles. Single actors were matched up with appropriate escorts and posed for photo ops for the fan magazines. Special care was taken with stars known to be gay, like Rock Hudson, to perpetuate the illusion of him as a hunky heterosexual. Some paranoid gay stars even entered into arranged marriages of convenience to protect the latch on their closet. Then, as now, many gays worked behind the scenes in show business, but they were usually just as discreet as the stars they protected.

Today much has changed. Now it's almost a badge of honor to be openly gay in Hollywood—behind the scenes, that is. The major studios now offer health benefits to same-sex partners of their employees. There are many openly gay writers and producers who have managed to increase the visibility of gays and lesbians on TV and in the movies. They hope that increased awareness will lead to increased tolerance. But they are realistic about the struggle. Among well-known openly gay performers, there are only a few lesbians, most notably singers k. d. lang and Melissa Etheridge and actress Amanda Bearse (neighbor Marcie on *Married, With Children*). These brave pioneers have paved the way for others to join them, and even though their careers do not seem to have suffered, there hasn't been a stampede to follow in their footsteps.

One who has is Chastity Bono, daughter of Cher and Congressman Sonny Bono. Chastity, a pal of Rosie's, has been appointed entertainment media director for the Gay and Lesbian Alliance Against Defamation. She will monitor how gays are portrayed on TV and film. Cher, who struggled at first with accepting her daughter's sexual orientation, eventually supported her and spoke out at the National Coming Out Day Rally in Washington, D.C., in October 1996: "It's the most difficult thing to achieve: to love people who are different than you, who believe differently, who look differently."

Among the openly gay men in showbusiness, one of the most

outspoken is writer and actor Harvey Fierstein. When asked in 1996 if he was interested in hosting a talk show, he replied, "Haven't you heard? I do have my own talk show. Except I use a different name: Rosie O'Donnell. Actually, I love Rosie and I'm thrilled for her success. I can't wait to be a guest."

What many people in and out of the gay and lesbian community wish for is a wholesale coming out, a veritable deluge of openly gay people who would encourage everyone to come forward. Another courageous soul who is sticking her toe out of the closet is Ellen DeGeneres, star of the very popular sitcom, *Ellen.*

TV Guide reported in September 1996 that Ellen Morgan, the character portrayed by Ellen DeGeneres would finally be coming out as a lesbian during the 1996–97 season. While the report may have been leaked by the show itself as a way of testing the waters for such a bold move, there is no doubt that that is what Ellen DeGeneres wants to have happen. Her manager, Arthur Imparato, had this to say: "If you look hard at the whole series, there are a lot of elements over the years that could be laying groundwork for that storyline."

On the season premiere, Ellen began to sing the song from *West Side Story*: "I feel pretty and witty and *gay*" (written before "gay" meant anything other than cheerful). In Ellen's version, she paused before "gay" and inserted "hey." On the October 2 episode, Ellen stepped out of the closet in her new home and said, "Yeah, there's plenty of room, but it's not very comfortable." Later in the episode she learned her parents were divorcing, and her character had this intense emotional reaction: "Put yourself in my place. What if I said something shocking to you. Like my whole life had been a lie, and I'm really—left-handed." Her manager also said that "Ellen is trying to break new ground and do something that has not been done before on television."

These puns and games and inside gay jokes amuse those who are knowledgeable, but DeGeneres's fans in the gay and lesbian community wish she would come forward. And what they really want to know is, if Ellen Morgan does escape the closet, will Ellen DeGeneres follow her alter ego?

ABC announced they were moving *Ellen* from her family hour time slot to 9:30 P.M., which would certainly help the story line be accepted. Inroads have already been made in prime time. *Roseanne* married off two gay men, and *Friends* did the same for two women—all without public outcry. If Ellen DeGeneres–Ellen Morgan does accomplish this feat and live to tell a happy ratings story, it ought to go a long way toward encouraging other entertainment figures to do the same.

In the midst of the speculation about this move, Ellen DeGeneres made the rounds of the New York talk shows. When she stopped by to visit her buddy Rosie at her talk show, they didn't avoid the issue but seemed rather to engage in a rehearsed script about it. They both delivered their lines tongue-in-cheek and struggled at times to keep a straight face.

ROSIE: "So, lotsa rumors in the press about Ellen Morgan—let's straighten the whole thing out—what's gonna happen to Ellen Morgan?"

ELLEN: We were really trying to build this up slowly and reveal it in a way that would change people's opinions—we do find out that the character is *Lebanese.*"

ROSIE [*not looking all that surprised*]: "Just out of the blue?"

ELLEN: "No, there have been clues....You've seen her eating hummus, and a big, big fan of Casey Kasem and Kathy Najimy."

ROSIE [*pauses and looks thoughtful*]: "Hey—I'm a big fan of Casey Kasem. Listen—" [*she pushes a button on her digicard console and Casey Kasem blasts out, "You go girl!" Rosie continues,*] "Maybe *I'm* Lebanese."

ELLEN [*smirking*]: "You could be Lebanese."

ROSIE [*nodding*]: "I could be Lebanese myself—I didn't know that."

ELLEN: "That's odd, because sometimes I pick up that you might be Lebanese."

ROSIE [*nodding yes*]: "Yeah. Well I think that's great—a lot of networks wouldn't take the risk."

ELLEN: "Half of Hollywood is Lebanese."

ROSIE [*nearly cracking up*]: "Really? People don't know."

ELLEN: "We have to change people's perceptions about the Lebanese."

ROSIE: "And you're doing a good job."

Though the Lesbian-Lebanese wordplay was fun and daring, one can only imagine the confusion this thinly veiled coming-out party might have caused in the minds of those viewers who are way out of the loop and wondering how a blonde could be Lebanese. It would also seem to indicate that Rosie has her hand on the doorknob to the closet and is turning it.

Lots of Rosie's fans believe she's a lesbian. Many more wonder. And others just don't care. In the Rosie chat rooms on America Online, her sexual orientation is frequently a hot topic for discussion, which the online monitors try to squelch. She also makes the lists of famous lesbians in AOL's gay area, Planet Out. Although it isn't really anyone's business but hers, she does have an opportunity to make a huge difference in the social history of our country.

During the summer of 1996 and again in January of 1997, Rosie was outed in the tabloids. She was reported to have been living in a lesbian relationship that had soured. There were photos of her on vacation and on her motorcycle with an alleged girlfriend. A more reputable newspaper, the *Philadelphia Inquirer* (not associated with the tabloid *National Enquirer*) made it public on August 8, 1996 and named her alleged female lover: "Couple du jour: Rosie O'Donnell and a singer-slash-dancer who she met doing *Grease*."

In January 1997 the *National Enquirer* reported Rosie was dumped by her alleged live-in girlfriend of two years. The woman will reportedly retain visitation rights with Parker, who she helped raise from day one. Whatever the whole story, it does seem that being the unseen partner to a famous closeted lesbian would not be much fun. Rosie doesn't take female dates to premieres and awards shows; if she has a girlfriend, she's not on Rosie's arm for the official show business occasions.

What a difference a show makes. Later, on the day she appeared on Rosie's show, Ellen DeGeneres strolled onto David Letterman's set to the tune of "I'm a Girl Watcher." But when she tried to evade Dave's direct questions with her coy Lebanese routine, he shook his head and said "No, you're not," and refused to let her evade the question. Letterman turned into a bulldog; he forced her to give him genuine answers—and for once his badgering of a guest seemed appropriate.

DAVE: "Help me out here. I understand that sometime in the near future, your character on the show will become a homosexual, will function as a lesbian."

ELLEN [*laughs, stalling*]: "She will function as a lesbian!"

DAVE: "You know what I mean. You know how they do—"

ELLEN: "Well, however the lesbians function, yes [*laughs nervously*].

DAVE: "Nothing worse than a dysfunctional lesbian."

ELLEN: "No!"

DAVE: "Get yourself a functioning lesbian—take it from me. Make sure all those lesbian functions are operational before you take off. Make sure the seat back is in its upright and original locked position."

ELLEN [*feigns being impressed*]: "You know some of the lingo—that's lesbian talk."

[*Then she tries to convince him she doesn't know what will happen on the show and tries to divert him with the Lebanese bit. He rejects that routine entirely.*]

DAVE [*insistent*]: "But is it going to happen? And if it does happen, well that's great!" [*He seems sincerely enthused.*]

ELLEN [*nervous*]: "You're like in hard news right now." [*Feeling the pressure, she fidgets, stalls, and seems to be gauging the audience reaction, which is loud applause, so she blows them a kiss.*]

DAVE [*very sincere*]: "I hope it happens—I think it'd be great."

[*Ellen nods affirmatively.*]

DAVE: "I love different stuff on TV, because so many times the stuff on TV can be the same...and I like lesbians. I've always liked lesbians. [*Ellen is cracking up.*] And I think America likes lesbians."

ELLEN: "I think it's been proven that America likes lesbians."

DAVE: "This would be breakthrough television—what are you waiting for? Let's do it!"

ELLEN: "All right." [*She shouts*] "Now! You got me all pumped up!"

DAVE: "Let's do it. I'll sign off on that—and we'll see her in the lesbian function."

ELLEN: "Oh, it's going to turn into *Red Shoe Diaries*."

[*After the commercial break Dave wouldn't let go of the subject and demanded absolute clarification.*]

DAVE: "I want to see the lesbian on the show. Will that happen?"

ELLEN [*worn down*]: "Yeah. I'll make sure."

DAVE: "Because if you don't, I'd like to have a lesbian on this show....Don't string us along here."

As she did on Rosie's show, Ellen gave as much subtext as she gave substance. Time will tell if Disney/ABC has the courage to let Ellen sally forth from her closet.

One of the underlying issues in all of this is the unwritten rule that the mainstream media will not out a gay or lesbian celebrity. Most stars have powerful publicists whose job it is to shield them from invasive questions.

In the print media, publicists try to secure the best interviewer for their clients, one who will be compatible with them, and one who will follow certain edicts when necessary. It is common for writers to be told that certain topics are just off-limits. Television and radio talk-show hosts are also clued in as to what questions their guest will not answer. Granted, some barge ahead anyway and risk sounding strange if the guest takes the "no comment" route. A host who did that could also expect that the guest might not return to his show. So what evolves is the tacit agreement: Don't ask, don't tell.

This code of silence is easy to spot in action. Just watch Dave or Jay interview single young women over the period of a week or so. They will almost always inquire about their personal lives—who they're dating, what kind of man they like—and to some degree, flirt with them. At times, Dave actually seems to get authentically carried away by the charms of some guests—Isabella Rossellini comes to mind. Then watch them interview Rosie or Ellen or any closeted stars. Leno and Letterman will never ask them about their personal lives. Because they know better and because they follow those rules.

At least Rosie doesn't trot out faux boyfriends, gay hairdressers, and the like, for escorts and photo ops. When you think how often the love lives of "het" celebrities are documented in the press, there is a curious dearth of dating data about Rosie.

That's because Rosie pays a publicity staff a lot of money to keep it that way. Rosie's publicist, Lois Smith, appeared on a panel recently on the PBS issue-oriented *Charlie Rose Show*. They were discussing the media invasion of privacy, in part because of the Clooney boycott. Speaking about her clients, Smith said, "I want a little mystery, a little inaccessibility. People are entitled to some privacy; you don't have to reveal everything." She was joined on the panel by several writers and magazine editors who went on to discuss the constraints placed on them by people like Smith. They all agree the process is akin to brand management of a product.

Then Lois Smith went on to speak specifically about Rosie. "I represent somebody who is going through exactly this same process right now [a media feeding frenzy], and I'm doing everything I can to put the brakes on—but every publication known to God and man wants to do Rosie O'Donnell—hot, hot, hot."

The managing editor of *People* magazine replied, "She's been on our cover two or three times already, and she's done very well [in newsstand sales]. There's intense curiosity, a public itch about her."

Rosie has discussed this very topic, both in regard to herself and to her guests. "There are issues that celebrities don't want to bring up, and I can understand why. They ask beforehand, and I call and say, I would never bring up this tabloid story or that reference. And I won't do it, in the same way that I wouldn't want an interviewer to do it to me."

So what has Rosie herself said publicly about her personal life? Not a lot. She's always ambiguous and evasive when pressed on the issue. Her stock answer is: she's single and doesn't have time to date. "I'm as vague as I need to be or want to be, for the time being," she said in 1996, which leads to speculation that she may out herself in her own autobiography.

Here are her earliest known feelings on the subject. After telling a joke on *The Rosie O'Donnell Show* about the six-year-old boy who was suspended from school for kissing a girl, Rosie demonstrated what may have been a prophetic game that she played as a child. Rosie and her best pal, Jackie Ellard, gave each other pretend "cootie shots" to vaccinate each other against the evils of kissing boys.

On a more serious note, in October 1996, Rosie spoke eloquently to actor Peter Strauss about what she wanted in a relationship—and apparently has yet to find. Strauss appeared in the TV drama *Rich Man, Poor Man* when Rosie was an impressionable fourteen year old. It apparently made a lasting impression on her, as she could quote lines from it twenty years later. Rosie asked Peter if he remembered saying these words to his love interest: "We were meant to be together, it's inevitable, it's ordained." Rosie went on to say, "I want that one day in my life, for somebody to say, 'We were meant to be together, it's ordained.' That's what I look for, still, to this day. I'm waitin'."

Speaking of her college days, Rosie made it clear she feels lucky to have survived. "If I were a gay man, I'd probably be dead by now," she said in 1994. "When I was in college and sexually active, no one was that careful." In her defense, that was 1980–82, and AIDS had not yet modified sexual behavior. During the many years she spent on the road playing the comedy circuit, Rosie didn't seem to make much time for relationships.

But by 1992 she sounded like she had had a lot of experience: "I don't believe it's like a puzzle piece with only one specific part that fits. I think there are many people, and you go and you go, and you go, and you love your way through your life." While promoting the sex farce *Exit to Eden*, Rosie was inspired to say, "I think it's really important to live out your sexual fantasies."

When asked directly about her love life, she gives pat answers such as these in 1992: "I'm single, dating, and available." And "I'm single and searching for someone who will complement me." Although the following year she apparently had some success. "There's no one special, but believe me, I'm looking." Then, unable to contain her happiness, she continued. "Actually, I lied. I'm in love."

She is on the record about her difficulties when she feels a relationship should end. Shutting people out of her life is a "huge issue" for her. "To know the pain of being left makes it nearly impossible to do it to someone else," she said in 1993. "So with people I get involved with, it's usually forever—I keep them in my life."

That same year, she and Madonna did a joint interview in which Madonna asked her which way she would choose to break up with someone: phone, Express Mail, or fax. Rosie replied, "Definitely fax. But as you know, sweetheart, I'm not very good at breaking up. My relationships tend to linger on in never-ending sagas."

Madonna replied, "That's why we get along so well."

Later, Madonna asked her if she was dating more, now that she's famous.

"No," Rosie answered, "you know me, I'm hardly the dater."

Madonna pressured her on the issue, certain that more people must be coming on to her now.

"As you know," Rosie explained, "I am really sort of brain-dead when it comes to that."

As proficient as Rosie has become in the realm of her career, she seems to lag far behind when it comes to relationships. She did speak candidly about the problem several years ago. "I always need to be kind of in control, and I have this sort of omnipotent force in my career—and near impotence in my private life. As much as I know exactly what I'm doing in my career, I have that *not knowing* in my private life. I don't know which apartment I should buy, who I should get involved with, whether I should get committed, if I should stay monogamous. . . . I never know. I'm in a constant state of confusion, so I don't have that power or control in my private life."

Rosie has also been forthcoming about her ongoing therapy. "Just because I have stability in my career doesn't mean I don't have the same insecurities as everyone else. Do you think I've got it all together? Are you out of your mind?"

More obliquely, she conceded in early 1994 that there was no major romance in her life at that time. "That's the stuff I'm still working out." When asked if she saw balance between work and pleasure entering her life anytime soon, she replied, "After some more therapy, perhaps."

Rosie does have some degree of confidence about her ability to attract a partner. "If I'm interested in someone and want to have a romantic relationship with them, I feel like I can entice them with my wit, or my intellect, or my essence."

Simply put, Rosie O'Donnell is a driven woman: driven to achieve career success; driven to leave a lasting body of work; driven to create financial stability, all at an early age. She has accomplished all of that, and more. What she can't seem to do is slow down. But she does understand the problem. "I'm a workaholic who isn't happy without a twenty-four-hour day." That kind of drive has served her well in her career, but it has cost her stability in her personal relationships.

She seemed ready to tackle the issue in 1994. "I think I need to figure out why it is I distract myself from having a real private life by working constantly. And when I've figured that out, I think then it'll be time to find someone."

She explained the problems encountered by an itinerant actress: "If you're on a film set—three months in Seattle, say, and then three months somewhere else—you don't have the constant time you need to work on a relationship." Which is one reason she wanted to do *Grease* on Broadway. It would keep her in one place for a while and create an opportunity for her to devote more time to her personal life—and to pursue the one thing she said she really wants— "a deeply committed relationship."

What is startling in all of these quotes is the exclusive use of ambiguous pronouns. Rosie is highly skilled at avoiding the use of "him" or "her." This is the speech of someone who is extremely guarded when discussing her personal life. Try talking about your life for a day without using gender-specific pronouns. Then try and imagine doing it for fourteen years. Check out this lone example of a male reference—a highly evolved allusion that's really an evasion, from 1993: "Because I started doing stand-up comedy when I was sixteen, I rarely dated. Now I'm getting into that area of my life.

It's generally men who are much stronger and don't have a problem with power issues that are attracted to my kind of strength."

"Attracted to my kind of strength," not "attracted to me" or that "I'm attracted to." Very skillful, and difficult to believe accidental. It is part of her sexual mask.

To compensate on her talk show, where she regularly reveals so much of herself, she has adopted some elaborate set pieces to deflect attention from her personal life, or lack thereof. The most notorious is her silly, overblown crush on the safely married Tom Cruise. And when she tires of talking about "her Tommy," she reminds us of her teenage crushes on the young male singing sensations of her era: Donny Osmond, Bobby Sherman, and David Cassidy. She's had them all on her show and swooned on cue as they sang to her. She certainly puts a lot of effort into overacting the role of a heterosexual; it's just not very convincing.

The sum total of all this is a portrait of someone who generally feels inept when it's time to become intimate with another human being. Yet Rosie is clearly someone who feels deeply about things and yearns for that magic connection, that mystical feeling that she and her love were meant for each other. Notice that it doesn't matter if you know what the gender of her lover is. These longings and frustrations are universal.

That said, Rosie beams in loud and clear on "gaydar." As any card-carrying gay or lesbian person knows—(and there really are people who carry and hand out cards in an effort to educate that say: You have just had an interaction with a homosexual)—"gaydar" is how they identify each other, or at least the likely prospects. Imagine the discomfort of approaching a straight person in error, and you can understand how this unique form of personal radar came into existence. Gaydar consists of a checklist of signs and signals that identify someone as gay. And while there are many possible tipoffs that gays beam out to one another, these are some of the checks Rosie would receive next to her name if she was examined by "gaydar."

- Owns two motorcycles
- Onstage attire (when not playing a movie role that has a prescribed wardrobe) is strictly very tailored pantsuits
- Offstage attire is chosen solely for comfort and practicality—sweats and shorts and not skirts

- Only wears makeup onstage
- Doesn't shave her legs
- Or her chin. In fact, in some lesbian circles, a chin hair is a cool thing
- Doesn't wear much jewelry; made a fuss when her wardrobe woman made her wear a bracelet on her show
- Doesn't obsess much about her weight; doesn't feel she must be thin to be presentable or desirable
- Takes little interest in her hairstyle, leaving all that up to her "hair guy." In short, she is not at all interested in looking attractive to the opposite sex when she's off the clock
- Not into cooking or many other "femmy" things. She'd rather shoot hoops than do needlepoint, for example
- As a kid, the ultimate tomboy
- Still a self-confessed jock
- Not afraid of power tools
- Doesn't call a handyman for every little thing she needs done
- Had zero interest in conceiving a baby the old-fashioned way
- Told Willie Nelson this was her favorite song of his, then winked as she hit the digicard button: "For All the Girls I've Loved Before."

Granted, many heterosexual women share some of these traits, and sharing these interests or lifestyle choices does not mean a woman is gay. These are just some of the classic things that some segments of the lesbian community often have in common. There are, of course, many lesbians who choose to conform to more "het" standards of self-expression and who easily "pass" for straight. There is, however, no doubt that if Rosie just strolled into any lesbian bar, she would not look the least bit out of place. She would fit right in at any Sunday potluck and on any softball team. She would be immediately accepted as a "sister friend."

Ultimately, it is up to Rosie to set the record straight. She has signed a multi-million-dollar book deal with Warner Books, which would be an ideal forum for her to do so. With gay rights such a hot political issue right now, she does have an opportunity to become the poster girl for the cause. As a single, adoptive mother, she can be a great role model—with or without a partner. Melissa Etheridge and her partner are doing their share of groundbreaking, by going public with their pregnancy.

After all of this has been said, whether or not she comes out as a lesbian really has no bearing on her ability to entertain and make us laugh, though the new range of comedic possibilities is enticing to think about. On the whole, her fans seem mature and open-minded enough to accept her, whatever her sexual orientation, and it would be nice to believe that her ratings wouldn't suffer if she did divulge that she was, indeed, "Lebanese." The bottom line is, all her fans want is for her to be happy, to find a well-deserved loving partner and enjoy life.

↬ 6

Her First TV Role

When Brandon Tartikoff offered Rosie her first acting job, it was, ironically, on the TV series *Gimme a Break*. Though it didn't prove to be an especially positive experience for her, it was on a popular, long-running show on a major network. Rosie was hired for its sixth and last season on NBC, 1986–87, which included moving the show to two new nights and time slots. During its run, the show aired in ten time slots on four different nights—no wonder fans of the show were challenged to find the program!

Gimme a Break was essentially an old-fashioned kind of sitcom, founded on the premise of so many of Rosie's childhood favorites: widower dad needs help raising his brood. The twist this time was that the fill-in mom for this white family was played by black actress Nell Carter. As Nell Harper, she dispensed equal measures of love and wisecracks to the police chief's three daughters. Later in the series, after the death of the chief, Nell took over as both parents, added some more "orphans" to the clan, and moved them all from California to New York City. The new location provided an array of exotic ethnic supporting players, including Maggie O'Brien, Nell's upstairs neighbor, played by Rosie. "I was Rhoda Morgenstern with an Irish accent," Rosie said soon after the show ended.

Although she rarely had many lines to learn, Rosie did enjoy an acting apprenticeship of sorts. She certainly had every opportunity to learn all the basics—camera blocking, hitting her marks, working the camera, and so on. By most accounts, there was trouble on that set, and when star Nell

52

Carter became peeved she disappeared into her dressing room. Rosie had a tough time feeling accepted by a group that had been together for years, but she was eager to please and get along with her more experienced cast and crew. She was well liked and undoubtedly supplied some much-needed comic relief.

Rosie often shared her lunch with cast member and veteran actress, Rosetta LeNoire, who regaled her with stories of the glory days of the Cotton Club. As the goddaughter of Bill "Bojangles" Robinson, Rosetta spent time at the famed Harlem club as a small child, and she found an attentive listener in Rosie, who gobbles up showbiz history like M&Ms. Another lunch partner, actress Jackée, worked on the nearby set for the sitcom *227*. Even though Rosie was admittedly nervous at times as she learned the sitcom ropes, she was smart enough to spend time with anyone whose brain she could pick. She has always understood the value of personal friendships inside the business, and that has served her very well.

When Nell Carter appeared on *The Rosie O'Donnell Show,* she made veiled references to the trouble on the *Gimme a Break* set and told Rosie she often requested scenes with her because she wasn't among those causing her grief. Nell recalled that Rosie "was so quiet, and she just sat there." Rosie laughed and explained, "That's right, but I was totally scared."

Rosie weathered the stormy set, but in 1993 she cited the experience as "the most crushing blow of my career. My goal was to be on a sitcom, then I got on this show in its last year and people weren't real happy to be there. I thought, I've climbed this mountain and there's nothing there." Once again, her big break failed to lead directly to other projects. But it is hard to beat a weekly series for exposure, especially to those people who make casting decisions.

Although she did have to return to the comedy circuit for a while before her next TV project materialized, each time Rosie went back it was with more name recognition and better bookings. She also began to pick up some fun jobs that fit in well with her natural love of games and trivia. Still in her big-hair period, she appeared on the game show *Cross Wits* and humorously humiliated herself dancing to the show's theme song with fellow celebrity guest Charles Shaughnessy, later the star of the hit sitcom *The Nanny.*

Eventually, Budd Friedman, owner of the Improv, tipped her off to an audition for a veejay spot on MTV, the first cable music-channel. Rosie remembers how it went: "MTV put me in front of a camera, turned it on, then asked me which rock star I'd want to be locked in an elevator with, and what we'd talk about." Her response—Tina Turner (reasonable answer) and the new crowns on her teeth (strange answer). MTV passed, but execs at their sister network, VH-1, liked what they saw. Rosie's professional advisers and a chorus of other comics advised her not to take the job, believing it would be a leap into obscurity.

But Rosie wanted to believe that three *is* the magic number, and this must finally be the big break that would count. So in April 1988, at the age of twenty-six, she reported to work introducing Top 40 rock videos, on the kinder, gentler VH-1 cable channel. It was a full-time job, writing and performing twenty-four three-minute comedy segments seven days a week as interludes between the music videos. In those early days VH-1 was seen as uncool and the butt of many other comedians' jokes. It was, however, included as part of many cable systems' basic channel lineup and had terrific growth potential.

It was quite an odd gig. "The hardest part is not having an audience," Rosie said soon after her veejay debut. "I never know if I'm going over." One of the funnier gags she worked out involved having a dialogue with her cameraman, who gave his yes or no responses with a tilt or a shake of the camera.

"There's a lot of insecurity in a job like this," Rosie also said. But it was worth it, knowing she was beaming into 27 million homes—surely one of them would be inhabited by someone who would recognize her *real* talent! "VH-1 is perfect for me right now. I get to talk about my life, my weight, Whitney Houston's ego problems, whatever pops into my head. It certainly beats working for a living." And it was great practice for another TV show she was destined to host eight years later.

One of the oddities of the format was that the producers wanted Rosie to introduce herself every time she went on, which she felt was silly. So to amuse herself and those listeners who were paying attention, Rosie started introducing herself as different celebrities, as in: "Hi, I'm Chaka Kahn" and so on. Then one day, O'Donnell dared to claim she was none other than Mrs. Brady herself, Florence Henderson. Which prompted an irate call from Henderson's manager, who feared that viewers would expect Henderson to actually materialize on the show. So the VH-1 producers forced Rosie to end her impersonations.

Rosie did have a lot of freedom to say whatever else she thought would be funny or interesting. During the summer of 1988, Rosie, an avid sports fan, watched the Seoul Olympics with the rest of the world and began to comment about it during her segments. In particular, Rosie developed an obsession for American gold-medal diver Greg Louganis. She joked repeatedly that her dream was to have a dry-land encounter with him and his swimsuit. When Louganis heard about it, he decided to surprise Rosie during a taping. Right in the middle of a segment he strolled onstage clad only in his Speedo. Rosie screamed, turned beet red, and dove for him. He was a great sport and stayed to chat with her for several segments.

Her stint as a veejay, with its odd schedule, was a sort of trial by comedy fire. She recalled, "That was hard work, but it was very valuable. It taught me to draw on all my resources, to pay attention to everything, so I can use it. It was like high-impact comedy aerobics."

Despite Rosie's bouncy highjinks, eventually VH-1 decided to phase out all of their veejays, and since Rosie's contract had not expired, they offered to buy her out. Unlike the other veejays who went their own ways, Rosie was determined *this* big break would lead directly to something better. Sensing an opportunity to expand her horizons, she made them a brilliant counteroffer. Paul Barkley recalls the details of the wheeling and dealing:

"Rosie told them, 'Hey, I've got a better idea. Let me produce a stand-up show and you don't have to pay me any additional money, but if the show goes past twenty episodes, then you pay me money.' They thought they had nothing to lose, so why not? And *Stand-up Spotlight* ended up being their highest-rated show for several years. So it worked out well for her financially, and it also worked out real well for them."

The format was simple: Rosie opened each half-hour show with her own monologue full of her well-polished observational humor. That was followed by stand-up routines by two established comedians and one up-and-coming talent. This cut down dramatically on the amount of new material she had to perform each week, though her exposure was still tremendous because VH-1 aired the show as many as sixteen times every week.

Rosie spoke enthusiastically about the gig at the time. "I've spent years developing my own act, and now producing *Stand-up Spotlight* lets me cultivate new talent and help other people develop their careers. I love coming up with concepts, then working to make them happen. It's very exciting and a lot more fun than I ever imagined behind-the-scenes work could be."

Always networking. Rosie couldn't know when a contact would pay off, she just felt that sooner or later most of them would. And most of them did.

While many performers are content with just doing their onstage duties, Rosie seeks and thrives on having more control. She was born to produce. And she feels her suburban working-class background and down-to-earth sensibility helped make her a successful producer. "You have to know what things cost, how long it takes to do them, and have an instinct about what's going to work on-screen," she said, smiling. "The mall teaches all."

Paul Barkley went on to talk about how wisely Rosie used her new producing power. "She used that forum to bring up a lot of comics that were good to her on the way up, that maybe were ahead of her when she started. She always put on people that she had met along the way."

He also explained that there was a lot of competition and insider politics among the comedy clubs in L.A., and if you worked a lot at one club, then you would never get on a comedy showcase taped for TV at another club. Rosie wouldn't play those games. Barkley remembers her attitude. "I don't care where you work—if you're funny, you're on the show."

He also compared what she was doing to Jay Leno's experience hosting the *Tonight Show*. Being a cable show, without the cachet of the legendary late-night show, *Stand-up Spotlight* could feature some less-seasoned comics who might not be ready for a shot at every comic's dream booking. Jay Leno likes to be a nice guy, and he has met most of the comics who are working, so it is hard for him when he has to turn someone down.

Barkley has heard all about it. "Try telling a comic he's not right for the *Tonight Show*. Jay had a lot of difficulty, because he could only have three spots a week for comics, if that. Whereas Rosie would have three comics per episode, times twenty-two episodes—that's sixty-six people. Leno would be lucky to have one breaking comic a week."

Mark Ridley of Detroit's Comedy Castle said that "everybody who did her show told me they were treated like royalty. Even if they didn't get a break from working on the show, they certainly walked away *feeling* like they had just done the *Tonight Show*. She's very sensitive to other comedians coming up through the ranks."

Stand-up Spotlight featured clever opening credits, with a slick nightclub feel. Rosie shined a flashlight on the credits and then on herself in a routine that was fresh and memorable. Often clad in black slacks, a white shirt and a snappy red blazer, she was by now, a well-practiced host and performer and appeared at ease with her duties. One of her jokes from that era made fun of her pasty white thighs: "I'm just walking down the street this summer, wearing shorts and a T-shirt, and a guy drives by in a van. He stops the van, rolls down the window and goes, 'Yo, Casper! Get a friggin tan—you're blinding me with those albino legs of yours!'"

On a later show she did her now famous bit about which witch was which: "I meet a lot of celebrities in my life—Darren from *Bewitched*—I saw him in Ralph's Supermarket. I'm not sure if he was the first or second Darren—remember that? When you were a kid, they just switched Darrens and never explained why. I would always be looking at my father—'Daddy? Just checking.' See, it was scary."

And unlike her early days on the comedy circuit and her first sitcom experience—both of which sometimes frightened her—this job proved a delight. She even received her first award nominations (an American Comedy Award and a Cable Ace Award) for her work on *Spotlight*. The steady job also took her out of the comedy club rat race and allowed her to settle down into some sort of normal domestic existence. "I really enjoy performing, but the demands of that lifestyle can take their toll," Rosie said at the time. "Producing and writing have shown me there's a lot I can do and still spend more time at home than I do on the road."

Home for Rosie at that time was a modest house, on Bellingham Avenue in the Studio City area of Los Angeles, that reflected her unpretentious nature and the casual lifestyle she prefers offstage. Rosie prefers to lounge around in sweats, shoot hoops, and play Nintendo. "It's like kids live here—but it's me," she admitted, "and my silverware doesn't match. I think it's important for America to know that."

Describing her Studio City neighborhood, she said, "It's like the street I grew up on. Kids on Big Wheels and dogs barking at all hours. My house is very Long Islandy with a Laura Ashley interior." Casual acquaintances who see her decor are usually surprised at the frilly side of Rosie O'Donnell. "People go, 'I can't believe this is your house.' I go, 'Whatd'ya expect? I would live in a garage with tools?' People who know me really well go, 'Oh, this is totally you.'"

Rosie's work at VH-1, in fact, led almost immediately to greater exposure. Viacom, the parent company of VH-1, also owns the Showtime premium cable channel. Executives at Viacom were pleased with Rosie's performance. Wanting to cross-pollinate their cable channels, they signed her for several specials. The first one, "Showtime's Comedy All-Stars," hosted by Harry Anderson, aired in 1988.

Her latest accomplishment, which she shared with her audience, was expensive cosmetic dentistry—she had her top four and bottom four middle teeth crowned. "I'm sittin' in the dental chair goin': 'I'm gonna look like Christie Brinkley.' The dentist drills for like six hours, then he leaves the room. I take the little mirror that looks like you ripped it off the side of Barbie's Country Camper, and I look—I *am* the *Howling*—I have $8,000 worth of points in my mouth—$8,000! $8,000. It's a car! Okay, it's a Hyundai with a slutty radio, but it's a car."

Rosie also scored big laughs with a hot topic, drug abuse. "I don't drink anymore, I don't do any drugs....I had a real bad experience with drugs when I was like ten years old—I almost overdosed on Flintstones vitamins. It wasn't funny—I took two Wilmas and a Betty—thank God I had that Dino so I could come down." It is very funny in hindsight, knowing that she would later giggle her way to greater fame as Betty Rubble.

"Showtime's Comedy All-Stars" was followed two years later by a half-hour special that showcased Rosie with one other comic, Bill Engvall. It was called "A Pair of Jokers" and was taped at the Comedy and Magic Club in Hermosa Beach, California. This was a standard format for Showtime, which had already become known for its specials featuring newer comics. Rosie had fifteen minutes to strut her stuff. First she apologized for her thick accent. "I hate having a New York accent, because I think no matter how intelligent you are, people think you're an idiot. I *can* speak without a New York accent," she continued, using a generic, well-enunciated news-caster voice. "But in order to do it, I have to open my eyes really wide and actually think about everything that I'm saying. But the problem is, I can't do this for very long—I start to feel like a contestant in the Miss America Pageant." Then she smiled real pretty: "I have the IQ of toast. My talent is eyeliner."

Another joke jabbed at the reigning First Lady. "Nancy Reagan is a strange-looking woman. I think Nancy Reagan looks like a human Pez dispenser. I think if you pulled her head back, a Pez would pop right outta her neck." Finally, she made fun of the sport most often joked about. "Golf is not a sport. Golf is men in ugly pants walking. And just to make it even more dull for the viewing audience at home, the announcers whisper—so they won't wake up the people sleeping in front of their TV sets."

One reviewer said, "Of the two, O'Donnell comes across as the more inventive and funnier." The specials were more small steps in her upward climb to the top. Of the network and the opportunity, Rosie said at the time, "It shows they're behind my work, and it's a reminder that comedy has an enormous audience today."

The fantastic growth of the audience base for comedy in the 1980s coupled with the twin explosions of cable television and comedy clubs eventually produced a glut of comedic entertainment. In 1990 you could turn on the TV and find a comedy show at almost any hour of the day or night. One reviewer at the time put it this way: "Comedy is no longer seen as relief from everyday life, a respite from the stress of workaday activity. Cable TV is turning humor into just another unavoidable part of existence, an unrelenting fact of life from which drama now beckons as a welcome alternative." Given this glut of programming, it's not surprising that the quality began to decline sharply.

Chick Perrin of the Comedy Connection shares his theory on the change. "It's just typical of Hollywood—they overkill everything. The very thing that made comedy a hit in the eighties was the thing that killed it in the nineties. We see people that I don't even know on HBO specials, and they suck. So it's just a big cycle. They always kill the golden goose."

The very economy of putting on comedy shows meant there weren't enough good comics to go around. As a result mediocre talent got pushed to the head of the line. In turn many paying customers stopped going to the clubs, especially when they could stay home and watch all the comedy they wanted on television.

The chains of clubs that thrived for a while soon suffered, because they failed to realize that each city is a comedic microcosm, and a comedian who thrives in Indianapolis could bomb in Newark or Miami. Some clubs also started "papering," or giving away free or discounted tickets just to fill the club, hoping to make it up in bar tabs. It didn't work. The clubs that survived had hands-on local management who paid close attention to whom they were booking. Jan Maxwell Smith of Igby's spoke recently about other changes: "At the height of the stand-up boom, a headliner could make between $2,500 and $3,500 a week. Now, those same people are making $1,500 to $2,000 a week, because their competition is gone and there are only a few clubs left, and they're not able to pay eighties prices."

So when Rosie, then twenty-eight, took time out in 1990 to return to Commack and attend her tenth high school reunion, she had reason to feel good about herself. A former classmate recalls the event. "She showed up, and of course she was getting a lot of attention. Everybody was really glad to see her. She's a fun, loving person. When I watch her show, it just amazes me that she's so good. She's got the talent, and she always had it."

Rosie depended less and less on the clubs—for income or visibility. Also she had turned to producing as lucrative backstage work far ahead of the upcoming wave of comics who realized that was an optional way to survive. Soon, comics were all over prime-time television—in front of the camera heading up sitcoms and behind the camera as writers and producers. Paul Barkley explains how that trend affects the clubs. "You see guys that were doing stand-up, and you ask what they're doing now, and they go, 'I just wrote for Tim Allen's new movie—I got two million for that.' Guess they're not going to come back here for two hundred dollars."

And though things were going well for Rosie at VH-1 and she continued to do *Spotlight* for several more years, she never gave up on her real dream—acting. Her next opportunity probably wasn't a premise she would have created. The Fox network offered her a costarring role in their sitcom *Stand By Your Man*. Still, it was an *acting* job, and a starring part, too. Her costar was Melissa Gilbert, the former child star of another of Rosie's childhood faves, *Little House on the Prairie*. The show was actually a rather dark comedy, presenting Rosie and Melissa as sisters, living together while their husbands did time in prison for bank robberies. Rosie's character rejoiced because her two-timing lout of a husband ended up behind bars: "I'm thrilled. Artie's in prison with a tattoo that says 'Rap Sucks.'"

It was also a fish-out-of-water premise, with Rosie as the mackerel who moved from her New Jersey trailer into sis's fancy mansion. Rosie and Melissa got jobs at a Bargain Circus discount store and hung out with an illiterate biker named Scab. Audiences didn't stand by the show for long, and after a four-month run in 1992, *Stand By Your Man* went off the air.

People magazine panned it mercilessly, citing the crass humor as one of the show's biggest problems. Referring to her lack of a social life (even though she's still married), Rosie's character quipped: "I haven't turned a man's head since I cut one on the cross-town bus." About that time, Hillary Clinton got into trouble with Tammy Wynette for appropriating her song title "Stand By Your Man" in reference to Bill's wandering eye. As *People* wrote of the sitcom, "Wait till Wynette gets a load of this. Grade D +."

Another critic griped about the casting of Melissa Gilbert as Rosie's sister. Rosie had wanted Fran Drescher to play her sister, but the network executives said they sounded too much alike. As Rosie later said of their complaint, "Hello-o-o-o, we're sisters! So they hired Melissa Gilbert—we're often mistaken for each other, me and Melissa," she added ironically.

Rosie had other problems at the time, as well. As she said in 1996 in a frank interview, she was brought to her senses about a potential problem. "When I was a young comic I used to drink a lot. All the male comics I was working with were a lot older than me. Instead of going back to the motel and be awake and afraid, I would stay and drink with the waitresses after the show and try to get sleepy."

She continued to drink until 1992, when a friend told her she drank too much and pointed out the alcoholism in her family. "I was so mad. I said, 'Are you implying that I'm an alcoholic?'" Her friend was a therapist who gently pointed out that Rosie seemed to have a problem. "So I stopped drinking totally for several years, just to show her I could. And I think it's good that I did, because if I had continued along the way that I was, I seriously feel that it would have become a problem for me."

Rosie would later joke about it. Upon meeting someone from Nova Scotia, she told her, "I have relatives there, the O'Donnell family—check the local pubs!"

What helped ease the pain of the sitcom's demise for Rosie was that she was in ever-growing demand for specials, charity gigs, and guest appearances. In 1992 she helped out on Gloria Estefan's Hurricane Relief show, which Showtime aired as a special. She also appeared on *Women Aloud,* an innovative cable program that featured female comics speaking their mind, without holding much back. It was a natural for her, and if someone else hadn't thought of the premise first, perhaps Rosie would have. She also guested as herself—always a sign you've arrived!—on *Beverly Hills 90210.* And for an even bigger thrill, she got to be a presenter at the Emmy Awards.

But what really made her feel good about herself was the premiere in 1992 of her first movie. And it was an unqualified hit.

Paul Barkley remembers having breakfast with Rosie the day before she left to begin filming *A League of Their Own.* "It was weird—we were just sitting there having a conversation and I go, 'Boy, tomorrow you go to Chicago to work with Madonna and Penny Marshall—your whole life is going to change.' And she goes, 'Yeah, I know, it's amazing.'"

And change it did.

~&7

A League of Their Own

Despite her achievements Rosie at age thirty still needed to live her biggest dream, to be in the movies. "I always wanted to be an actress," Rosie has said again and again. "Barbra Streisand was my hero, idol, god, queen. I wanted the funny roles. I wanted to be Laverne....those were my dreams as a kid." How strange to be directed in her first big movie by Laverne (Penny Marshall) herself. Success would be sweet revenge for Rosie, who had endured far too many people telling her to give up on herself, that she would never make it.

One of the great things about being an actress is that your whole life becomes relevant and useful. Every skill you ever learned, every sorrow you ever felt, every goal you ever reached, can be tapped into to build a characterization. When Rosie's agent sent her the script for *A League of Their Own,* she knew this was her really big chance. "I thought if there's one thing I could do better than Glenn Close and Meryl Streep, it's play baseball." Though girls hadn't been allowed to play Little League ball when she was a kid, Rosie still learned the game in her neighborhood. "I started playing baseball when I was five, there were twenty-three boys on my block and six girls—we almost had our own league." That experience would pay off.

Before being cast in the period film about the All-American Girls Professional Baseball League, every actress had to pass tryouts to prove she had athletic ability and the potential to come up to speed as a ballplayer. To evaluate the women, the producers hired veteran U.S.C. and Olympic coach, Rod Dedeaux. "I really have a passion against faking baseball in movies," he said, "and the producers assured me they wanted realism." Recruiting took place in Los Angeles, New York, Chicago, Toronto, and Atlanta.

Every able-bodied actress in Hollywood tried out for this movie. Lori Petty, who played Kit, the pitcher, recalled the tryout fever. "If they had just watched baseball on TV, they felt 'I can play'—because they wanted to be in the movie so badly." The tryouts were held at the University of Southern California, and coach Dedeaux and his assistants videotaped and graded each woman on hitting, running, catching, throwing. Rosie was cast to play third base. "I was the only one who could throw the ball from third to first, so I got the job."

The role of Doris Murphy was originally written much differently, but once Rosie made the team, it was rewritten. "We changed the script to make a part for her," director Penny Marshall said, speaking about Rosie. "She had a wonderful quality. And besides, she could play baseball."

Meanwhile, Madonna, who had never played baseball in her life, was also eager to land a part in the film. Real life Major Leaguer Jose Canseco was spotted leaving Madonna's apartment at 3:00 A.M. one morning. Pepper Davis, a former women's baseball star and consultant to the movie, set the record straight. "He was giving her baseball tips, but nobody believed it. She wanted to be in the movie in the worst way, so she called up Canseco....The papers made a big flap out of it." Seems that wasn't necessary after all—director Marshall was more worried about auditioning for *her.*

The real pressure for Rosie began after she was cast. Penny Marshall told her Madonna might join the club and asked her to help charm the unlikely candidate. "Be funny," Marshall urged Rosie. "If she likes you and she likes me, she'll do the movie."

Rosie remembers that just before that fateful first meeting with Madonna "I was nauseous for two hours." Rosie had recently seen *Truth or Dare,* the candid documentary film about Madonna on tour, and decided humor was the best icebreaker. In her own stand-up act, Rosie claimed that the first thing she said to Madonna was, "I have a vibrator." And that Madonna's quick response was, "Panasonic?"

Though Rosie had sought movie stardom all her adult life, when it finally seemed attainable, she was both nervous and prepared. "When I got cast in *League*, I knew something was starting. And when Madonna was cast as my best friend, I thought, 'Well, here we go.'"

No coercion was needed to sign up Tom Hanks to portray Jimmy Dugan, the coach of the Rockford Peaches. "Look, the whole reason I did this movie was because it was going to be a blast," Hanks said afterward. "Come on—play baseball all summer with a bunch of girls? Please! Help me. And get paid to do it? Fine, I'm there."

The only casting crisis came when Debra Winger, who had originally been chosen to play the lead, heard that Madonna had made the team. Reportedly, that didn't set well with the temperamental Winger and she bailed out, well into the training portion of the rehearsal period. Tracy Reiner, who played Betty Horn, recalled the challenge Winger's last-minute replacement faced. "Geena Davis had the roughest time because she didn't do the whole initial training with us...and the catcher's supposed to be the best player. She came in not being able to play, and we were months ahead of her."

Davis was up to the task, however, and worked extra-long hours to perfect the illusion that she was the star of the team. After receiving endless advice and coaching, she did eventually draw the line and posted this note: NO ONE MAY TELL GEENA HOW TO PLAY ANYMORE.

The movie is set in 1943, when the ranks of professional baseball were being depleted as the "Boys of Summer" went off to war. The story focuses on several teams in the new Women's League and the difficult transitions the players make as they leave behind families and jobs for the uncertain world of professional baseball. Each team was a melting pot of women from all over the country and from varied social and economic backgrounds. The clashes that ensued fueled the story of their first season living and traveling together.

The actual women who were brave enough to buck tradition and play in the new league were true protofeminists, an aspect of the film that appealed to Rosie and Madonna. Those pioneers performed with considerable zeal and spirit and proved that women could be just as tough as their male counterparts. In sports, as in many areas, the early contributions of women have often been forgotten or marginalized. Most people had never heard of this league until the movie came out.

A highlight of the process for Rosie was meeting Faye Dancer, one of the ballplayers who inspired her character. Early on, Penny invited the actresses and many of the original players to her home for an informal session of sharing experiences. Rosie loved looking through their old scrapbooks. "Faye is a tough, spry woman in her early seventies, and she shared wonderful anecdotes with me. She's a great lady—I love her."

Since many of the original players were on the set as consultants and extras, it became really important to all the cast members to live up to their reputation. Director Marshall said, "I know that our actresses were trying their damnedest to *be* their idols—who were the original league players."

That meant grueling practices that nearly stopped the film before it got started. One of the coaches said that the toughest thing to teach was convincing arm action. Tom Hanks laughs when he recalls that particular challenge. "A lot of them *still* threw like girls." Pepper Davis gave credit to some of them, however. "You had some darn good ballplayers out there: Robin Knight, Freddie Simpson, and Rosie O'Donnell." Coach Bill Hughes said of Madonna (who had to be shown on which hand to wear her glove): "She had a burning desire to excel at the job. Nobody, *nobody*, works like she does. Wore me out."

Rosie was amazed at how much one little tip from a pro could improve her game. "I was in batting practice, and I'm hitting away, and Pepper said to me, 'Move your right foot…point it up.' So I move my right foot, honestly, an inch forward. Oh my God—boom! You know? And Pepper just nodded and walked away."

There was no acting when it came to the injury list. In fact, all of the bruises seen in the film are real; no makeup artist was required. Learning how to slide into a base proved to be too much for most of the women. That and the authentic vintage equipment they used, such as the shoes with the huge metal spikes.

Tom Hanks remembers one day on the set in particular: "There was a slip 'n' slide concussion day." One after another, the actresses went down with concussions, whiplash, abrasions, gashes and stitches, broken noses, and sprained ankles. At one point the imprint of a baseball was visible on Geena Davis's arm. The one person who had no trouble learning to slide was Madonna. She was fearless. She did all her own sliding in the film and mastered the technique of sliding headfirst with seeming ease. Geena Davis declined to do any sliding and so was especially impressed with her. "It's pretty fun [sic] that you can see it's really Madonna doing it."

Rosie has said what she enjoys most about making movies is the collaboration: "It becomes a big family." And some family members get to play two roles. It seems that Penny decided one day she needed someone to play Rosie's father, and sizing up the various people on the set, she spotted Eddie Quin, the key grip. Because he looked and sounded a bit like Rosie, he was chosen. Penny simply told him: "Go over there by the bus and do something funny—hurry up, it's getting cloudy." And so a bit part is born.

Geena Davis also had a sense of family and had only good things to say about her experience: "I found it an incredibly bonding experience. I think adversity breeds bonding." The adversity included being away from home for a long time, in really hot, humid weather, as well as the physical demands of their roles. "We all really got along together and supported one another....Women are good at that kind of thing," Geena believes.

Still, all families have their feuds, and this one was no exception. Rosie, as usual, tells it like it was. "It's hard to avoid the petty fights, and they definitely occurred. And anyone who tells you they didn't is lying." She went on to say how insecure most actresses are, herself included. "There were little cliques that formed and unformed.... *This* one was mad at *that* one because she didn't get invited to the slumber party. We all reverted to our adolescence, because we were locked together for twenty-two weeks, working six days a week."

What she alluded to was her instant bond and friendship with Madonna, which inspired some envy among the other cast members. Also, only the big stars (Geena, Tom, and Madonna) lived in splendor in large secluded homes during the three months they endured Evansville, Indiana, in the summer of 1991. The rest of the cast had to scramble to find short-term rentals. It's safe to say Madonna won't be welcomed back to Evansville anytime soon, since she told *TV Guide* that living there was like being stuck in Prague. The house she was living in *didn't get MTV.*

Rosie, on the other hand, was in pig heaven. "My whole life I've been on the road, which is why I loved Evansville," she explained. "There was a movie theater, a mall, and a McDonald's. That's all I need to be happy." Besides, she had her new best friend to hang with. "We'd see every movie at the multiplex. We even paid to see *Cool As Ice,* so that tells you how the summer was." Lori Petty remembers going out every Saturday night, no matter how tired they were. "There were a couple of dance bars that we would go to and just dance and dance and dance and kind of let all of that out."

Tom Hanks elaborated on their hangouts. "There was one gay bar that, uh, became a hangout for the, uh—you know, Madonna found it." Leave it to Madonna to find the most interesting place in town. An extra on the film recalls another caper that made the local papers. "Some drunken farmers kind of let themselves into Tom Hanks's house and persuaded him to go on a hayride. He didn't make much of a fuss, but he did have guards at his house the next day."

Rosie remembers that shortly after they met, Madonna invited her to take an advance peek at some of the pictures for her infamous *Sex* book. "She brought out some photos, and I remember thinking, Whoaaaa! I told her, 'Yeah, those are your breasts and that's you naked, all right,' but she was talking about them as casually as I might talk about snapshots of my family at Thanksgiving." What came next, really threw her—Madonna invited her to be in the book, too. "Right, I'm going to be pages forty-eight and forty-nine," Rosie said sarcastically. If it was a test to measure how flappable she was, Rosie must have passed, because their bond continued to deepen.

Though their friendship is now legendary, it began because of the painful uncommon experience they share. During their first meeting, Rosie said to Madonna, "My mother died when I was ten, and I totally understand what motivates you." Madonna, who also lost her mother to cancer as a young girl, says of her friend, "Rosie and I speak the language of hurt people. She is very protective, loyal, and maternal with me." In June 1996, Rosie said of her friend, "We have a sisterlike relationship that has continued to this day."

For Rosie, making the movie was a terrific experience. After all, she loves baseball, though it must have been frustrating to play with so many women who were really just learning how. Despite her great desire to be in the movie, Madonna was not such a happy camper once she made it to the set. In a 1993 interview, she asked Rosie which she would rather do—make another baseball movie with an all-female cast or have her teeth drilled. Rosie's choice was not surprising: "I would say make another female baseball movie, because I was hoping there would be a sequel." Madonna was willing—if it was shot someplace else and was *not* about baseball. Rosie reminded her, "If we didn't do that movie, we never would've become friends." Madonna finally agreed with her. "Meeting you was the best thing about doing that movie."

One of the things that upset almost everybody was Penny Marshall's directing style. She had a very naive concept of how this movie could be shot. She believed that if the scene called for the pitcher to pitch one ball, then a strike, then one that could be fouled left, and finally one the batter could get a line drive off of, then her cast ought to be able to do all that, in that order, time and time again so she could get her master shot. Tom Hanks knew she was dreaming. "It's not going to *happen!* It was just ludicrous amounts of fun."

This approach was clearly impossible, though one time, luck was on their side. Geena remembers one day when the light was fading fast, she was up to bat and not clear about what she was supposed to be doing. Between her mumbling and her thick New York accent, Penny is hard enough to understand under the best circumstances, but when she yelled at the cast through a megaphone it was nearly impossible. Geena remembers hearing Penny shout "—the ball!" And she's thinking, do *what* to the ball?

"The camera started rolling.... I'm just hoping I hit something—and I hit a very decent line drive toward second base." Pleased with herself, she threw down her bat and tore off toward first base, when she noticed a lot of commotion over at second base. "And I'm thinking, 'Oh, my God, have I hit her?' Anyway, they say 'Cut!' and everybody's congratulating me." Turns out the script called for her to hit a line drive to second and hit the second baseman in the head. Geena finished the story: "Unbeknownst to me, I had done the absolute perfect thing. I thought, 'Man, I am a genius!'"

Rosie remembers the endless retakes. "It was 'Do it over, do it over.' A million takes. On the whole, ninety-nine percent of it was 'Get this specific play, get this hit, get this reaction, get this throw.'" Geena divulged how they finally simulated her all-important homeruns. She would take a slug at the ball, then Penny would film her reacting like she'd hit a homer, when in reality there were two beefy crew members behind her with a giant slingshot they used to shoot a ball over the fence.

Tom Hanks remembers that a whole lot of footage was shot each day. "They'd say, 'Penny, there's two and a half hours of dailies tonight,' and she'd groan and roll her eyes." Rosie remembers it that way, too, "Penny would be, 'Why did I say I would do this film?' She would say it all the time."

Increasingly desperate to get the shots she needed, Marshall resorted to all kinds of ploys, as Rosie recalled: "Penny would just turn the camera on me and say, 'Rosie, go over there and do something funny.' Well Penny, what do you want me to say? 'I don't care, do anything.' Then she would ask for some pork. She's a lovely woman, but she eats bacon all day."

Another day, frustrated with how difficult it was to get the shots she wanted, Penny had the bright idea to just let the cast play a real baseball game and she would simply film it and use whatever footage she could. Not a bad strategy if she was working with real ballplayers. But she was not. Geena recalled that on that day Penny got really mad. "None of the actor-pitchers could get the ball over the plate (they did stand the regulation sixty feet away), and if they had, none of the actor-batters could have hit them. So people were just throwing balls endlessly for hours and hours, and Penny's yelling, 'Hit the damn ball!'"

One way all the cast members relieved the growing tension and frustration on the set was to entertain the extras between takes. With 5,000 extras in the stands, they had a captive audience. Penny encouraged her actors to do this because she needed the extras to keep coming back day after 106 degree day—and sometimes stay all night. As one extra recalls, "One night we worked really, really late and everybody was dragging. So Penny picked up a megaphone and started cracking jokes." Not only that, the extras were required to dress as if it was autumn. One extra remembers "Rosie spraying Madonna with a hose because she was bitching about how hot it was." It was probably the wackiest show in the country at the time. As the experienced stand-up comedian of the bunch, it fell to Rosie to be the ringmaster of these impromptu performances. For a sure crowd pleaser, Rosie liked to belt out her version of Madonna's hit, "Like a Virgin." When she was done, the diva herself would blast out of the dugout and wrestle Rosie to the ground.

As her fans know, Rosie's repertoire is endless. "They'd hand me the mike, so for thirty minutes I'd sing the *Brady Bunch* theme and do stand-up, then I'd introduce Tom and he'd do some bit, then I'd get Madonna out there. Everyone participated." When the mercury soared, hose fights really amused the crowds. Geena Davis got into the act, too. "We'd do goofy stuff. My favorite thing to do was sing 'Bohemian Rhapsody.'...Rosie knew the words, so we would sing this at the top of our lungs, and now it's like this gigantic hit." Tom Hanks enjoyed the puppet shows over the dugout walls and the bat-balancing contests. The funniest stunt had to be when the cast spelled out "Evansville" with their bodies.

But no one took the auxiliary entertaining more seriously than Geena. It must have been the heat. What else could explain her obsession with putting on the musical, *Jesus Christ Superstar?* Actually, her idea was *Jesus Christ Superstar Goes Hawaiian.* Geena admits she was over the edge from the tension on the set. "Every morning in the makeup trailer I made everybody practice and I cast everybody in parts."

Tom Hanks also had a particularly good time at the training table. "I got really fat....I got to know the craft service guys very well. They had a great spread, too, I might add." Rosie concurred. Although Penny had wanted her to lose twenty pounds for the film, she thinks she actually gained weight during the shoot. "Not on purpose. It's just craft services, you know? There's like an eighty-foot table with every kind of carbohydrate they can find...from 5:30 A.M. until you go home at 10:00 P.M., complete with hot dogs and sandwiches and donuts and Twizzlers and Pop Tarts— need I go on?"

Actually, Rosie had different intentions when she started the movie. "I had fantasies at the beginning of the film that by the time we wrapped I'd be a lean, mean fighting machine, one hundred twenty pounds of sinewy muscle. However, that didn't occur." When asked how she liked working with fellow chowhound Hanks, she replied, "He is the best. Very family oriented, professional, and prepared; the crew loves him—that's always a good way to tell who is okay."

Rosie's first scene in the film was an especially funny one. She is busy showing off her bat balancing when sisters Geena and Lori meet pals Rosie and Madonna at the League tryouts. They discuss their odds of making the team, as there are clearly lots of hopefuls there.

MADONNA [*acting really tough*]: "Some a youse are gonna have to go home."

LORI [*playing defense*]: "Whadya mean some of *us?*"

MADONNA [*whispering to Rosie*]: "Do it."

[*Rosie, obeying her command, whips around and pitches a fastball as hard as she can, point blank at Geena, leading the viewer to expect a black eye at best. Instead, Geena is cool as a major league catcher, and nabs the ball barehanded without flinching.*]

Rosie did get some of the big laughs in the film. When the women were being shown their new uniforms for the first time, most were dismayed to realize they were expected to play baseball in dresses. Very short wool dresses that were quite shocking in the 1940s. Then Rosie quips, "Whadya think we are—ballplayers or ballerinas?"

Another scene had all the "girls" getting makeovers and going through charm school. It seems there were too many tomboys on the team. Though she played a brash, former roadhouse bouncer, Rosie did have one of the sweetest scenes in the movie. On the team bus, she spoke about her past and how she wasn't treated like other girls, because she could play baseball well. They made her feel "wrong and weird and strange—or not even a girl, just 'cause I could play. I believed them, too, but not anymore. I mean, look at us—there's a lot of us, and I think we're all right." She then tears up the photo of her lout of a boyfriend back home and throws it out the window in a wonderful moment of liberation.

At one point, the team decides to do their part to attract bigger crowds by performing crazy stunts during the game. Madonna suggests that maybe she could "accidentally" let her bosoms fly out of her uniform, to which Rosie replies, in a classic case of art imitating life, "You think there's a man in this country that hasn't seen your bosoms?" Geena does the splits as she catches a fly ball; Madonna makes a catch in her hat; and funniest of all, Rosie dives into the stands to catch a foul ball and comes up with a hot dog in her mouth—*and* the ball in her mitt (which only took ten takes to get!). Doris Murphy was an in-your-face kind of player and would have won the award for most team spirit (and Rosie's portrayal of her might hint at why she was voted Most School Spirited in high school). Years later, Rosie revealed that clever editing went a long way toward making the actresses look good. "I'd catch the balls for everyone, and they'd edit it in."

In the summer of 1992 premieres were held for *A League of Their Own* in New York and Los Angeles. Rosie and Madonna attended the New York bash together, which was held at Tavern on the Green in Central Park. Party crashers crept under the tent and helped themselves to food, drink, and party favors and had to be ejected by eagle-eyed publicists. When asked at the party how she had liked making the film, Rosie replied, "The amount of practice we had to do was not fun for me. I'd rather lounge around watching Oprah Winfrey than have to do laps around a field in hundred-degree heat." At the L.A. premiere party, director Marshall recalled over hot dogs and fries, that her job was toughest "during the women's cycle. *Everyone* got a little testy at the same time." As this was Rosie's first premiere party as an actor, she was thrilled to stargaze at all the celebrities in attendance. "I'm a big groupie," she said at the time. "I'm a fan of all these people.... Christine Lahti was at the premiere, and I was like, 'Oh, God.' I'm a huge fan of Christine Lahti."

Many of the fans who stayed for the closing credits had to get out their Kleenex. Original members of the real league were shown playing a reunion game at the Hall of Fame ballfield at Cooperstown. One reason this movie did so well, grossing over $107 million domestically, and touched so many people was that many women in their mid-thirties and beyond never got the chance to play team sports in school and missed out on all those female bonding experiences. Rosie was lucky that she did have opportunities to play sports growing up.

As she hit the road to plug one of the most eagerly anticipated movies of that summer—and at $50 million, the most expensive baseball movie ever made—her publicist warned Rosie that during interviews "you can't tell those people *the truth.*" Not advice Rosie is ever apt to take. Rosie remembers her infamous appearance on *The Arsenio Hall Show* with Madonna in tow. For Rosie, who was also a TV veteran by then, it wasn't all that different than doing stand-up, so she wasn't too nervous about it. Madonna, however, had an attack of nerves backstage waiting to go on. Pal Rosie tried to calm her down: "So I go, 'Why are you nervous? These people slept on the concrete outside to see you.' But you know what? This wasn't her venue. If I had to go out there and sing 'Don't Cry for Me, Argentina,' I'd be shaking, too."

The film opened to big box office takes, but mixed reaction. The review from Canadian magazine *Maclean's* was typical: "The result is a long, well-spanked fly ball of a movie that shows promise, but drifts foul." Roger Ebert stuck his thumb up with an insightful review in the *Chicago Sun-Times.* He said the film "has a fair assortment of stock characters...but it has another level that's a lot more interesting." He found its look at an early chapter of women's liberation to be refreshing and said the movie has "a real bittersweet charm." Even though Geena Davis's character, Dottie, is the best player in the league, her true allegiance is to her husband. And though she clearly lights up and comes alive when she's playing ball, when her husband returns from the war, she quickly leaves baseball. Ebert believes this interesting ambiguity about women's roles in that era is probably in the movie thanks to Penny Marshall. A male director "might have assumed that these women knew how all-important baseball was." Ebert went on to say that "Marshall shows her women characters in a tug-of-war between new images and old values, and so her movie is about transition—about how it felt as a woman suddenly to have new roles and freedom."

The film received a rather glowing review from *Sports Illustrated.* Despite what Tom Hanks said about the throwing prowess of the cast, *SI* thought they were great. "Nobody in *A League of Their Own* throws like a girl. In fact, everybody throws better than John Goodman did in *The Babe.*" They go on to rave about Geena Davis being a natural baseball talent, and then have this to say about others in the cast: "Madonna, as centerfielder 'All the Way' Mae Mordabito, and Rosie O'Donnell, as her third baseman sidekick, keep the team and the movie, loose." The writer for *SI* thought the film did get bogged down when it aimed for sentimentality. While he thought the movie "says something nice about sisterhood, both in the relationship between Dottie and Kit and in the larger sense of the team," he also cringed at the reunion scenes that bookend the movie. There seemed to be a gender split on that issue. Most women loved that part of the film, while male reviewers were often repelled by that sincere display of emotion. *SI* summed up the film in baseball lingo: "Doesn't quite go the distance but gets credit for a victory."

Rosie generally earned good notices for her part. One reviewer said, "As Madonna's foil in *A League of Their Own,* O'Donnell nearly stole the show." *Us* magazine said Rosie "captured the attention of casting directors by proving herself to be an adept ensemble player, someone who always knew when it was right to blend in and when it was time to mug."

The film's impact on women proved enormous. Four years after its release, the movie is still a hot topic on Rosie's America Online message boards. Fans fill folder after folder with comments. From a woman in Arizona, "I have watched this movie twenty times and still cry at the ending." Another woman writes: "This movie depicts only what I have dreamed about. As a child growing up my dream was to be the first girl Phillies player."

All in all, the film made money, the stars got good reviews, the audiences were treated to a palatable helping of sports history, and Penny Marshall made her point about women pioneers.

Rosie came away with a huge hit for her first film, and two close friendships that continue to this day. In addition to bonding with Madonna,

Rosie connected strongly with Marshall. She often jokes that her job is to "interpret" for Penny, whose monotone delivery can be difficult to decipher. The two friends went on to exploit their personaes in a series of wonderfully wry television commercials for K-Mart. In 1996, as a guest on the second installment of Rosie's new talk show, Penny revealed how the spots came into being. "They called me and said you would do it if I would do it." Rosie added, "And they called me and said that you would do it if I would do it." Penny had the last words: "So we're stupid. We're doin' it!"

Even people who mute commercials or channel surf during them stop to enjoy these gems that are often better than the programs they interrupt, most likely because Rosie had a hand in writing them. Rosie also loves to tease Penny on her show about her greedy shopping sprees every time they tape a new batch of commercials. "We're ready to shoot—where's Penny? Oh, she's in Housewares." According to Rosie, Penny brings a flock of assistants and carts off piles of stuff, worth about ten grand. But mostly, Marshall finds the process enjoyable because of Rosie. "I love anyone who can improv, and Rosie can improv. Plus she understands my mumbling, so she's a friend for life."

League cohort Tom Hanks also appeared on Rosie's show to plug his first directorial effort, *That Thing You Do!* Of course they reminisced about the fun they had shooting *League.* Tom started off by surprising her with "my favorite moment" from the film, which showed Rosie stumbling and falling as she ran onto the field (she tripped over a microphone cord, she claims). He showed it several times, even in slow motion, teasing her mercilessly. Rosie had a belly laugh at her own expense and remembered that "Penny wanted to kill me. 'You ruined the whole ta-a-ke,'" she mimicked in her perfect Penny impression. Rosie got revenge by showing a clip of Tom in drag in his infamous TV series, *Bosom Buddies.* It was clear that the two stars are good friends, especially united by Rosie's close friendship with Tom's wife, Rita Wilson.

Later, Tom told how the men on the set were awed at working at Wrigley Field. Rosie made it clear that she was not among that group. "All the men were running around like 'I can't believe it,' picking up dirt—and all the women were [she whines] 'When do we go back in the studio?'" Tom recreated the excitement of the experience in his telling of it. "Men were weeping.... [he cries mock tears] I'm standing right next to the ivy in Wrigley Field." Whereas Rosie wanted to know, "When's lunch?"

Tom later revealed that as a youngster he was just as much of a TV freak as Rosie. He proved it by singing the theme song from *Underdog,* one that even Rosie didn't know. Then they launched into a duet of the theme from *Super Chicken.* When Tom was able to finish the entire song on his own, Rosie passed her crown to him, "You are the King of Useless Crap."

Another *League* costar who appeared on her show was Geena Davis. Geena had been scheduled the previous week, when a fire at Rockefeller Center shut down taping for a few days. Though she had a two-week Hawaiian vacation planned with her husband, Geena graciously waited around New York another four days. She told her host, "Nothing's too big a sacrifice for you, Rosie."

These two also shared amusing memories about making the picture together, but Rosie revealed how much she really learned from Geena on that film. Rosie told how she spent a lot of time observing the acclaimed star, who at that time was fresh from her success in *Thelma and Louise.* "I think to myself the first day, she's not even acting—she's like doin' nothing. That girl has to *act* a little bit more."

Rosie even amused herself, recalling how little she knew about acting at the time. "I didn't want to say anything, being that you have the Oscar and everything. Then I saw the movie [*A League of Their Own*]—and I went, 'Wow! News flash! That's how you do it.'" Referring to her own performance in the film Rosie said, "I was a little bit over the top....I was Stallone." Geena graciously assured her that she had been just perfect in the part.

On an earlier taping of her talk show, Rosie featured some of the original players from the All-American Girls Professional Baseball League. Known as "Pickles" and "Pepper," who were advisers on the film, they helped Rosie demonstrate a trick she learned while making the movie: pitching two baseballs at once. Rosie said of the film: "I think it really pays tribute to these women, and for that alone I'm very proud of the movie." Rosie also said this was her favorite movie that she's been in "because I love to play baseball and I got to play every day, and I think it's the best movie I've been in."

Rosie was now on a trajectory to her own stardom.

❧ 8

Best Friend Madonna

Who better than Madonna to tutor Rosie on the highs and lows of fame? In some ways, her friendship with Madonna mirrors the roles Rosie so often plays: that of best friend and confidante to the more glamorous leading lady. "I think I'm just very best friend-ish. I think everybody thinks I'm the kind of girl they'd like to go have a beer with. Madonna provokes people in every way, forces them to look at who they are and what they're about and their sexuality and their feelings about interracial things. That's her essence— she's provocative. I'm really not. It's hard to know what your own appeal is. I think it's relatability, if I was to sum it up in a word."

In the stratosphere where Madonna dwells, it can be enormously valuable to have a real friend who can always be counted on to give you honest feedback. Publicists and agents and managers don't like to slap the goose that lays their platinum eggs. But Rosie has never been one to mince words. Rosie sometimes serves as a reality check for superstar Madonna, as she explained in this anecdote. "On the set of *League,* Madonna had this boom box. Somebody threw a ball at it, and she goes, 'Hey! You break that, and you're buying me a new one.' I said, Madonna, you have more money than most third world countries."

After they finished making *A League of Their Own* their bonding continued in the shopping malls of America. "She doesn't like the way I dress," Rosie said in 1992. "She says I'm a Gap outlet reject—and it's true. I'm a nerd. What can I say?" Wardrobe is probably one area where they should go their separate ways. It seems doubtful that they'll ever be the kind of girlfriends who swap clothes.

Madonna explains their relationship this way: "My friendship with Rosie has nothing to do with image. I cannot explain the mystery of what happens when you become best friends with someone. I can only say that we are tortured by the same things, we laugh at the same things, and I love her madly!"

Even after *League* came out, Rosie still did some stand-up gigs, and one night when she was performing at Igby's in Los Angeles, Madonna decided to catch her set. The owner of the club, Jan Maxwell Smith, recalled how intensely Rosie guarded her friend's privacy. "She said, 'Make sure no one knows that Madonna's going to be here. Put her in the back!' Then when she came to the door, I didn't even recognize her, she was so dressed down, without makeup."

Madonna was also sensitive to the situation and didn't want to distract the audience from Rosie's spotlight, so she slipped in after the set began and left before it was over. That, of course, is the downside to fame—losing anonymity and the ability to live spontaneously, without your antics ending up in the tabloids.

Knowing the most famous woman in the world has helped O'Donnell keep her feet on the ground as her own fame has increased. (They were each other's date to Oscars one year.) Rosie explained, "Before I met her, I saw [the film documentary about Madonna] *Truth or Dare* and related so much to what I saw. I related to the family stuff and the Catholic stuff. That was the initial connection between us."

Madonna provides a different kind of reality check for Rosie. "Since meeting people like Madonna and Bette Midler, I know they're real," Rosie said. "If you're going to use stars to mentor you, just know it's an illusion. Who they really are is not what it's about—it's how their work affects you. I know that now."

One very unusual aspect of Rosie's friendship with Madonna is that being a sizable woman who can wield a fist if she needs to, Rosie sometimes plays bodyguard when they are out in public. In a dual interview, Madonna once asked Rosie what she liked best about working with her, and she replied, laughing, "I would say my initiation into the Bodyguards of America Society."

Rosie leaps to defend her friend in other ways, as well. In 1994 she gave this response to criticism of Madonna in the press: "She is much kinder in person than she ever lets the press know." More recently, Rosie talked about how their friendship has helped her understand the influence of the press on the lives of celebrities. "Coming to know and love Madonna as a human being brought me to a different awareness of what that kind of media image does to someone. She is not the persona we see and hear. She's more vulnerable than that."

By 1996, the new Maternal Girl had mellowed a bit, and Rosie was relieved that she was adopting a kinder gentler public persona. "After the Letterman thing, when she said "fuck" a thousand times, she stopped acting like that. And I say to her all the time, 'It's so nice to not have to apologize for being your friend anymore,' because she's been letting her real self be seen. She's really a wonderful person, and I have a tremendous amount of respect for her."

Rosie chose a food analogy to describe their different images. "Madonna is some exotic food, and I'm just a peanut butter and jelly sandwich." Madonna says they do have plenty in common. "We both have a longing for strong female role models. We like to be the center of attention and make people laugh. We both like to sing, though obviously my voice is more mainstream than hers. Our personal lives are a mess. And we both love candy." Friends can teach you things you may not have learned, but should have. Madonna once told Rosie, "I learned to share my candy with you.... It was a breakthrough moment." A love of music is another important connection between them. When asked in 1996 if she was ever going to record a duet with Madonna, Rosie replied, "I'd love to, but she wouldn't let me. I love to sing, but I'm not a good singer."

Having Madonna for your great friend and making no secret about it, inevitably led to a few comic references in Rosie's act. Good friends usually do not keep much from each other, and these two are no exception. When asked during her stand-up act if she had ever seen Madonna naked, Rosie replied, "I have seen her naked. Yes. In fact, probably everyone who knows her has seen her naked. Strangers have seen her naked! Probably three people at this bar have seen her naked! If I had a body like that, I'd probably be naked most of the time, too."

Before long, there would be dramatic changes in both their lives that would bring them even closer together, to their memories of their mothers, to their own centers.

⭓ 9

Sleepless in Seattle

Although Rosie's performance in *A League of Their Own* was well received, she was worried about being typecast as a loud-mouthed tomboy. She has made ten more movies and has yet to play another tomboy. Loud-mouthed, perhaps, but no other character has been a clone of Doris Murphy. In fact, Rosie has stepped into a whole lot of different shoes since she hung up her cleats. She's portrayed everything from a prehistoric housewife to an undercover cop; from a newspaper editor to a nun; from a nanny to an assistant district attorney. What is consistent in most of these characterizations is a no-nonsense approach, and at times, that in-your-face, don't-give-me-any-crap attitude.

Many writers have tried to pigeonhole her as the prototypical best friend, a designation she doesn't mind at all. She calls it the "sassy best friend with a heart of gold." Another time she called it the "second banana who's got all the funny lines, the Eve Arden role." She points out that she's played best friend to some fairly awsome women. "In my first movie, I'm best friends with Madonna; my second movie, I'm best friends with Meg Ryan. That's not a bad career right there." She's become adept at spotting it in any script she's given. "I'm not insulted....I have no aspirations to do Shakespeare. This is exactly what I'm equipped to do and what I like to do. Kathy Bates should do Kathy Bates, and I should do the Rosie O'Donnell roles, which are the kind of shticky comedy, Bette Midler-ish sort of things."

Friends in high places, such as actress Kate (Mrs. Steven Spielberg)

Capshaw, said in 1996 that when she thinks of casting Rosie, she imagines the kind of roles that Shelley Winters did in the 1950s. "They both have that strength of body and face, yet you always feel that bareness, that fragility underneath," Capshaw said. Perhaps those kind of roles, that demand much baring of the soul to play, are parts that Rosie could grow into as she matures and develops more faith in her acting range.

So far, she has shown no aspirations in that direction. Part of the problem may lie in Rosie's increasing fame. When asked what she dislikes most about fame, she replied, "Losing the ability to watch people and develop characters from that. Now people watch me. I am no longer anonymous, and that's tough." Rosie said in 1994 that she wouldn't turn down a leading role if it was right for her, "but I'm not aspiring to take Meryl Streep's roles. The people I relate to are like Vivian Vance. That's Betty Rubble. I see myself as Rhoda, not Mary Tyler Moore."

When asked if the transition from stand-up comedy to films was difficult, she replied, "Kinda, but I was lucky to work with great people who helped me—Geena Davis, Tom Hanks, Penny Marshall." Though comedy was a route into show business, it was never the destination. "I never wanted to be a stand-up," she said in 1994. "I didn't idolize Joan Rivers. The people I idolized were Barbra Streisand, Bette Midler, Carol Burnett— women who performed as well as did comedy. To be a monologist really bored me. To say, 'Did you ever notice this?' as opposed to *becoming* the person who noticed it. My goal was not to be Johnny Carson but to be Carol Burnett."

When it comes to the craft of acting, she has confessed that she has no secrets. "I hate to say this, because I think real actors are going to be miffed, but I don't really prepare. I read the script and think who the character is to me." Then again, she hasn't been given roles that required her to stretch too much beyond her emotional experience. "My movies have been funny and light and little pops, with well-written and well-defined characters. I haven't had to delve into who I think the person really is."

This is what she likes about acting: "The best part is creative fulfillment and tons of cash and fun, fun, fun. The worst part is always worrying if you will ever work again."

Jeff Arch, the writer who came up with the first script for Rosie's next film, *Sleepless in Seattle,* recalls pitching the first draft without success. The plot has the young son of a widower (Tom Hanks) trying to find a new wife for his father. The woman the boy selects (Meg Ryan) does not even meet them until the final scene of the movie. One producer said, "I love foreplay, but I can't handle ninety minutes of it. Nobody's going to make this movie." Arch recalls, "All I knew when I thought of this thing is that if I got these people to the top of the Empire State Building on Valentine's Day, somehow I'd have a hit." Four rewrites and three writers later, Nora Ephron was tapped to direct her own final rewrite. By then the property had evolved from one that nearly everyone had turned down to one that everyone wanted to produce. Arch describes the final product as "Body by Arch, Fashions by Ephron."

Nora Ephron remembers Rosie's audition very clearly. "I had never heard of her. I'm unbelievably embarrassed to say that I did not know who she was. She was supposed to stay for ten minutes, and almost an hour later we were still there. The script was in the process of becoming, and after she finished reading what was there, and I went and printed out more that was in the computer, she started talking about her life and her family—it's all right there, amazing."

Later that day Nora said to her children at dinner, "I saw this woman, I don't know if you've heard of her, she's on VH-1. And they looked at me like, 'You're even older and more washed-up than we've dreamed,' and that was it." Rosie gives the kids all the credit for her casting. "The reason I'm in this movie is because of Nora's thirteen-year-old son, who told her 'She's funny, Mom, you should cast her.'"

In *Sleepless in Seattle* Rosie plays a newspaper editor at the *Baltimore Sun* and Meg Ryan's boss—and looks so professional in a great wardrobe and a wavy hairdo. Since director Ephron had herself been a journalist, "she had a clear idea of what she wanted," Rosie recalls, "and I just did what she said."

Nora's sister, Delia Ephron, who also worked on the picture, called Nora "the bossiest person on the planet," when she stopped by Rosie's show to promote her novel. Rosie had to agree with her. They laughed about how Nora's directorial personality is far reaching. Rosie remembers the many dinners they had while filming *Sleepless,* and how Nora always ordered for everybody.

The reviewer for the *Los Angles Times* said Rosie was "so deadpan she was beyond droll." Rosie explained why. "Nora kept saying, 'Bring it down, bring it down.'" She had also learned a lot from *A League of Their Own,* and was concerned about coming off too big and loud. "I tried to remember how Geena Davis brought everything down and internalized everything. That's really what I tried to do in this film, because there was no room for that sort of bigness."

All that underplaying did not come naturally. Nora also coached her about her thick New York accent, telling her that her character "graduated with a master's from the Columbia School of Journalism, [so] you don't speak like you're from the street." Rosie was grateful for the guidance. "She really helped me. I noticed in my stand-up act my accent is much thicker. It's not on purpose, it's out of nerves. When I get nervous it becomes much more Fonzie and Sylvester Stallone-ish. Nora wouldn't let that happen, for which I'm glad."

Writer Arch took some of his inspiration from the fifties weeper *An Affair to Remember* and even uses the actual movie as a plot device. What critic Roger Ebert calls the characters' "romantic compass." Rosie and Meg Ryan are cocooning with a bowl of popcorn and yet another viewing of their favorite movie, and they agree that "men never get this movie." Rosie's character affirms her belief in romantic fate with this speech: "You want to hear about destiny? If I hadn't married Martin, I never would have bought the house with the dead tree—on account of which I got divorced—on account of which I hit a car—and met Rick while buying a neck brace." The truth is, the two actresses had a hard time identifying with it, as they both found the old film outdated.

"We would be hysterical laughing at the film," Rosie recalls. "It was ridiculous. If I had seen it when I was younger and more impressionable and not quite so cynical, I probably would have been moved. But being thirty when I saw it, it didn't get me."

Another plot point that Rosie disagreed with was the quick recovery of Tom Hanks's son from the death of his mother. "When I read the script, I went, 'Well, this is a movie,'" she laughed. "Because this isn't how it really happens—having been in that situation. *Sleepless in Seattle* is how you wished it would have been, not how it actually was."

The boy is the catalyst for the plot, calling a radio talk show seeking a new wife for his dad. This leads to a national letter-writing campaign, joined by Meg. Unbeknownst to her, the letter she receives in reply was written by the son, not the father, and is rather lacking in literary flair. But as Rosie says to appease her, "So he can't write—big deal! Verbal ability is a highly overrated thing in a guy, and our pathetic need for it is what gets us in trouble."

Meg Ryan has spoken about the fun they had filming together. Apparently Rosie never stopped doing her comedy routines, she just had a different venue—and a captive audience. "Whenever I saw that I'd be working with Rosie that day I knew I'd be having a blast and that my stomach would cramp because I'd be laughing so hard," Ryan said later. "Rosie is so amazingly quick, and I had so much fun, and I'm so happy to know her." A pattern was forming: on-screen pals becoming off-screen pals.

As the reviewer for the *Washington Post* wrote, "I think a lot of people will fall hard for this movie....Actually, this is what this movie is about: Should we follow our hearts or our heads? Heed our passions or be sensible? The movie seems to urge that we not settle for less but, instead, give in to romance and open our lives to chance encounters and magic."

Roger Ebert wrote in the *Chicago Sun-Times* that "*Sleepless in Seattle* is as ephemeral as a talk show, as contrived as the late show, and yet so warm and gentle I smiled the whole way through." Though the reviews were mixed overall, Rosie generally received good notices for her part. The *Washington Post* said Becky was "sharply played by O'Donnell" and that "everyone around Ryan is much better developed, particularly O'Donnell, whose sweet-tart persona really registers in the role of Becky." Long Island's *Newsday* said of the movie: "The bell-ringing, sweaty-palmed, heart-pounding, can't-live-without-you love Ephron is aiming for is such a universal dream that even the suggestion of it goes a long way." And of Rosie they wrote that "she has the bulk of the best one-liners, and her performance is a joy." *Time* magazine dubbed Rosie "charming."

The lovefest continued, when director Ephron said of Rosie in an interview: "When you meet her you want her to be your friend. She's genuinely decent and funny and good and incapable of doing anything false." In 1994, Rosie was asked: who's the nicest person you have met in show business? Her reply: "The nicest person is Meg Ryan."

Ultimately, it is the audiences who vote at the box office. *Sleepless in Seattle* scooped up $17 million during its first weekend, and went on to gross over $126 million domestic and $65 million in rentals. The head of TriStar Pictures said, "This is a film with absolutely no violence and no strong language. People say they are clamoring for this kind of movie, and this just shows that if you put it out there, they will come." Though the film has no surprises—it is predictable every step of the way—audiences still exit the theaters smiling *and* grasping their hankies. And Rosie received her first nomination for an *acting* award, an American Comedy Award, for her second movie.

While making *Sleepless in Seattle,* Rosie never once set foot in the Emerald City, as the locals call their favorite city. For her next movie, *Another Stakeout,* she finally did make it there, or to an upscale Seattle suburb. Portraying Gina Garret, assistant district attorney in Seattle, she is assigned to supervise police detectives played by Richard Dreyfuss and Emilio Estevez, returning to duty in this sequel to their 1987 film, *Stakeout.* Basically an episodic caper, the story brings together characters on a surveillance detail who don't like each other very much. The conflict comes from differing approaches to police work. This version was a comedy, with the occasional bad guys appearing for dramatic tension. Later, Rosie admitted to telling a rather large lie to get the part. "They said to me, 'Can you drive a souped-up stunt car?' and I said, 'I've had a souped-up stunt car for *years!*' I didn't even know how to drive a stick shift at the time."

By most accounts, this was another happy set, and the three stars improvised a lot. Of Dreyfuss, Rosie said, "Richard is very confident and very over-the-top and big, but it all worked. He encouraged me to be bigger. If I thought it was too big, he'd say, 'Do one for me.' I'm glad he did, because those times ended up being the funny parts of the film." She went on to say, "Richard is the nicest and the smartest guy I have ever worked with. He is a dedicated dad and a remarkable friend."

Of Emilio Estevez, she said, "My favorite actor I have ever worked with—I adore him, and we have the same strange sense of humor. We laughed the whole time." In fact, they laughed a little *too* much and upset the director when they ruined takes with their highjinks.

This is how Emilio explained it: "If I looked at Rosie, I was just gone. Same with Richard. The director wasn't happy, but we had a good time." Rosie related how they all went out drinking one night and partied a bit too much, considering they had a 5:00 A.M. call the next morning. Rosie said you can tell they all had hangovers, but she won't divulge which scene they were shooting.

And when they weren't laughing, they were typing. Seems that the entire cast and crew were members of America Online and addicted to their computers. Rosie credits them with transforming her into a Nethead. "They turned me on to it, and now I am hooked." A nineties kind of set. Hot chat and cool websites dominated their backstage activities. None of the eighties drug scene, snorting blow in the trailers.

As Rosie played her, Gina Garrett had plenty of appealing quirks and a campy retro sensibility (there's a bit of June Cleaver lurking beneath some of her bits of business). Well meaning and earnest, not easily flustered, she was a good match for her loose cannon cohorts. In one hilarious scene, on the ferryboat trip over to their stakeout location, Rosie decided that Emilio Estevez would look younger and be more believable as Richard Dreyfuss's son if he shaved his mustache.

EMILIO [aghast]: "Forget it. I don't think you understand the relationship a man has with his facial hair."

ROSIE [rolling her eyes]: "Oh, please—I'm not asking you to cut off your penis."

EMILIO [belligerent]: "Well maybe you'd like to try."

ROSIE [impatient]: "Oh, don't be ridiculous."

EMILIO [upset]: "I have had this mustache for thirteen years. How long have you had yours?"

[Rosie inhales sharply, puts her hand to her mouth, and turns away. Later, Estevez is shown shaving off the mustache.]

The three are posing as a family vacationing together in a rented home, conveniently located next door to the house where they hope their missing witness is hiding. Early on, Rosie gets a bang out of listening to the tapped phone conversations. The surveillance subject, played by Kathy Moriarity, is discussing the breakup of her friend's marriage, and Rosie becomes involved as though she's listening to a soap opera. Soon she knows all the players' names.

ROSIE [disgusted]: "Larry's a pig."

RICHARD [defensive]: "Oh, and Kate's an angel?"

ROSIE [lecturing]: "Kate's a woman, Larry's a man. Need I say more? I rest my case. [Getting very excited now] This is really fabulous—I mean this whole thing of being able to hear. I feel a teeny bit guilty, but I'm really enjoying it."

Later, the three stars fight over the various bumbles and foul-ups that led to their predicament. Rosie has invited the surveillance subjects over for dinner.

ROSIE TO RICHARD [*really steamed*]: "You pathetic Steven Seagal wannabe—walking around all dressed in black."

[*Emilio laughs.*]

ROSIE [*turning to Emilio*]: "You think it's funny? Well you're even worse than he is....You're just a flunky, you're a sidekick. He's Fred and you're Barney. He's Johnny Carson and you're Ed McMahon."

EMILIO [*huffy*]: "That's it! No one calls me Ed McMahon.

The guys threaten to leave, she cries, they give in, the story goes on. When the neighbors arrive, Rosie serves them some of the funniest concoctions ever seen in a movie: hard-cooked eggs and black olive pieces carefully assembled to resemble penguins and an armadillo-shaped meatloaf with corn-flake scales. At one point, Rosie slips up and mentions the name of their friend she had heard them discussing on the phone. To cover the gaffe, she quickly invents an excuse.

ROSIE [*sweating*]: "I have the ability to *see* things. I hate to say this—some people even say that I'm psychic. It's strange—ideas, images, thoughts, names just pop into my head....I can't even watch *Jeopardy*—I know all the answers." (This is an inside joke for Rosie fans because she did appear on celebrity *Jeopardy,* and she won.)

This ploy works and then the action steps up as Emilio is bound and gagged and carried off in the trunk of a car. Obligatory chase, expensive car gets trashed, all stars end up in a slough in the dark, but they catch their witness. Then the really bad guys show up, guns are fired, Rosie tackles the hired assassin, he slugs her and takes her hostage. Archie, the dog, saves the day. Seems Rosie's character wouldn't think of leaving her beloved rottweiler in a kennel, so she brought him along for comic relief. (In truth, he was not Rosie's favorite costar. "He was very big, very wild, very young, and not well trained, and I was afraid of him," she recalls. "When I went to grab him when he was barking at the cat, he tried to bite me three times!") So Archie attacks the killer, pushing both him and Rosie into the pool. As Rosie climbs out, she is shot. Barely able to speak, she asks Dreyfuss if they got the killer (of course they did). Then she asks one more question.

ROSIE [*bleeding and really wet*]: "Am I gonna live?"

RICHARD [*being nice for once*]: "Yeah."

ROSIE [*passing out*]: "Excellent!"

Not eager to become an action heroine, Rosie remembered shooting that scene. "The dog was crazy and slobbery. At the end when I get shot, he was supposed to lick me. I had to put steak all over my face. Yechh! It was a nightmare. It was the most difficult part of the film, without a doubt. Hands down."

Yes, but she *did* get her name "above the title" for the first time. Of the film Rosie said, "A lot of people missed that movie. It just screams 'video.'"

Again, the reviews were mixed. One *Washington Post* review was written in the form of a sequel-to-do list, ending with: "Release film in summer when, you tell self, audience will pay price of admission just to sit in air-conditioned room. Book in Multiplex showing *Jurassic Park*. Pray for spillover."

The *New York Times* huffed: "The film is not only a sequel to the same team's *Stakeout*, but also to approximately nine out of every ten comic-cop movies made." They further enthused: "*Another Stakeout* defies criticism. Everyone who goes to see it will probably know what to expect. There's no need to say more."

The *Hollywood Reporter* proved more generous: "Director John Badham, goosing every scene with chases, including numerous dog-after-cat episodes, milks the plot bone to the fullest."

Roger Ebert, who has seen enough sequels to dread them, was pleasantly surprised by this one. Once he got over being upset at the uncomfortable drink holder-armrests, he said, "The movie started to grow on me," he wrote in the *Chicago Sun-Times*. "O'Donnell is good at standing her ground and speaking her mind, and the plot makes just enough sense to hang the gags on." He summed it up this way: "Movies like this are chewing gum for the mind. This one holds its flavor better than most."

And once again, Rosie was honored with a nomination for an American Comedy Award.

Next in order of release, came three forgettable films. In two of them, Rosie had tiny bit parts, not even big enough to be called cameos. In the third, she had a leading role that might have lead straight to the unemployment line, had that movie been released on schedule.

In *Fatal Instinct,* a spoof of every sultry adultery movie ever made, Rosie has one brief scene with star Armand Assante. The parrots do most of the talking. Only the truly obsessed Rosie fan would watch this film just to see her few seconds on screen.

In the well-received comedy about the movie business, *I'll Do Any-*

thing, Rosie has a tiny part as a makeup artist who gets to fluff powder under Nick Nolte's chin while he prepares for a screen test. This time she gets a funny line, at least, and looks adorable, wearing huge gold earrings and a beret with a big flower on it. Nolte, nervous about his big test, asks her and her coworker to leave him alone because "I need to focus a little." Rosie raises one eyebrow *way up* and exits with her pal, saying, "Have you seen the pastry truck? Has that guy been by? Let's *focus* on a danish."

The film that could have ended Rosie's career, *Car 54, Where Are You?* was actually the first movie Rosie ever made. One of a long line of films trying to cash in on the nostalgia for old sitcoms, it wasn't released until three years after it was finished. It was so bad, it could have ended her acting career. She did say, "It was a bad movie and not a lot of fun to do." In fact, in 1996 she said it was the worst experience she had ever had in show business. When asked why it took so long for this movie to be released, Rosie replied, "It stunk." In one scene, Rosie gets tossed into a garbage dumpster, and, in another, in the bedroom with David Johansen as hubby Officer Gunther Toody, Rosie, portraying Lucille Toody, has to get on top and bounce the bed for all it's worth.

Diehard Rosie fans looking for a campy, so-bad-it's-funny film might enjoy it, and it's probably worth renting just to see her outlandish, low-rent wardrobe. In one scene she wears a frilly black and white party dress and her hair piled on top of her head in cascading curls. In another, she's clad in a pink feather-trimmed robe while she fixes breakfast. Rosie's also decked out as a matron of honor at Fran Drescher's wedding while the final credits roll.

In this movie, Rosie plays a really raunchy-mouthed Brooklyn housewife who thinks her husband, Gunther is cheating on her. In one of the few scenes where she probably had fun, she launches a head of lettuce at Gunther's head. She imagines him cheating on her with police groupies—an idea she gleaned from watching *Geraldo.* Later, she tries to take advice from Sally Jesse to get her husband to talk to her more often. Ironic that the future Queen of Nice Talk should play a trash-talk addict in her first film role.

Rosie rarely looks relaxed in front of the camera, which is understandable given that this was a substantial part and her first film. Rosie explained years later, "You learn on your first movie....I didn't know how to hit a mark. You have to walk to a specific spot, and I didn't know how to do it. So they put a sandbag down for me. You can see it—I'm walkin', then all of a sudden—(she lurches) it was horrible."

Still, it wasn't that Rosie was so terrible, it was simply a bad part in a worse movie. Rosie was interviewed on the set of this flaky flick and revealed her first impressions of movie making: "I was so excited to finally be in a movie. I thought I was gonna be working, working, working, but most of it is waiting, waiting, waiting."

She also found it difficult to adjust to delivering lines in a vacuum, since there is no laughter allowed on a set, it's difficult for an actor to know if she's being funny. "I'm used to telling a joke and getting a response," Rosie explained. "I wanted to look around at a cameraman and see if he was laughing. It was very hard to make the change." Mercifully, this movie has been relegated to one-copy status in the five-day rental section of your local video store. The only good thing that happened to Rosie as a result was her friendship with Fran Drescher, who played Velma Velour, a floozy in a red wig and an even redder feather boa.

Here's one sample review from the *New York Times:* "As Gunther's wife, Lucille, the funnier Rosie O'Donnell is used mostly for one-note hollering, in crass domestic scenes that play like John Waters without the taste." In 1996, Rosie had this advice for her fans: "You shouldn't rent it. If you do, I'm sorry, and I owe you $1.50."

Rosie's next two roles were unforgettable. For the first one, she'll be loved by generations of kids for bringing to life a favorite cartoon character. For the other, she'll spend the rest of her life trying to live it down.

A cute picture of the small child we now know as Rosie, the Queen of Nice.

This is where Rosie grew up—her childhood home at 22 Rhonda Lane in the "Names" section of Commack, Long Island, about fifty miles east of New York City. (Photo by author)

Rolling Hills School, along with Sawhill Elementary, is where Rosie attended classes before graduating to Commack High School South. (Photo: Anthony Catarelli)

Christ the King Roman Catholic Church, established in 1959, three years before Rosie was born, is where Rosie and her family worshipped. (Photo: Anthony Catarelli)

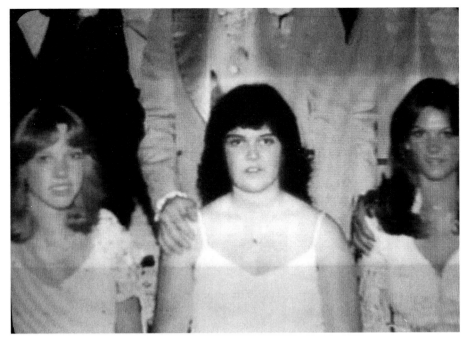

Prom night at Commack High School with Rosie and friends.

This is where Rosie went to high school. Originally called Commack High School South, it has since become Commack Middle School, and all high school classes have been consolidated into Commack High School North. (Photo: Anthony Catarelli)

G.O. SHOW

Yearbook pictures of the school's General Organization Show with Rosie at lower right and upper left.

Rosie as President of
Student Directors

The Commack High South Drama Society, showing Rosie in the back row, fourth from left.

In addition to "Class Clown,"
Rosie was voted "Most School
Spirited" girl.

In this yearbook picture, Maureen, Rosie's sister, is in the middle row, fifth from the left.
Rosie is next to her.

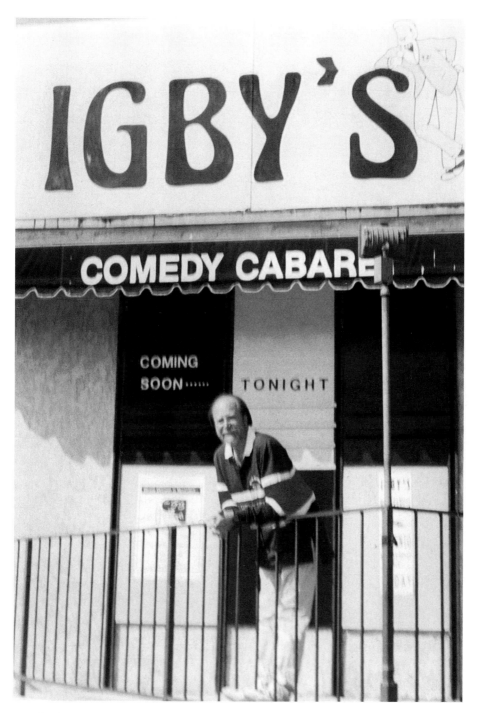

Her first big-time stand-up engagement in Los Angeles was at Igby's, shown here with owner Jan Maxwell Smith out front. (Photo by author)

Rosie's new home in Nyack, New York, overlooking the Hudson River, formerly belonged to legendary stage actress Helen Hayes. (Photo by author)

✑ 10

Becoming Betty Rubble

How nice for Rosie that the sting of *Car 54*'s eventual debut could be overshadowed by the release later that year of the hugely popular *Flintstones*. Though severely criticized by most reviewers, the film proved to be a box office smash, grossing over $130 million domestic and $70 million in rentals. Though yet another spin-off from a TV show, or more accurately *shows,* this movie was made with a big budget and high style, and with as much storyline as you'd expect from a cartoon. *The Flintstones* debuted in 1960 as television's first animated prime-time series. A huge hit, it ran until 1966, and with its many further incarnations (nearly thirty at last count) it has probably never been off the TV screen. For that reason alone, it was *the* kid flick to see in the summer of 1994.

There was, however, trouble in Bedrock before the cameras even rolled. Anytime it takes thirty-six screenwriters to finalize a script, something has to be terribly wrong. (As the showbiz trade paper *Variety* wryly pointed out, "Almost as many people signed the Declaration of Independence.") It shouldn't have been that tough. The premise has always been the same— the Nortons and the Kramdens travel through time to prehistoric suburbia, squabble, kiss, and make up. The resemblance to the *Honeymooners* was so obvious that when the TV show first aired, Jackie Gleason threatened to sue the show's creators, Hanna-Barbera. According to a close friend of Gleason's, "Jackie's lawyers told him he could probably have *The Flintstones* pulled right off the air. But they also told him, 'Do you want to be known as

the guy who yanked Fred Flintstone off the air? The guy who took away the
show that so many kids love, and so many of their parents love, too?'"

That's an important point that the screenwriters overlooked. The TV
show was as much adult satire as it was a kid's show. The movie failed to
expand on the original story and offered no ironies or new insights into the
characters. Instead, the committee of writers cobbled together a tired plot
about office politics and embezzling schemes. (One reviewer called it
"primitively plotted and glacially paced.") However, a huge sum of money
was put to good use on the sets. It is no accident that nearly every visual
pun looks like a toy commercial. Nor is it an accident that the set looks like
a theme park—nearly everything you see was exploited in one way or
another. When asked if she could expect a cut of the money made from
Betty Rubble dolls, Rosie replied, "I certainly do—coming soon to a Happy
Meal near you."

Rosie has avidly collected Happy Meals figurines— "I have like
hundreds"—so she was thrilled to join the unique club of actors who have
inspired them.

Rosie recalls having a good laugh when her agent told her there was
interest in her for the part of Betty Rubble. "I thought, *are you kidding me?*
She's this tiny little petite thing, and I'm not exactly similar to the cartoon
rendering." As Rosie tells the story, director Brian Levant's wife saw her at a
charity event and told him Rosie would make a good Betty. "When I
auditioned, I did the Betty Rubble laugh. That got me the part. When I read
the part and everyone laughed, I thought 'Okay.' But I didn't lust after it my
whole life, no." (The two actresses she beat out for the role are Janine
Turner, from *Northern Exposure,* and Tracey Ullman.) Later on she
admitted that she hadn't watched the show as a kid. "It really was hard for
me to get into Betty. But I've assimilated it all and really think I've captured
her essence." She certainly captured the trademark laugh, which she still
enjoys using.

Rosie has said this film was the most fun to make. She got to meet and
work with Elizabeth Taylor, who played Wilma Flintstone's mother. On Liz's
first day on the set, however, none of the actors was brave enough to
approach her. Except Rosie. "Someone had to break the ice," she reasoned,
"so I went up to Liz and said 'I really love your perfume.'"

The next day Rosie found a crate of the stuff in her trailer, courtesy of
her new pal. Later in the shoot she told *Entertainment Tonight* that all her

recent success "feels like someone else's life. It feels like any minute somebody's going to come in and say, 'Guess what? It was all a big joke—what do you think you're doing working with Elizabeth Taylor? Get the hell off the set.'"

She also got on well with the rest of the cast: "It was like going to Disneyland every day. The cast and crew were great." And the feeling was mutual. One crew member recalls that "in between takes Rosie would break out into show tunes. She was always cracking jokes and singing."

Another crew member, a camera assistant, also has great memories: "I think Rosie is wonderful. She's almost like a female Robin Williams, always joking and doing things, always entertaining everybody." She went on to say that Rosie didn't confine her joking around to other cast members. "She was good to the crew....She talks to you, she doesn't talk down to you. She's just like a pal."

A still photographer on the film remembers one awful night when Rosie saved the day: "We had an all-nighter to film when Fred's car crashes through Slate's office. Everybody was running on a short fuse—everybody but Rosie. She really helped people get through that sixteen-hour night."

In 1996 when asked about the experience, Rosie said, "It was the best job that I ever had in the movies. I got to go barefoot, and I only had one dress in the whole movie." (But what a dress.)

The worst part for Rosie was filming in the tremendous heat and dust at the quarry. The film was shot at Vasquez Rocks in Agua Dulce, California, near Los Angeles. This dramatic setting with rocks jutting out of the desert floor has also been used as a location for *Star Trek* and *Star Wars*. "It was very, very, very, very hot. A hundred and five some days, and we were wearing suede." The colorful, fanciful sets even became a tourist destination on their own, attracting over 100,000 visitors.

In all of her movies, Rosie has only played a mother once, and one of the sweet ironies is, as Betty Rubble *she adopts a son.* Her funniest lines come early on, as she meets Bamm-Bamm (the boy raised by wild mastodons) for the first time. "It just hit me," she tells Fred and Wilma, "From now on I'll be spending twenty-four hours a day attending to the every need of a helpless little boy." Then she glances at Barney playing on the floor with the Flintstones' daughter, Pebbles. "Then again, maybe it won't be such a big adjustment after all." That line is followed by the famous Betty laugh. Though her desire for her own child was growing, it would be another year after the release of this movie before Rosie became a mom in real life.

Ignoring the bad buzz on the picture, Rosie looked stunning at the Hollywood premiere, clad all in white from head to toe. She and her costars partied afterward at Planet Hollywood and brought some memorabilia for a charity auction—one of La Liz's fur-trimmed costumes and some of her stone-age perfume bottles.

Sadly, the bad reviews were funnier than the movie. Reviewers enjoyed trying to out-pun one another with their put-downs. Here's a sampling:

"Yabba-dabba-boo."
"The movie suffers immediate comic extinction."
"The gags are as old as the Ice Age."
"Yabba-dabba-doodoo."
"An avalanche of corny rock jokes."
"Yabba-dabba-don't."

Roger Ebert praised the set, but not much else. "A great-looking movie, a triumph of set design and special effects." The reviewer for *Time* magazine was one of the few who seemed to like it. Of the stars he said, "All tread a nice, comically persuasive line between caricature and naturalism." Referring to the previous summer's megahit, *Jurassic Park,* he wrote, "Once again, prehistory has been good to the film's producer, billed here as Steven Spielrock."

Entertainment Weekly took a thoughtful approach to the film. "Does it say something about the infantilization of American cinema that an absurdly literal-minded big-budget version of a goofy cartoon series is now our idea of a major motion picture event? You bet it does." Admitting that he enjoyed the film, their reviewer went on to say, "If Rosie O'Donnell is hardly a double for the svelte Betty, that's forgotten the moment she duplicates Betty's delighted rapid-fire giggle."

In her no nonsense way, Rosie advised, "When you go to *The Flintstones* you get a cartoon. If you want to be inspired or challenged, this ain't the film to go to."

One of the better lines appeared in the closing credits: "No dinosaurs were harmed in the production of this motion picture." Despite the adult critics, the film was popular with youngsters. Rosie was named Favorite Movie Actress for her part as Betty Rubble and honored with Nickelodeon's Kid's Choice Award.

When Garry Marshall, who had just directed *Pretty Woman,* told Rosie he needed her to star in *Exit to Eden,* Rosie took a leap of faith and did it. Rosie plays an undercover cop who chases a smuggler to a remote island resort designed for sexual adventurers. Once there, she has to dress like the other vacationers, which required losing about thirty pounds to fit into the scanty wardrobe. She had met Marshall while making *A League of Their Own* for his sister, Penny. (Garry Marshall acted in that movie, portraying the league owner and candy magnate, Walter Harvey.)

The role of Detective Sheila Kingston, a Los Angeles undercover cop was originally cast with Sharon Stone. When Stone backed out at the last moment, Marshall called Rosie himself, and promised "I won't embarrass you." When she found out who she was replacing, Rosie was astounded. "I couldn't imagine the producers at this meeting saying, 'Shall we go with Sharon or Rosie? Sharon or Rosie?' I asked my agent how many people were offered the role between me and Sharon Stone—ninety?"

In truth, Garry Marshall admits there were a few others, but none was as adept as Rosie at "mixing the comic with the erotic. We were trying something very new, and we needed someone with whom the audience could identify to ease them into this slightly kinky, slightly threatening world." He went on to say that Rosie has a kind of hip innocence that "helps take the edge off the sex in the movie. Yet she's still sexy, and for the first time in her career, she even has a romantic thing going."

As Detective Sheila Kingston, Rosie was expected to wear some classic leather fantasy outfits. "I took that movie as a way to approach problems that I had with my body image, knowing full well that I had to wear that outfit, and knowing full well that it was going to be tough for me. Emotionally it was very hard." When asked how she liked her studded bondage wardrobe in the movie, Rosie replied, "Well, at first I was freaked out and scared and embarrassed, but then I kinda got used to it—and I did rather enjoy it."

The first day was the worst. Then after that "the camera crew started making wisecracks, like, 'Wow, you look really hot!' And I'd say, 'I do?' After a while I started strutting around, going, 'Yeah, I'm pretty in this, aren't I?' I mean, there are some gorgeous people around who aren't ninety pounds."

Marshall recalls how brave she was. "She was taken aback by having to wear some of the skimpy costumes, but she did. She doesn't worry about how she looks all the time. That can be very refreshing in Hollywood."

Rosie said she didn't think she would have played this role for any other director, but she had confidence in Marshall because he was the man who took "a story about a prostitute who winds up dead in Hollywood and turned it into Cinderella for the eighties [*Pretty Woman*]." Years later, Rosie met up with another star of the film, Hector Elizondo (*Chicago Hope*), who teased her about her infamous attire. "The last time I saw you, you had on what you would call crotch floss." To which Rosie had no immediate response.

What intentionally funny lines there are in this mess belong mostly to Rosie. Early on, she and undercover partner, Dan Ackroyd, are selecting their getups to take on their assignment to an S&M fantasy island resort. She tries on a dirty blond wig and mugs for him, "Debbie Gibson?" "In a less than perfect world," he replies. The running gag is that he's the prudish one and she's a bit more adventurous, prone to tormenting him with details of her bodily functions, such as: "I'm ovulating, Fred!" Later on she wonders aloud to him how one decides to become a dominatrix. "Do you wake up one day and go, Hey, I feel like being bossy?"

Dan tries on a full leather bondage suit and comes out of the dressing room to survey his image in the mirror. He even scares himself, "It's like Elvis goes to hell!"

Loosely based on an Anne Rice novel, the main problem with *Exit to Eden* is that it is a mixture of several genres that do not belong together. As the writer for *Playboy* magazine said in his review, "Fans of Anne Rice's intensely erotic novel will find the kinky soul of it missing from the movie adaptation." Overlaid onto the fantasy island story is a silly undercover-cops-chasing-smugglers story. Sometimes the film seems like a comic cop caper, then a buddy picture, then a sex farce, and then suddenly a serious love story.

Once Rosie and Dan get to Eden, she does get off a few good lines. In one scene she is finally questioning one of the people they followed to the island, and when he becomes agitated by her questions, she tells him, "Relax, breathe—pretend I'm Oprah."

Later she has to rescue the same guy (who is now assigned to her as her slave) from the evil clutches of the smuggler, played by supermodel

Iman. Rosie is decked out in her bondage outfit for the first time and tries out some verbal discipline on her suspect as she exits the room with him in tow. "You—with me—now. Get up, take off the robe—I like that thong thing—walk tall. Tell me I look gorgeous from behind."

Soon after, Iman sneaked up on Rosie and attacked her from behind, beginning the infamous fight scene between them. Both barely clad in leather dominatrix getups, they rolled around on the floor until Iman kicked Rosie in the head with her spiked heel. Rosie actually needed stitches in her scalp.

But she got even with a return punch to Iman's gut. Dan jumped into the fray and helped subdue Iman. In one of the few hilarious moments in the movie, Rosie mirandizes Iman in Iman's own bizarre accent.

Talking about the scene later, Rosie said, "Iman totally beat the crap out of me." Rosie had first told Iman, "Don't worry, I won't hurt you," thinking she was some fragile model. Rosie didn't know that Iman lifted weights every day. "I am very strong," the tall beauty said. "Once they said 'Action!' it took Rosie *and* Dan to keep me down. The next day [Rosie] was all black and blue, and there was not a scratch on me."

Hand-to-hand combat skills aside, Rosie was great at getting what laughs could be tweaked out of the weak script. Reportedly, Rosie's role was enlarged after a critical test screening revealed she was the best character in the film. Perhaps that's when it was decided Rosie should also contribute the voice-over narration, which does seem like an afterthought to try and tie all these disparate pieces together. She does get the last words, however: "So what did I learn from this case? No matter what your sexual preference, true love is still the ultimate fantasy."

Not surprisingly, reviewers were merciless in their criticism:

"Sodden Emmanuelle-lite caper."
"Sad-assed thing that is neither sexy nor funny."
"Makes about as much sense as the outtakes from *Ishtar*."
"You don't have to be a masochist to sit through *Exit to Eden*, but it helps."

For once, Roger Ebert cut Rosie no slack. "I'm sorry, but I just don't get Rosie O'Donnell. I've seen her in three or four movies now, and she has generally had the same effect on me as fingernails on a blackboard. She's harsh and abrupt and staccato and doesn't seem to be having any fun. She looks mean."

The reviewer for the *Chicago Tribune* was in a minority with her opinion. "Only O'Donnell gets a fair shot at turning her unlikely presence in a sex enclave into comedy. Her barking delivery ('No, I don't feel like having my toes sucked right now.') and choice of bedtime reading (*The Bridges of Madison County*) sparks the occasional laugh." *Newsday* was a bit kinder: "In an unmitigated critical bomb, Rosie emerges as the next top female comic in films today. Rosie has tremendous appeal. She turns tin into gold, and in *Exit,* O'Donnell has nothing but tin to work with."

Here's Rosie's own review: "I thought it would be a funny Garry Marshall, light *Laverne & Shirley* romp through S&M....Who knew?" And as far as reviews go, Rosie has learned not to trust even good ones. "If you start believing that, you change who you are, and you start performing for them. You start thinking, 'Let me be good for the reviewer,' instead of the audience. I think that's the downfall of a lot of artists."

Again Rosie emerged with a new friend, costar Dan Ackroyd. She has been a lifelong fan of *Saturday Night Live,* so it was a real thrill for her to get to know one of the legendary original cast members of the show, especially since they discovered they have many interests in common.

There is one funny story about the film that Rosie happily tells on herself. After the film was in the can and in the editing process, director Garry Marshall decided he needed to shoot some new scenes. Rosie, however, had gained some weight in the interim. She claims you can see her knock on a door in one size then walk into the room a very different size.

Rosie notes, "If Garry Marshall called me tomorrow and said, 'We're doing *Exit to Eden Part 2,*' I would do it, because he's the nicest guy, the funniest and most generous man you're ever gonna meet in show business, and he creates a real environment of family on his films." She went on to describe a scene she was shooting playing an exotic dancer. "I'm humping a pole and this guy is looking at me lecherously and he's pretty good, and I said, 'Who is that guy?'" Turns out it was Garry's dentist. "That's the people he casts in the film! His hairdresser, his mother's friend from Brooklyn, whatever."

By the end of that experience, Rosie had acted in eight movies, six with substantial roles. Despite the debacle of her last film, she was still in demand for even more parts. She could have continued on in the same vein indefinitely. Character actresses like Rosie can make smooth transitions as they age and do not need to experience the trauma of relinquishing ingenue status. She had bought a nice little starter home (though modest and unpretentious, it cost $332,000 in 1990) in the San Fernando Valley and made a comfortable life for herself.

She said at the time, "I find that living in L.A., your whole life is centered around show business, and the more successful you become in it, the harder it is to get away from it. Living there, it doesn't stop. Every dinner. Every lunch. More and more meetings. It feeds on itself, and before you know it, there is no balance. All you have is work and very little life."

Rosie remembers one event that really affected her. She was seated between Walter Cronkite and Dennis Hopper at Swifty Lazar's Oscar party. "Faye Dunaway walked by and Cronkite started talking about *Bonnie and Clyde* and how he'd known the real Clyde. On the other side, Dennis Hopper was telling me about his wild days and who he'd been with. It was like being in two worlds....I went home and felt sort of depressed."

To keep her sanity, she sold her California home at a huge loss. (Property values took a big dive after the Northridge Quake.) Rosie then moved back to New York, where she had kept a two-bedroom apartment on the Upper West Side. "In New York, they could care less. People see me and go, 'Hey Rosie, how ya doing?' I go, 'Hi!' and it's over. They don't go, 'You know what? My brother was a grip on your movie and I wrote a script. Could you get this to David Hoberman at Disney, because I'd like a three-picture deal.'"

What she did once she got back to New York astounded everybody.

⌁ 11

Grease, Her Broadway Role

A s a teenager, living so close to New York City, it had been relatively easy for Rosie to cut class, take the train into Manhattan, and catch a Wednesday matinee. "I would memorize the theater directory, and I'd tell all the ushers at the theaters that I was going to be a star," she recalled. So despite her booming film career, Rosie set her sights on a childhood dream—to star on Broadway. "To me, there is nothing like the thrill of going to a Broadway show, when the lights go down and you have that orchestra in front of you. I always get goosebumps. It's the reason I went into show business in the first place."

Her agent thought it was a terrible idea and said, "More people see you in one movie than will ever see you in a two-year run of a Broadway show." Many friends warned against it, including Tom Hanks. "You'll get so bored you're going to want to kill yourself after two weeks." Even her therapist thought it was career suicide. "My therapist had a field day with it. She called it self-sabotage." Rosie then launched into an imitation of her therapist: " 'What's wrong with you? Things are going well and all of a sudden you want to do something you don't know how to do. Why? Why?' It's one hundred forty dollars an hour to hear her say 'Why?'"

None of them understood her motivation, what it meant to Rosie to be on Broadway, The Great White Way. For her it meant show business success.

When Rosie heard that legendary Broadway actor-choreographer Tommy Tune planned to produce a revival of *Grease,* she called his office and let him know of her interest in the part of Betty Rizzo. Rizzo is the bad girl who lures the good girl down the wrong paths in this tame, high school love story set in the 1950s. Tune told Rosie she had to audition for it. "I'm no singer, but there are many actresses who do musicals whose strength is not their voice," Rosie said, naming Tyne Daly and Lauren Bacall. "I knew I could play Rizzo."

Rosie described the audition on David Letterman's show: "Tommy Tune sat in the back like Flo Ziegfield, in the dark, and I was scared to death." After singing two songs for him, she was asked, "You can dance, right?"

"Oh, yeah, I can dance," she lied, hoping they wouldn't make her prove it.

Director Jeff Calhoun remembers her audition well. She downplayed her singing and dancing abilities, "but then she started rattling off these numbers—that she'd been in two movies that had grossed more than $100 million and how her name would help us sell tickets." She made everyone there laugh. "There was just this quality she had," Calhoun said.

Rosie's candor won her the role. "I will give you a hundred percent and sell tickets," she promised them. "They believed me." According to columnist Liz Smith, "Rosie's audition was so spectacular that all other Rizzos were vanquished, and she was offered the role on the spot."

She was also very realistic about what she was doing. Rosie knew it was one of the few roles she felt equipped to play. And she would finally find out what it was like to be on the other side of that magical curtain. "I know it's not Shakespeare. It's not even one my favorite musicals," she said right before the New York opening. "But ever since I was a little kid I wanted to be Barbra Streisand and, like that stupid song says, 'to hear the roar of the crowd.' There's nothing like it."

There were other good reasons to take this leap of faith in herself. She discussed some of them in a 1994 interview. "I did three movies in a row, and if you're a comedic actor you get into a niche in everybody's mind. And then when you're hot, you end up doing a lotta bad movies for a lotta money, 'cause they offer you so much money." She went on to cite Whoopi Goldberg as a good actress who appeared in a number of films that didn't advance her career. Rosie tried to learn from others' mistakes.

"I thought taking *Grease* for a year would remove the chance for me to do that. It's very hard to turn down that kinda money. You figure, it's three months, what does it matter? It's three million dollars. My God, I could put my nieces through college." She reckoned that after a year off from Hollywood, she'd be in a better position to reevaluate her options.

"I really respect Rosie for wanting to do *Grease*," Jeff Calhoun said. "She's making a financial sacrifice most film actors won't make. But she is also a businesswoman, first and foremost, who knows exactly why she does what she does." The director also stressed appearing in *Grease* would not be an easy time for a previously pampered movie star. "This is blue-collar work. No trailers, no one doing your makeup for you."

After doing so many films on location and away from home, Rosie was seeking more quality time for herself. "I'll be in New York until November and have more time to spend on myself," she said soon after the show opened there. She would also be living near friends and family, which is always a centering influence on her.

At the initial rehearsal, associate choreographer, Jerry Mitchell, gathered the cast, and rattled off the first dance sequence: "We're going to do step-touch, step-touch, hip, hip together, back, and up. And two, and three, and go." And everyone started dancing. Everyone except Rosie, who instantly realized she was way over her head. "I was like, 'Excuse me, what was the first part? The step what? *Hello?*' And they practically had to tutor me," she admitted, grateful for the generosity of the cast and crew. "I've been nurtured and really held together by this wonderful cast."

To add to the problems, this was Jeff Calhoun's first directing effort, and he wasn't sure at first how to handle his star's nerves and her stage inexperience. He soon found himself "walking on eggshells around Rosie. I knew she was nervous, and I was intimidated." Then one evening they went out for several pitchers of beer and reached an understanding. "Rosie basically gave me permission to do my job," Calhoun explained.

Though Rosie took voice lessons to prepare for the role, she was still not singing up to her potential. Calhoun believed she could actually become a very good singer with more training, but there wasn't time. The director had taken a huge risk to allow Rosie to sashay onto that big stage in a pink-and-black baseball jacket and sing the satiric "Look at Me, I'm Sandra Dee." So he very gallantly staged both of her solo numbers so that they end with the chorus of singers backing her up. "I wanted to protect her, so she never has to end a song by herself to applause," he said.

Another ally was musical director, John McDaniel, who conducted the numbers from the orchestra pit. He is good natured and generous, and

Rosie and McDaniel formed a strong bond that continued on to other projects. Once she relaxed into the role, they began to make each other laugh at the slightest suggestion, which in a live stage show is not necessarily a good thing. Rosie tells it this way: "Every night in the middle of my ballad I'd look at him and he'd be laughin', and I'd start to laugh. Sometimes I'd have to turn around, so this is what the audience [who paid $65] saw—" She then demonstrated the effect, and all you could see were her shoulders moving up and down. "Once I start laughin', especially if I'm tired, there's no helpin' me."

At the time of the New York run, Rosie was candid, as usual, about her abilities. "You're not going to say ouch when I sing, but you're not going to be wowed the way you are with Sam Harris and Billy Porter, who get standing ovations every night."

When asked if she had ever sung before *Grease,* she replied, "No, and some say I still haven't." Nevertheless, it must have been another huge thrill for her to do the cast recording, and to finally have a CD with *her* picture and name on it. In fact, her voice sounds clear and fine on the CD.

This production was one of many exceptions. The part of fifties bad girl Betty Rizzo is very much the supporting actress role, yet because Rosie was the biggest "name" in the cast, she received special billing. There were others with bigger parts, but it was Rosie who packed the house. In a departure from the usual staging, Rosie refused to smoke cigarettes onstage. "I've never tried a cigarette. I'm repulsed by it," she said. She found another fifties pastime for Rizzo to indulge in—she dazzled audiences with her shocking pink yo-yo! When asked if that was her idea, she replied, "Yes. I'm thirty-two years old, and my character is seventeen. I used the yo-yo and the bubble gum to make myself look younger."

Considering Rosie's physical size, putting her in the role of Rizzo was the first of many creative casting decisions. Rizzo has always been portrayed as a more classically seductive character, and despite some grousing by the critics, Rosie made the role her own. (*New York* magazine declared, "O'Donnell delivers her lines with the proper deadpan hauteur, but a fat Rizzo?")

Some of the costumes took a bit more effort. "It takes the dresser, Carol, *and* her mother to zip up the corset I wear for that hourglass, fifties sort of figure," Rosie told *Vogue* magazine. She did, however, train for the part, and with rehearsals and then eight demanding performances a week,

Rosie did pare her 5'7" frame down to 150 pounds, which for her is very small. She also claimed she gave up beer for the duration.

Soon it was time to pack Rizzo's trashy clothes and sassy attitude and set off for three months on a seven-city tour as a way to prepare for the Broadway debut. Rosie thought she was ready for it. After all, she had paid her dues many times over on the grueling comedy circuit. "I never thought three months on the road would be that hard," she admitted near the end of it. One of their stops was in Detroit, a city she found "sort of sad, at least the area where the theater is was quite depressing." But on the whole, the audiences were very supportive of her. "Nobody is really expecting me to get up there and be Whitney Houston. They know what I am and what I do," she explained when the tour came to Boston.

Many of the cast members were veteran practical jokers and relieved some of the inevitable monotony. They were especially fond of getting Rosie's goose during one of her big scenes. "I had to open this cooler," Rosie explained, "and I was supposed to be really sad that I'm pregnant, and I'm supposed to take out a soda and have my big moment. But they would put like a Cabbage Patch doll in there with its head off and blue gunk coming out of it."

They returned to New York in April and headed for the Eugene O'Neill Theatre (freshly painted shocking pink, no less) to prepare for opening night. John Arnone designed the wildly colorful Day-Glo sets. The witty costumes, featuring iconic telephones, flamingos, and Scottie dogs, added to the fifties ambience. At times the show had the feel of an impromptu production, with the actors making their own props, as in the scene where Rydell High students came onstage carrying big yellow pieces of cardboard to symbolize a school bus.

For her part, Rosie smiled and smirked from every ad touting the show. And she delivered—$2 million in advance ticket sales before the show even opened.

On May 11, 1994, Rosie stepped out onto a Broadway stage and "ramma-ramma-lammed" into a dream come true. As the wisecracking leader of the tough girl group, the Pink Ladies, she snapped out her lines like so much bubblegum. (These girls weren't tough enough to be called a gang.) With a very thin plotline, the show is held together by its music. In the ensemble number "Greased Lightnin'," Rosie sings one of the stranger rhymes in the history of Broadway musicals. To her boyfriend, Rosie expresses her feelings about what he can expect to happen in the backseat of his jalopy: "Hey Kenickie, you won't even get a hickey."

Rosie's first solo was "Look at Me, I'm Sandra Dee," in which she dons a blond wig and makes fun of the lead character, the good girl, Sandy. It doesn't seem to matter that half the audience doesn't know Sandra Dee was a '50s starlet. In her other big number, "There Are Worse Things I Could Do," Rosie wisely chose to act more than sing. In it she expresses remorse for her inability to befriend Sandy. There is a subplot that gives Rizzo one of her better lines, "I feel like a broken typewriter—I skipped my period." Rizzo, the bad girl with a good heart, fears she is "PG," but before the third act is over, she declares a false alarm in time to join in the grand finale.

The opening night audience was clearly there to have a good time, and they whooped and hollered at nearly every joke. But the really big moment of the night came during the curtain calls, when Rosie stepped to the edge of the stage and gave an emotional speech to the audience. Her voice soon choked with tears, causing another huge round of applause. A friend who was there remembers her saying: "This is such a wonderful night; it's a dream come true. The only sad part is that my mother didn't see it." Later when told she ought to make the curtain speech a nightly ritual, Rosie replied, "I couldn't do that every night. I only broke up because I saw my family sitting there, and they were crying."

After the performance, Rosie joined her fellow cast members at Roseland for the opening night party. Columnist Liz Smith raved about her appearance that night: "Rosie is truly lovely looking up close (she has pale, exquisitely freckled skin)." Rosie did, however, look rather overwhelmed by the blur of flashbulbs and the glare of the TV cameras, but this was what she had wanted. The performance she gave at Roseland was just as impressive as the one back in the theater. She mugged, she posed, she cracked jokes, and had a blast befitting Broadway's newest star.

Soon after the opening, Rosie said, "It's very scary singing to the public every night, because I don't think of myself as a singer." It didn't take her long to realize how hard she had to work in a Broadway musical. "I'm committed to nine months of this, then I give birth to a complete collapse."

Rosie actually hated *Grease's* message. She didn't realize it until she was in rehearsals, but she has been very vocal about it many times since then. "In *Grease* there are a lot of offensive lines. It's quite sexist, very homophobic, very racist," she said pointedly. "I don't even like the message of the play: If you're a nice, normal girl, change yourself into a trampy, slutty girl to be accepted by the cool boy." She has said that whenever she sees young girls in the audience, she wants to shout at the end of the show: "Don't believe it!" In its defense, Rosie also called *Grease* a lighthearted romp through another era, and she pointed out that not every aspect of a project has to meet her own moral standards.

The reviews ranged from savage to generous. Referring to the terrific advance sales, the Hollywood trade paper, *Daily Variety* said, "O'Donnell must be doing something right, even if it isn't singing or dancing."

Showing a generosity of spirit, the writer for the *New Yorker* said the show "offers a lot of pleasure....All the actors are likable and sing well as a group and in solos." About Rosie, she wrote: "O'Donnell, making her Broadway debut as the tough-talking Rizzo, is the very soul of likability, she's so game and seems so happy to be part of this enterprise that even though she doesn't project very well and doesn't have much of a singing voice, you're on her side."

Of Rosie's road show performance, the *Boston Globe* wrote, "She has the brazen delivery of Ethel Merman...she burps, she boogies." The *Washington Post* was blunt: "The less said about her off-key, blaring singing, the better."

When asked right after the Broadway opening if she took reviews personally, Rosie replied, "Not really. I find most of them amusing." What matters to her is that she knows she is connecting with her audiences. Two years after she had moved on to bigger venues, Rosie received this fan letter on America Online:

"My friend and I went to see you in *Grease,* and afterward you stood out in a thunderstorm until everyone had been addressed. It was great that you care so much to do that! Thanks! *Grease* was awesome! You definitely made the show!" That kind of heartfelt review from a youngster who had saved her allowances for a balcony seat meant more to Rosie than anything a professional critic could say about her.

One of the fun aspects of doing a Broadway show is that celebrities in the audience often come backstage afterward to chat and offer congratulations. During one memorable performance, Rosie was taking center stage for one of her solos, when a little girl in the audience shouted out, "Mommy, that's Rosie!" The ardent fan's mommy, who just happened to be her friend Demi Moore, shushed her daughter, telling her to be quiet because "this is Rosie's big moment." Rosie spotted them from the stage and mouthed "hello" to the girl, who was obviously more used to movie sets—where you can always do another take. Meg Ryan, her friend from *Sleepless in Seattle,* celebrated Mother's Day by attending with her young son on her lap. She was heard to whisper to him, "Look, there's Rosie!"

Another perk of starring on Broadway is getting asked to be a presenter at the Tony Awards program, which Rosie did with great flair in June 1994. She and her copresenter, Bebe Neuwirth of *Cheers,* did a funny bit about a mezzo soprano and a ballet dancer and nearly stole the show. When asked if she was upset her show didn't win, Rosie replied, "No, I was shocked we were nominated after the bad reviews." She went on to say that she had a great time schmoozing backstage at the awards show. "It was fun in the Green Room 'cause I met a ton of people—Carol Burnett, Marlo Thomas, Gwen Verdon."

Rosie relaxed from the grueling nightly performances by joining the Broadway Bowling League. Lucien Hold, of the Comic Strip in New York, used to hang out with her back then. This is the routine he remembers: "They all do the show, go out for dinner, and then go down to the Port Authority on Thursday nights at midnight and take over the lanes. Rosie was just one of the bowlers like everybody else. I used to love to go down and shoot the breeze with her and her friends. There was no 'she's a star.' Rosie, even though she *is* a star, she's so down-to-earth that it breaks through. She doesn't carry an air around her that she's above other people. She's a pretty good bowler. She averages around one-sixty, which for anybody is decent. She's a talented athlete, and she's strong—she got that sixteen-pound bowling ball whipping down the lane pretty good!"

Six months of eight shows a week did begin to take its toll. Rosie finally admitted that "it does get a tad boring doing the same thing every night." Much later, Rosie admitted she desperately wanted to relieve the monotony. "Toward the end of the run I was so bored, I would literally do this during 'Hand Jive': I'd see my friends in the audience, and I'd go [mouths the words *We'll go to Joe Allen's after the show*] right in the middle of the scene." But then she explained what kept her going. "I love seeing the little kids wide-eyed in the audience. I remember *being* that kid, and that keeps it fresh for me."

A year after the run Rosie was asked if she would ever do Broadway again. "I don't think so, but you never know," she answered. "It is very,

very, very, very, very, very tiring and I'm not a trained singer." She has said many times that the only other Broadway role she feels she could perform is Sonya, the role Lucie Arnaz did in *They're Playing Our Song*. More recently she said, "My days as a singer are over—did they ever begin? I ain't no Patti Lupone."

In fact, her lack of extended vocal training caused her to develop vocal nodes. "When you really don't sing properly you develop like a callous on your vocal chords. So when you get tired or talk too much or sing too much, you get this hoarse, sort of Harvey Fierstein sort of thing goin' on," she told her television audience in 1996. "Unless I stop singing—and let's face it, that's not gonna happen."

With her run winding down, the producers realized they could probably keep the show going for a long time with similar feats of unlikely star casting. Following Rosie in the role of Rizzo was Maureen McCormick, much better known as the original Marcia Brady, star of one of Rosie's all-time favorite TV shows, *The Brady Bunch*. The two had met at the home of their singing teacher in Los Angeles. They took one look at each other and burst into a *Brady* song. That led to a friendship, and Rosie later recommended Maureen to replace her in *Grease*. Rosie also sublet her apartment to her for her six-week run. "I think Rosie is the funniest woman alive," McCormick said, noting that Rosie had become "like a sister to me."

That certainly brings the circle all the way around from Commack to Broadway. After Maureen, Brooke Shields and later Sheena Easton did turns as Rizzo. Rosie had this to say about Brooke's performance: "I thought she was pretty good, really. It isn't a tough role to master, especially for me. I grew up playing Rizzo in my backyard (my sister always got to be Sandy)."

When the curtain closed for the final time on Rosie's Rizzo, it seemed certain that Rosie got exactly what she came for, another dream brought to life.

✒ 12

At the Top and on the Tube

One big reason Rosie's visibility and popularity continued to grow was that she is a hard worker, not content to sit idle for very long. Even while she was busy making films and performing on Broadway, Rosie made time for other TV appearances, benefits, and occasional comedy club dates. Those, especially, were a lot more fun now that she was a genuine star and opening in Vegas for her idols—such as country singing sensation, Wynonna, who even let her sing some back-up for her.

"I do gigs if somebody I like is working in Vegas and they want me to open for them. I love working in Vegas; a lot of comics hate it, but I love it, and I do it all the time for benefits," she explained in 1993. "But I'm doing jokes that I've been doing for years, and the audience can mouth them along with me. It's time for me to get a new act, and if I don't have the time to work on it, it's really unfair of me to go tour around the country and do the same old jokes that I've been doing forever."

Some of the gigs Rosie did were more for her own amusement, like appearing on celebrity *Jeopardy,* where she performed very well, undoubtedly surprising some of her former teachers back in Commack. For another déjà vu experience, she finally got to host *Saturday Night Live* in November 1993. It must have been very surreal to be in that famous studio at last, considering that she never missed the show as a child and received her first important attention as a performer doing Gilda Radner's "Roseanne Rosannadanna." Rosie also appeared on *Sesame Street* as Oscar's Fairy

Grouch Mother and, for a contrast, on *A Gala for the President at Ford's Theatre.*

At the end of the 1993–94 season, five of the top six shows were sitcoms captained by stand-up comics—and three of the five were women: Jerry Seinfeld, Tim Allen, Roseanne, Ellen DeGeneres, and Brett Butler. And most of them were not very well known until they landed their own shows. Given television executives' unrelenting desire to replicate someone else's success, it's not surprising that by that time, a visible comic like Rosie could have written her sitcom ticket, had she so desired. But by then, she was already making her mark in bigger and better things—movies.

She did do a few more guest shots the following year, on Cindy Crawford's MTV show and on the sitcom *Living Single*. But the TV highlight of 1994 for Rosie had to be her appearance as a presenter at the sixty-sixth annual Academy Awards. She exclaimed, "Look at me—I'm on the Academy Awards. Can you believe it? I've got the dress. I've got the jewels. I've got the breasts. And they all have to be back by midnight."

In 1995, Rosie also appeared on the Oscar extravaganza, though in a rather strange fashion. That was the year David Letterman hosted. As part of a prepared bit lampooning his own role—loosely described as acting—in the disastrous *Cabin Boy,* Dave induced lots of A-list actors to tape fake auditions for the movie. Rosie was in great company as she "auditioned" for the silly film. That year she also appeared as a presenter on Nickelodeon's *Eighth Annual Kids' Choice Awards* and received one of the awards. In fact, she had so much fun that year that she returned the following year as the host for the event. Rosie also did a guest shot on the short-lived sitcom *Bless This House.*

Most of her free time, however, was consumed with creating and trying out a new comedy act for her first one-woman TV special on HBO. This is a definite rite of passage for any comedian and a sure sign she had reached the peak of her profession as a comic. Starting in the fall of 1994, Rosie took her new act on the road to prepare for the one-hour special. In Boston she told reporters she had gotten rusty and needed to get her comedy edge back.

"Comedy is a combative art form," she explained. "If you're not trained and you go into the boxing ring, you're gonna get the crap kicked out of you. The audience is ready—they know you can deliver a good punch, so they're waiting for that punch—and if you don't have it, you're gonna get beat up."

She went on to say she had missed the comedy scene. "I think once you have a love for stand-up comedy in the beginning of your career, you always go back to it. Robin Williams, Billy Crystal, they always go back and do it in some capacity, no matter what they're doing filmwise. I kind of feel the same thing." She was definitely feeling anxious in Boston: "I'm actually a little nervous, because I haven't done a long show for quite awhile. It's going to be unfamiliar at first."

Reviewers in Boston picked up on her shortage of material, as evidenced by her riffing off of conversations with audience members. At one point, she spotted a critic in the crowd furiously taking notes. She gave herself an impromptu review: "She opened with a curse, then she talked about oral sex...and she's a lot fatter in real life." The critic for the *Boston Globe* wasn't too impressed: "I can't say there weren't laughs, but this was a real up and down ride, an act in need of better material and a sharper edge."

Four months later, Rosie was in Chicago for another round of tryouts. By then she had added more material and was close to being ready for the taping, scheduled for April 1995. Though her first appearance had been bumpy, Rosie said it helped that her sister, and sometime business manager, Maureen, was in the audience. "I saw her mouthing hints to me like Cliff Notes. She's going, 'Do the thing about Daddy.'" New material she put in the act included bits about growing older (she was by then thirty-two); wanting a baby; and a large section about her transformation from a regular person into a star.

To reporters in Chicago she said, "As much as I've achieved some sort of success in the film industry, I don't feel any different. And I think people have this illusion, including myself before it happened to me, that everything was going to change once you sort of made it."

Not true, she said. She still feels like she has plenty in common with the folks who attend her shows and movies. She added, "You become friends with who you work with, because that's life. But it's really no different than if I got a job at the high school teaching English, and I was hanging out with the art teacher and the janitor."

She does enjoy the perks that go with being a star. She no longer drives from gig to gig by car to stay in seedy motels or condos. "Now they fly you first class, and you get to bring three friends and go to a hotel and you only work on the weekend. It's a whole different thing than when I was young and staying at Motel 6. It was a very, very lonely existence then."

The critic for the *Chicago Tribune* liked what he saw: "O'Donnell's talent has always been that the audience can easily relate to her like she was an old friend from the neighborhood. She mixes that with a confidence and ease that marks any top-flight comic...always been a joy to watch...the type of comic that makes stand-up special."

To tape the HBO special, Rosie returned to one of her favorite clubs, the Comedy Connection, in Boston. This is the same club where she lied her way in the door to earn her first sixty dollars, so that circle was now complete. The end result, which debuted on April 29, 1995, was a big hit with her fans. In it, she didn't shy away from topical humor and had this to say about O. J. Simpson, whose trial was still dragging on. "How guilty is *that* guy?" she asked, referring to the infamous Bronco ride. "I think there's no way in the world that's how an innocent person behaves. Three years from now, I'm going to be sitting by O. J. at some dinner...nice to meet you. Listen, could I have the steak knife?"

Her successful TV special was followed by her first Emmy nomination for Outstanding Individual Performance in a Variety or Music Program. It was especially sweet because it recognized her as a performer—and as a writer—since she wrote the material for the special. Rosie was all jeweled up and eager to receive one of the statuettes the following September, but she did not win the award. She lost to none other than her idol, Barbra Streisand, who was also nominated for *her* TV special. From her front row seat, Rosie watched Barbra as she whooshed by to collect her trophy. Rosie was also nominated for an Emmy the following year for a guest appearance as herself on Garry Shandling's super spoof of late-night talk shows, *The Larry Sanders Show*. But again, no award.

In January 1996 she suddenly found herself performing in Las Vegas— filling in for George Burns at his 100th birthday appearance at Caesars Palace. Considering all of the comics that could have been chosen to substitute for the ailing legend, this was a high honor. George called Rosie and impressed her with his energy and mental acuity during their twenty-minute chat. Rosie said he was "completely lucid and funny" and told her jokes she couldn't repeat anywhere. He may have been stuck at home and unable to perform, but Burns still read the daily Hollywood trades, so he was well aware of the impending debut of her new talk show and wanted to discuss the marketing of it with her. Later that year Rosie spoke about her encounter with Burns. "I met him one time before he passed away. He was very sweet and kind. It was a big thrill for me because I grew up admiring him, and my parents loved him."

Next on her TV schedule was a favor to her pal, Fran Drescher. Rosie appeared in a cameo role as a quintessential New York City cab driver on Fran's hit sitcom, *The Nanny*. At last Rosie finally got to perform on a hit sitcom with a happy cast and crew. She was busy taking notes for her own show while she was on Fran's set. The following autumn, she again guest starred on a hilarious episode of *The Nanny*, but this time playing herself on the set of *The Rosie O'Donnell Show*, with Fran Fine in the audience shouting out child-care tips. And playing herself—as Rosie's old buddy from *Crosswits*, Charles Shaughnessy (Maxwell Sheffield) so gallantly pointed out— "is how you know you've really made it in showbiz."

In April 1996, Rosie hosted "Catch a Rising Star 50th Anniversary— Give or Take 26 Years," a TV special on CBS honoring the legendary comedy club. The special was taped the previous February in Aspen, Colorado, at the U.S. Comedy Arts Festival and featured an array of performers, including Robin Williams, Billy Crystal, and Richard Belzer, who had begun their careers at the New York City club. Although Rosie did appear at Catch a Rising Star, she was already established, and so she circumvented the grueling ordeal many young comics went through just to appear there. Comics often waited night after night hoping to perform, lucky to get a chance at two in the morning.

Rosie opened the special with a brief monologue in which she spoke about her early days on the road and how few women there were. She said club owners never booked two women together because it was a rarity in itself to have a female comic. Consequently, the few women on the circuit didn't get to know one another very well. Rosie recalled that "some emcees would introduce me— 'You're not gonna *believe* who we have comin' up next... it's a *female* comic!'—like it was some sort of estrogen freak show."

On the special, Rosie also told some jokes between the other acts, then finished up the show by singing a truly inspired and funny duet of "Finiculi Finicula" with Jon Lovitz. Her stage presence and confidence as a host contributed to a successful program. She was asked at the time if she found it difficult to clean up her act for network TV, and she replied: "Well, it's always a lot of fun doing shows for HBO, because you can just sort of do what you're thinking.... I have started editing nearly everything I say. It's really freakin' hard.'"

In late May of that year Rosie did another stand-up gig, at Resorts Hotel in Atlantic City. While this show was similar to her HBO special, Rosie was asked to tone down her material and eliminate profanity and most sexual references because children would be in the audience. One of her jokes from that era relates to her Catholic upbringing: "The Vatican has a new gift shop—if you break anything you don't have to pay for it, but they do make you feel really, really guilty."

During the summer of 1996, Rosie lived out another of her dreams when she guest starred on one of her longtime favorite soap operas, *All My Children.* "I've watched the show since 1974." She portrayed Naomi, a tough-talking, gum-snapping uniformed maid. Her scene begins with Rosie answering the door at the home of Adam Chandler to find Susan Lucci standing there.

SUSAN [*pulling the Walkman out of Rosie's ears*]: "Who are you?"

ROSIE [*yanking off Susan's dark glasses*]: "Who are *you?*"

SUSAN [*haughtily*]: "Erica Kane!"

ROSIE [*underwhelmed*]: "Whoop-de-do."

Later, the two actresses spoke about the experience. Rosie told Susan that she was "very nervous with you—you're Erica and everything—and I was thinkin', I'm gonna mess up." She went on to say how much harder she found this kind of acting than doing films. "You only rehearse it once, and you shoot it, and you'd better get it right." Susan assured her that she had done a fabulous job and invited her to return: "Naomi is definitely a character to be reckoned with."

But the most fun she had on other people's TV shows that year occurred while hosting *Saturday Night Live,* on December 14, with her partner-in-shopping, Penny Marshall, as her featured guest. It was the holiday show, in the twenty-second season of *Saturday Night Live,* and Rosie looked festive in expensive red velvet. As she stood there during the opening sequence, she remembered adoring Penny as Laverne, and she remembered fantasizing about standing right there, onstage in the giant studio 8H at Rockefeller Center. And here she was as the host, the star. Glamorous photos of *her* opened the show. The studio audience was standing and cheering for *her.*

Rosie and Penny began the show with a bad imitation of Sonny and Cher singing "I Got You, Babe." The singing, at least, was rescued by the entrance of the evening's musical guest, Whitney Houston. All three then participated in the first sketch, which was fairly amusing, as *Saturday Night Live* pieces go. Rosie played a nun choir director in a full-length habit with Penny as her tippling pianist. Whitney, of course, was the star pupil in the parochial school choir. They were attempting a rendition of "The Little Drummer Boy," which was disrupted by another girl trying to upstage Whitney. Rosie got off the best line of the night when she scolded the other girl (acted by Molly Shannon) for playing her drum too raucously: "You're drumming for Jesus Christ, not Judas Priest!"

Another skit parodied the low-key programming found on National Public Radio. Rosie, looking like a young Shelley Winters in a curly blond wig, portrayed an expert guest on "Delicious Dish," a cooking show. The premise alone was quite amusing to her fans, who know full well that Rosie's idea of cooking is dialing for pizza. The three women who appeared in this sketch were so unanimated they appeared to be comatose. The real laughs came because Rosie spoke slowly and softly in an unaccented generic voice—in a voice as far from her natural one as is possible.

Those viewers who managed to stay awake until 12:45 A.M. were treated to the sight of Rosie gussied up as the widow of a cop, wearing a wig piled high with curls and a magenta pantsuit with blue sequins. Like many *Saturday Night Live* sketches, this was four characters in search of a storyline. For the big finish, Rosie flashed her ample cleavage at another character. The sign-off to the show, however, was creative and festive as the cast skated around the rink at Rockefeller Center. The camera zoomed in for a closeup of Rosie, gliding off into a brilliant night.

As for stand-up comedy, Rosie will continue to return to it, as her schedule permits. It is her favorite form of self-expression. In July 1996 she said, "I prefer stand-up comedy because you're the one who is in control of what you say and when you say it, and also how much you work. If you do a movie, you have to go away for three months and work up to fifteen hours every day. It's very tiring. If you do a Broadway show, you say the same thing every night. It gets very boring. With stand-up comedy, you can change it every night, and if you don't feel like working, you don't book yourself for that night."

Rosie is often asked for advice by aspiring comics and actors and she always gives the same advice: "I say, 'Quit. You'll never make it. There are thousands out there trying to make it.' And I hope they go home and say, 'To hell with her—I'm gonna make it.' Because if you don't have that kind of internal fortitude, there's no way you're going to be able to survive this business."

She has only one regret about her comedy career. "I never did Johnny Carson."

᪲ 13

The Joys of a Single Mother

In addition to being motherless daughters, Madonna and Rosie both longed to be mothers themselves. Knowing too well what it feels like to be without a mother, they were both committed to giving a child the kind of loving experience they had missed. Rosie's longing was so great she could not bear to watch movies about orphans or talk shows that featured homeless kids. "I watch Sally Jesse Raphael, and she has all those kids who need to be adopted," she said in a 1994 interview. "I'm hysterical, thinking, I can put bunk beds in the spare room!"

For Rosie, who came from a large Irish Catholic family, there was no doubt that she would become a mother someday. She just wasn't sure about the logistics. "I always knew I'd be a mom. I didn't know the specifics of when or how kids would enter my life, really, I just knew that I would be open to whatever way they presented themselves," she told a writer from *Newsday*.

This wasn't some starry-eyed misty vision, either. Rosie knew full well from spending time with her brother's and sister's children what raising a child meant. That, she said, "eliminated any fairy-tale image of bringing home a little Cabbage Patch doll. I was there every day for the first few years of my nieces' lives. I knew it was all about getting up at night and getting thrown up on."

She was also realistic about her options. She was clear that she didn't want to take the artificial insemination route. Though very serious, she couldn't help putting her comic spin on it. "That's a freaky concept to me. I don't want to have coffee with a stranger."

Given the absence of men in her life, she also wasn't eager to take the traditional route. "If I was with a man I wanted to have a child with, I would have gotten pregnant, but I really had no ego investment in recreating myself. Nor did I feel the need to dive into my gene pool and go fishing there, because there is a tremendous amount of illness in my family, a tremendous amount of alcoholism."

That pretty much left adoption as her only choice. Friends of Rosie's had adopted a child and were happy with the result, and they put her in touch with a lawyer to help her get the process started. In recent years many show business couples have adopted children with happy outcomes— Tom Cruise and Nicole Kidman; Jamie Lee Curtis and Christopher Guest. Also, a number of actresses feel secure enough to raise a child on their own and have adopted youngsters without a man on hand, including Michelle Pfeiffer, Diane Keaton, Donna Mills, Amanda Bearse, Sheena Easton, and Kate Jackson. "Modern Hollywood has become very family-friendly," says Joan Hyler, a former agent at William Morris and ICM. "If you're the star of a $75 million movie, the care and feeding of your spouse and children becomes very important to a studio." Perks for those actresses are staggering, and certainly make it easier for female stars to play both roles.

Today's adoptive mothers are earnest about this step in their lives. Michelle Pfeiffer, for example, has made it clear that if she can't work out a satisfactory shooting schedule for her films that allows time with her children, then she has no desire to be an actress.

Rosie described the steps toward adoption for her: "I filled out the forms, I was fingerprinted, and I waited." Unlike many celebrities who claim that their fame and wealth had no impact on their adoptive process, Rosie, as usual, tells it like it is. She shared her feelings about it with NBC's Katie Couric: "Of course it made it easier. It's not like I didn't have to go through the process, but to deny that who I am didn't help things along would be a lie. The truth is, having money helps in every situation. The price of stardom is a loss of privacy. But aside from that, the money that comes with stardom makes life easier in every other way, I can't deny that."

Her fame also speeded up the process: "I'm very conscious that most people wait much longer to adopt. But you wouldn't say, 'No thanks, I don't want that baby.' I think you get the child you're supposed to have in your life."

When asked what she thought of the process, Rosie replied, "Mine is a closed adoption, with full disclosure at the age of eighteen. I think the process is wonderful, and I hope to get the word out about the many children who are in need of a home."

The long-hoped-for birth of her child finally occurred on May 25, 1995. Rosie first saw her new son when her lawyer brought her a photograph taken when he was just an hour old. She called her sister, Maureen, to share the news—and her concerns. "I said, 'My son is a smushed-up tomato, all red and blotchy!' She said, 'All babies look like that.' Now I think he's the most gorgeous child I've ever seen."

When he was just two days old, Rosie proudly took her new baby home. "As I held him in my arms the first night, everything just naturally fell into place. It completed me in a way that nothing else could have."

It also reconnected her to her mother and her mother before her. Rosie spoke about how she had idealized her mother because her image of her is frozen in time. "The first time I ever thought of my mom as a full human being was when I held my son, and I realized she felt all these things for me and my siblings…and that's when I started seeing her as a woman, as opposed to a child's version of mommy."

Rosie tells two different stories about how she named her son. Early on, she said, "I didn't name him after anyone in particular. I wanted a name that would work if he were a surfer or a Supreme Court judge. So Parker it is." Parker Jaren is the full name.

A year later, when actress Kirstie Alley appeared on her talk show, she told her a different story. "My son is kinda named after your husband—Parker Stevenson—I liked the *Hardy Boys* as a kid and decided back then if I ever had a baby boy I would name him Parker."

When she was twelve, Rosie had a crush on the young *Hardy Boys* actor Stevenson. As an adoptive mom herself, Kirstie seemed happy for Rosie and had a good laugh at their unusual connection. For the time being, however, she mostly calls him "Boo Bear." She asks, "Do you think he'll need therapy?"

Unable to turn to her own mother for advice, Rosie swears by a helpful book by Anne Lamott, called *Operating Instructions*. Rosie also received tremendous help from star pal mothers, Rita (Mrs. Tom Hanks) Wilson and Kate (Mrs. Steven Spielberg) Capshaw. Rita even brought *her* mother along to help during the first days of Rosie's motherhood. Rosie needed all the wisdom these women could offer, because she started off with a real challenge. "I had a seven-pound baby. My sister's babies were ten pounds. To me, he was this tiny little boy. He wouldn't eat. I was so scared. But Rita's mother got him to drink a whole bottle."

The older woman soon calmed Rosie's nerves, telling her "You can't kill him! Don't worry."

Kate Capshaw seemed to know where to get whatever it was that Rosie needed, and how to get it delivered quickly.

"I have to give her credit," Rosie recalled. "She provided everything I needed in any way, shape or form. During the first three months, I thought she should establish 1-800-Call-Kate for new mothers." One day Rosie mentioned that she didn't think she had the right size diapers, "And suddenly you'd hear *beep-beep-beep,* and a truck would be backing up. And a delivery man would say 'Here's ninety-five thousand diapers from Ms. Capshaw.'"

Other star buddies came to Rosie's aid when *Sleepless* costar Meg Ryan gave a baby shower for Rosie at Meg's Los Angeles home. Among the attendees were Carrie Fisher and former catcher to her third base, Geena Davis.

It was soon obvious Rosie had made the right decision in becoming a parent. "It's the best thing I ever did—I should've done it a long time ago," she said.

When people continued to ask her why she traded her film career for a baby, she would inquire, "Do you have kids?" When they would say no, she would reply, "That's why you're asking." Rosie says about the mothering bond, "It's about experiencing a wealth of emotions."

One of them is pride. "I took a picture of him every day for a while," she confesses, "but I only do it every month now." Though Rosie is very protective of her son's privacy and rarely allows him to be photographed for public consumption, she does carry snapshots of him and willingly shows them off. While displaying them for one reporter, she cooed, "Here he is looking like a baby model. He's got little green eyes. Sort of blond hair. He's very attentive, and he likes to laugh all day."

Although Rosie didn't care what gender child she adopted, in 1997 she did share her ideas about why she ended up with a boy. "I have a lot of issues to work out about men. I had some stuff with my dad that was never really resolved. I think that the adoption helps me to connect in a way that I wasn't able to before. I'm so in love with this child, who is a male and his own person."

Though little Parker is being raised without a father, he is not without men in his life. Rosie has three brothers whom she sees regularly, as well as male friends—one, known as TheR0Bobby on America Online, even baby-sits. When people quiz her about it, and they always do, Rosie reveals, "This baby would have been raised in a single-parent household had he been kept by the birth family. There are many structures that make up a family—and we're definitely a family."

Becoming a mother has also brought Rosie even closer to her sister, giving them more in common. And she told her friend, comic Margaret Smith, who also recently adopted a baby boy, that motherhood brought back her childhood. "I know with my son, I do things that I remember my mom doing."

Fiercely determined to raise her son by herself, she did experience one big shock. "I was surprised that a human being can function on as little sleep as I did for the first three months." Of waking up every two hours, she said, "...that's how they torture people in other countries!" After she had logged three months as a mom, Rosie was asked if it was harder or easier than she had thought it would be. "It is harder and more wonderful than I ever expected. Last night he slept for seven hours straight. Yippeeee!"

By the time Parker was a year old, she noted, "Beforehand I was much more of a pessimist, about my life and maybe my longevity....my mom died when she was young, and I always thought that might be my fate. Since having my son, I don't think that anymore. I think I'm going to live to see him grow up. It's like you grow another heart, like someone kicks down a door that was sealed shut, and then the whole world—sunshine, flowers—falls through. I have such joy that I didn't think was possible."

Just before Parker's first birthday, Rosie was finally able to celebrate Mother's Day "without feeling a lingering, omnipresent gloom. It was the first time I literally wasn't overwhelmingly sad, where I felt joy and levity and something close to pride." At about that time, Parker gave his mother a very special gift. Rosie's realistic preparation for motherhood included knowing there would be good times that would make it all worthwhile. "I knew about the joy that would come, that wondrous moment when he looks up and says 'Mama,'" which Parker said for the first time right on cue for Mother's Day.

Rosie also discovered that other women treat her differently now. She talked about how difficult it can be for her to go out alone in New York, now that she's so recognizable. But when she's out with Parker, it's a different story. "Now, when I take my son to the park, mothers stop me as a mom, not as somebody on TV or in movies. They ask how old he is, how he's doing. I'm able to connect with people on an innate maternal level. My fame has been superseded by my parenting, which I love. I'm in the sorority now."

Unlike other star moms, Rosie did not hire nannies and assistants to share the work load. "For the first ten months of his life, there was no nanny," Rosie said, explaining her desire to be a hands-on mother. Though she eventually had to have help to do her daily television show, Rosie made it clear that the help doesn't come home with her. "The nanny will not live in my house. I'll get my son up, we'll have breakfast, we'll go to work. He'll be in his own environment."

One of the things she sometimes does at breakfast is watch tapes she made the night before of her favorite shows. "When you have a baby, it curtails your TV viewing hours," Rosie explained. "I used to stay up late— 2:30—now by 9:30 I'm fightin' to stay awake."

So she sometimes watches *Chicago Hope* or a friend on Leno or Letterman when Parker wakes up at 6:00 A.M. Though her hours have adjusted to make room for Parker, she's very satisfied when her long day is done. "You feel a sense of purpose and a sense of accomplishment at the end of the day when he goes down for a nap. You really feel like—wow—I did it! He's happy and he's sleeping and he's fed and he doesn't have a cold and he's clean—and I'm exhausted!"

Eventually, Rosie incorporated being a mother into her comedy act. One of her best lines: "I adopted and I had the epidural anyway." She also makes jokes at her own expense about how she has become competitive with other mothers in that classic way that women do. "You get like mom-competitive and protective and snotty—you wouldn't think I would do that, but I did." When she finds herself with a bunch of civilian moms at the park she can't help doing her share of bragging—even if she has to stretch the truth to do it. When asked by another mother if Parker spoke in complete sentences yet, Rosie replied, "No, but he's getting his doctorate at Columbia!"

Early on, Rosie was asked if Parker was funny like her. "So far he seems

A lady in red at the opening of *Exit to Eden* in October of 1994 in Hollywood. (Photo: Gerardo Somoza/ Outline)

Rosie played a cop again in the movie *Another Stakeout* with costars Emilio Estevez and Richard Dreyfuss. (Touchstone, courtesty Kobal)

Rosie hammed it up with RuPaul at the premiere of the movie *To Wong Foo, Thanks for Everything, Julie Newmar.* (Photo:Gerardo Somoza/Outline)

Rosie in the film *Beautiful Girls* (1996) with Timothy Hutton. (Miramar Pictures, courtesy Kobal)

Looking glamorous in black at the premiere of *Beautiful Girls* in January 1996. (Photo: Thomas Lay/Outline)

Arriving at the premiere of *101 Dalmations*, Rosie shows off her "dalmation-esque" footwear in December 1996. (Photo: Steve Sands/Outline)

Mugging for the camera with her sunglasses, January 1993. (Photo: Michel del Sol/Outline)

Rosie demonstrates her hidden talent for juggling orange things. (Photo: Bonnie Schiffman/Outline)

Rosie performed on the Showtime Special for hurricane relief in September of 1992. (Photo: Frank Micelotta/Outline)

Rosie with Kevin Spacey at the Teddy Bear Auction. (Photo: Gerardo Somoza/Outline)

Rosie O'Donnell and Spike Lee were designated two of *Newsweek* magazine's 100 Top Newsmakers of 1996. (Photo: Thomas Lau/Outline)

Rosie shows off her Pink Ladies outfit in the 1994 Broadway production of *Grease*.

Rosie looked elegant at the 1994 Academy Awards ceremony. (Photo: Jeff
Slocum/Outline)

pretty funny, but it's hard to tell, because he's only a year old. He's very cute though, and he says 'Mama' twenty-four hours a day."

By the age of seventeen months, there were early signs he had caught the acting bug. Rosie was awakened at three in the morning by the sound of Parker crying on his baby monitor. She was a bit suspicious though, because the cries sounded insincere. But being diligent, Rosie trudged down the hall to check on him. As soon as she entered the room, he stood up, smiled, and said "Hi!"

Though Rosie has stuck to her policy of not divulging too much about her son, she did give a progress report in October 1996 to her friend Naomi Judd on Naomi's new interview show: "He's seventeen months old now. He's saying 'Mommy' every day—regular, loud, and frequent." For a moment, the comic became quiet and serious, as she spoke with heartfelt emotion about him. "I realize what a profound gift he is every day. He's given me a greater capacity to love and be loved—that I never knew existed." Rosie went on to say that her life had changed in ways she couldn't have imagined. "I knew that I would love my child, but I had no idea that it would fill me with such a sense of completion."

In 1996 she spoke about the dramatic changes in her emotional life. "My son has given me a greater capacity to feel things—and less capacity to control my emotions. I have no control, no on-off switch anymore. Now I cry in movies. I cry watching TV all the time."

Fans have besieged Rosie with advice on virtually every aspect of motherhood. One woman, with relevant experience, wrote: "I was adopted when I was six months old. I have always felt special. With your wonderful personality and being a great lady, your adopted son will also feel special."

Rosie is determined to raise Parker in a down-to-earth manner, while also protecting him from the outside world. For one thing, he only watches PBS— "but not out of snobbery," she is quick to explain. Rosie knows all too well what kind of TV shows are on in the daytime. "Nowadays a kid watches afternoon TV—it could corrupt him for life," she says. "I don't think that I would encourage my son to watch too much TV."

When asked what she most wants to give Parker, Rosie answers quickly, "Safety." Acknowledging that we live in a world that can be rather scary, she explained, "You know, the world can always be unsafe, but your home has to be a safe place. And growing up, mine wasn't. But he has a safe, loving home where he's known and accepted and loved. And that's really important to me." One thing she does to keep prying eyes away from Parker is host a play group for six other toddlers at her home every week.

Rosie has taken some amusing precautions to protect him and avoid having his face splashed across the tabloids. Once when a friend was visiting with her own baby, they spotted a man with a camera standing in Rosie's yard. When she asked him what he was doing, he said, "I'm sorry, but they offered me so much money. I'll leave, but people will be back." Rosie told how she let him take some photos, hoping to appease him. What he didn't know, was that the pictures he took were of Rosie and her *friend's* baby! Later, on Letterman, Rosie embellished the story, and joked that she had hoodwinked the photographers with her puppy wrapped up in a blanket.

Rosie has worked with many child actors, and knows firsthand what they are up against. "I try to tell the parents of kids in movies that fame is a difficult thing for adults to handle. It's impossible for children. All these showbiz kids who end up holding up drugstores and going to the Betty Ford Clinic—fame warps reality—sometimes forever." As for Parker, she says emphatically, "I'm going to tell him what my parents told me. When you're old enough to drive yourself to the audition, then you can go."

Rosie was asked what she would want if given the proverbial three wishes, and she responded: "That all kids were safe and loved. That we had a cure for all diseases. And for three more wishes."

When asked if she would like to adopt more children, she is clear about that, too. "Yes, I would. I'd love to have a bunch of kids...at least two or three more." She went on to explain that "I'm one of five kids, and I have very close relationships with all my siblings. When you grow up in a big family like that, I think you realize the comfort that provides. So I'll have at least two children. That's a guarantee." About her beloved son, she speaks eloquently. "It's like you throw a wish up, and you hope that it gets caught. And mine did."

↶ 14

Harriet the Spy

Motherhood changed forever how the thirty-two-year-old Rosie viewed her movie career. After Rosie ended her run in *Grease* she returned to film work and made a group of movies in which she had small but pivotal roles. The first one to arrive in theaters was *Now and Then,* the maiden output from Demi Moore's production company, Moving Pictures. Rosie was attracted to the script because it was all about friendship between girls, a topic not often explored by Hollywood. It is a coming of age story for the young girls, who also solve a mystery during the film, and a passage into maturity for the older versions of the characters as they reunite for the birth of a child.

When this movie opened in fall 1995 there were several other so-called female-bonding movies around, enough to suddenly look like a trend.

The main reason so few films like this ever get made is that men rarely attend them and these movies seldom make much money. The other part of the equation is that many women won't go to a movie alone, even if it sounds appealing to them. Also, many women are just too busy to go out to the movies, even with a friend. And it is the all-important first weekend's grosses that can make or break a film. It takes a blockbuster like *First Wives Club* to become an exception. Women are forever lamenting the sorry state of films and how they are rarely relevant to their lives, and yet they do not vote with their pocketbooks when one does come along. Demi Moore clearly had those women in mind when she developed this project:

125

"We [the characters] do get together and bond, and for me the idea that you can create a friendship that grounds you, that you can return to, is important for all of us."

In *Now and Then,* two quartets of actresses play four characters at age twelve and as adults. The publicity for the film overplayed the importance of the better-known adult cast, who only appear in brief segments at either end of the movie. Filmed on location in Savannah, Georgia, the adult stars—Rosie, Demi, Rita Wilson, and Melanie Griffith—were only there for the last week of shooting. Most of the film focuses on the growing pains and challenges faced by the young girls in the summer of 1970. "The adults had to study us," explained Gaby Hoffman, who played the young Demi Moore.

Reviewers were split over whether the adult actresses were believable as the grown-up versions of their talented counterparts. The critic for the *Chicago Tribune* wrote about the young half of the cast, "…in funny ways so much like the actresses they're supposed to grow up and become, that it's fun watching them." Rosie's younger self was portrayed by Christina Ricci. When she was asked if it was fun working with her, Rosie replied, "Yes, it was. She's a great girl. I was a fan of hers from *The Addams Family,* and I was very happy to play her as a grown-up." In general, Rosie said this was "a really fun movie to do."

Some of the pleasure came her second day on the set, when the big girls were sitting around bonding over a discussion of jewelry. Rosie, who didn't know her costars well yet, just sat and stared with her mouth hanging wide open as the other three women compared jewelers, reeled off phone numbers from memory, and shared tips on where to get the best diamonds. Rita, Mrs. Tom Hanks; Demi, Mrs. Bruce Willis; and Melanie, at the time Mrs. Don Johnson, had apparently hit their husbands up for some bigtime rocks. Seems Bruce was in the mood to buy Demi a 10-karat diamond ring, and her pals knew just where to send him. Of the experience Rosie said later on her talk show, "And I'm thinkin', one of these things is not like the other." Demi then showed her the very huge ring in question, to which Rosie exclaimed, "Oh, that is scary!" Demi nodded but said she figured she had earned it: "All I know is I pushed three babies out for it."

The young girls in *Now and Then* make a pact to always be there for each other in time of crisis. There are some poignant parallels between the character Roberta and Rosie. Roberta's mother died when she was young, giving her a rather defiant streak, and she was also a rugged tomboy. In the movie, Roberta never leaves home without a picture of her mom. She also enjoys faking her own death and scaring her friends. Demi Moore is the voice of the narrator who ties the stories together: "None of us ever experienced a loss like Roberta, and we didn't understand her jokes. She kept trying to make death funny—maybe to make it easier for herself."

The crisis that reunites the girls as adults is the birth of Rita Wilson's first child, to be attended by OB/GYN Rosie O'Donnell, in yet another irony. By this time, Rosie was openly yearning for a baby of her own, and in fact adopted Parker by the time the film opened. A classic Rosie scene occurs wherein she commandeers a limousine to spirit Rita and the gang off to the hospital for the delivery. After a fairly graphic birth scene, Rosie sheds a few tears and appears genuinely moved as she watches Rita embrace her newborn daughter.

Later, the women congregate in the treehouse of their youth to welcome the baby into their circle. Talk turns to relationships, and after Demi has described her many failures, Rosie says, "It sure is lonely all by yourself."

What you do not hear Rosie's character discuss is *her* personal life. Hers is the only character without much back story—because it was all left on the cutting room floor. Seems the movie that was released turned out quite different from the movie Rosie *thought* she made. Afterward she had this to say about it:

"The woman I played was quite assuredly a gay woman. I was very happy, because it was a movie for women and about girls' friendships, which I think there aren't enough of. The lesbian story line made it an interesting role to act and said something interesting about how people are accepting of each other."

She went on to explain how some of her dialogue was altered in looping; the name of her girlfriend was changed to a man's name. In fact, they originally shot a sequence where Rita Wilson says of Roberta and her partner: "They're thinking of adopting now. It's perfectly fine. It's very progressive." Rosie was told test audiences found it confusing. And to that she replied sarcastically: "And I'm like, 'Oh really?'"

The reviewer for the Long Island paper, *Newsday*, picked up the few references left in the film. He said of Roberta, "She excels at sports (her dubious sexual proclivity is delivered with something like a wink)." Too bad the filmmakers chickened out in the end. That lack of control and resultant frustration inspired Rosie to yearn for more control in her films.

The movie received mixed reviews, from ghastly to mildly positive. The same *Newsday* reviewer said of Rosie's performance: "O'Donnell has a nice wry delivery when the infrequently funny line comes her way." Other writers said: "Rather obvious and predictable, but thoroughly likable." And, "Not particularly deep, but it's a good-natured, sprightly comedy." Another liked the "absurdly funny birds-and-bees speech."

Next to be released was the ensemble piece, *Beautiful Girls*, which Rosie nearly stole with her long, passionate diatribe on why men are deluded by *Penthouse* Pets. Some reviewers even said that speech alone made the movie worth recommending. This film explores how a group of young adults feel about the life choices they have made in the decade since high school. In examining each others' lives, some characters are inspired to change direction and take new risks. Set in a small working-class Massachusetts town, the film was actually shot outside Minneapolis. As Scott Rosenberg, the gifted screenwriter of the film explained halfway through the shoot, "We came here because they promised us snow. We've had no snow! We've been making snow! Our tech guy is an expert on snow now. But everyone is very giddy and happy now because there's supposed to be snow on Monday." The winter weather plays a big role in the story, and it is difficult to tell the ersatz snow from the real thing.

Rosie plays her second character named Gina, this time the owner of a beauty salon where the other women in the story come for a shampoo and advice. (She also sports one of the most flattering hairstyles of her film career in this picture.) One of the best-written movies she has been in, *Beautiful Girls* is witty and insightful about man-woman relationships, and all the characters feel like real people. An all-star cast (Uma Thurman, Matt Dillon, Timothy Hutton, Lauren Holly, Mira Sorvino, and Martha Plimpton) comes together for their tenth high school reunion, in what critics have called "The Little Chill."

Beautiful Girls is a thoughtful exploration of heterosexual relationships and why they go awry. In an unusual show of support for the low-grossing movie, Miramax Films rereleased it in September 1996, seven months after its initial run. The reason given was to draw attention to Oscar hopefuls, screenwriter Rosenberg and actress Natalie Portman, who plays a precocious adolescent enjoying a mutual crush with Tim Hutton. His character in the movie has a fear of commitment, and Hutton believes that "everybody has a problem with commitment until they find the one person who makes the fear disappear."

Rosie's character lashes out at that fear in her famous speech to Hutton and Dillon, delivered as they follow her across a street and on a shopping excursion to the local drugstore. She tries to get them to understand some basic female physiology that their surgically altered fantasy girls refute. "Girls with big tits have big asses. Girls with little tits have little asses. That's the way it goes. God doesn't fuck around. He's a fair guy...it's not my rule. You don't like it, call Him."

Inside the store she opens a *Penthouse* magazine to its centerfold and tells them: "Well, it doesn't exist. This is a mockery, this is a sham—these are not real women, these are beauty freaks," which she goes on to explain, make real women feel inadequate. She adds, "No matter how perfect the nipple, how supple the thigh, unless there's some other shit going on in the relationship besides the physical, it's gonna get old."

She rants on that unless men change their thinking on this subject, the future of mankind is at risk. Despite the sincerity of her lecture, the guys seem unimpressed. As rosie walks away from them, they smirk, and comment on *her* body. Matt Dillon: "Great ass." Tim Hutton: "Nice tits."

This group of young adults is living the kind of inbred small-town existence one suspects can be found all over America. These twenty-eight-year-olds are not yet ready to grow up, still acting out life scripts written in high school. The reunion forces them to take at least one step outside themselves, and what they see doesn't thrill them. Rosie only appears in a half dozen scenes, but she does get in some funny Hollywood references. At one point someone tells her she looks like Kathy Bates, which is something Rosie frequently hears in real life.

Entertainment Weekly hated the film but loved Rosie. They said of Gina: "Played with gusto by Rosie O'Donnell like a stand-up comedian parachuted into Boys Town. She's the *Beautiful Girls* idea of what girls can understand only when they're not beautiful. She should take the bus outta town ASAP to a place where filmmakers don't rely on Elle Macpherson as a muse." The reviewer for the *Detroit News* also loved Rosie's performance. "O'Donnell offers an exuberantly profane guide to real women—no parts excluded—for the benefit of Dillon and Hutton. Both are thunderstruck.

Viewers would be, too, if they could quit laughing at O'Donnell's boisterous account of the truth beyond *Playboy.*" She went on to say of the film: "Anyone who doesn't take a moment or three personally would do well to get out more."

Rosie, who saw the film at a neighborhood theater in New Jersey with her sister, said there was a visceral response in the audience to her famous scene: "The women stood up and cheered. There was this huge uprising among these overweight, nonperfect women."

After her huge success in Bedrock, Rosie discovered a new direction with her acting roles. "When I did *The Flintstones* I saw the effect it had on little kids. It was really so pleasing to me to have a little six-year-old come up and go 'Betty Rubble!' I loved it, and I thought that was a great kind of career to have. So I always tell my agent, if there are any kid movies that you see, let me know. I would love to be the person who made only kid movies."

Rosie's wish came true when she received a call to play Golly in *Harriet the Spy.* A beloved children's book, *Harriet* is the story of a precocious child and aspiring writer who spies on her friends, family, and neighbors and gets caught keeping notes on their activities in a private journal. Golly is her wise nanny who inspires her to pursue her dreams. "I said yes right away. I didn't even need to read the script, because I had read the book [by Louise Fitzhugh] as a kid and loved it."

The call came from Nickelodeon, the wildly successful cable TV channel for kids and their baby boomer parents, with the nostalgic sitcom rerun fest that is Nick at Night. This would be their first feature film, and they wanted Rosie to be a part of it. Rosie explained why she loved the book so much: "It encourages young girls to be independent and artistic and intellectual and strong."

Though faithful to the book in many ways, the film does update some aspects. Golly, for example, is "much less prim and nannyesque than what readers remember," Rosie says. "Definitely a lot less proper." To play Harriet, they chose ten year old Michelle Tractenberg, already a star on one of Nick's kids' series, *The Adventures of Pete and Pete.*

Rosie liked the film's premise because it reminded her of the Disney movies of her youth. "It's not sugar-coated Disney," she explains. "It shows kids accurately in the nineties, how cruel they can be to each other."

Rosie remembers being inspired by the book when she was a kid. "I used to spy on my brothers...and I actually kept a diary, but I kept it in code—so that I couldn't understand it when I found it twenty years later."

Harriet's diary is found and read by her classmates, who then ostracize her for her catty comments. But Golly, her nanny, encourages Harriet to keep writing and to appreciate her individuality even when others turn against her. Certainly a message that resonated with everyone, especially with most children who have felt like outsiders. Rosie also teaches her tolerance: "There are as many ways to live as there are people in this world, and each one deserves a closer look." And she tries to instill an appreciation for perseverance: "Good friends are one of life's blessings. Don't give 'em up without a fight."

When asked afterward if she has spied on anyone lately, Rosie replied, "I live in New York City, and I do have binoculars near my window. Sometimes I look across the street, and I see other people looking at me with their binoculars."

Ten-year-old Michelle reported that one day Rosie started a cherry-pit fight on the Toronto set—and that Rosie won. "I couldn't help it," Rosie confessed, "because it gets boring on movie sets." Rosie also said she loved doing the movie because she got "free Gak [a colorful, rubbery substance children love to play with], and everyone tried to slime me." Near the end of the shoot, Rosie was asked how she liked working with so many children. "It's a lot better than working with grown-ups—the kids are great, they really are." Then she paused to add a little reality check. "They sure have a lot of energy—you're *very* tired after a day on *Harriet the Spy*."

Rosie was very popular because she willing to play with the young actors between takes. She said, "I'll have a big chiropractic bill after this movie, because they all want shoulder rides and airplane swings."

Most reviewers were kind to *Harriet* when it opened in the summer of 1996, and *People* magazine had this to say about Rosie's performance: "A sort of zaftig Mary Poppins without the airborne umbrella, she dispenses wise advice ('Sometimes a really small lie can be a really big help') as freely as a politician making promises."

Asked if being a new mother helped her with the role, Rosie replied that it did to some extent, "But I don't think I ever quoted Keats....When Harriet asks what it means I wanted to say, 'Hell if I know.'"

As with many of Rosie's movie roles, this one also contained ironies. Most poignant is the little motherless girl from Commack who grew up doting on Mary Poppins now *becomes* a mythical nanny figure for a whole new generation of kids. Especially with so many latchkey kids out there, this is an important archetype for children. The other, more frustrating, irony for Rosie is that while she had time to play with the child actors on the set every day, the schedule didn't give her much time to see her own newly adopted son. While she portrayed a nanny, someone else was watching *her* kid. She said, "That's a very big price to pay." Near the end of the shoot, she remarked, "This will be the last film I do until Parker is in school."

Those who went for popcorn in the middle of *A Very Brady Sequel,* also released in 1996, could easily have missed Rosie's brief cameo. Rosie and Zsa Zsa Gabor attend an auction together and bid on a horse sculpture that is important to the plot. Rosie doesn't have any memorable lines, but her appearance is startlingly funny. She's decked out like some Beverly Hills matron with more money than taste and makeup by Tammy Faye, including thick false eyelashes and shocking-pink lipstick. She is almost unrecognizable—until she opens her mouth.

Wide Awake, which was scheduled to open in December 1996, reunited Rosie with her companion-in-leather from *Exit to Eden,* Dana Delaney. Rosie finally gets to work out some Catholic revenge in this film, since she is cast as a nun-teacher. "Not a wacky nun," she is quick to point out. "I didn't get to sing or fly." Dana plays the mother of a ten-year-old boy who has a coming-of-age relationship with a little girl. It's also about the boy's search for God, and Rosie had this to say about her role: "I'm one of the nuns in his Catholic school. I saw it the other day, and I was really touched by it. I thought it was a great movie, and I'm really proud of that one."

Girl Hoops, which Rosie wrote and stars in for Disney, is planned for release in 1997. It's about a female former basketball player with a ten-year-old daughter. She is offered an opportunity to coach a team, and that causes her to face her past.

"I will miss doing movies," Rosie said emphatically in August 1996. "I will only do small parts like *Harriet The Spy* or *Now and Then* because of my schedule." When asked with whom she would like to do a movie, Rosie replied, "Whoopi Goldberg. I think she's really funny, and I think it would be great to see two funny women starring in a movie together."

Rosie's ultimate goal is to move *behind* the camera. Eventually she would like to do more writing and direct. "I don't have any desire to do the meaty kind of acting pieces. I'd much rather direct someone else doing that," she said in a 1994 interview. "I would rather not be the product, I would rather have a product to hand people."

She said, "If I were in Jodie Foster's position with that kind of power, I'd direct all the time. I don't think I'd act anymore. Not because I don't respect it, but creatively it doesn't fulfill me as much as I would like it to. When you're an actress, you're not selling the character. You're selling you. 'Like me. Buy me. Come see me.' And that gets toxic. Which is why I started writing."

But more than any other factor, even before he could speak, Parker began to call the shots in Rosie's career. His needs come first. So Rosie has her infant son to thank for her next great career move.

↩ 15

The Rosie O'Donnell Show

During the twenty-six days she was in Toronto filming *Harriet the Spy,* Rosie rarely saw her new baby. It's nearly impossible to be a hands-on mother with the grueling schedule of film production. She felt horrible and said, "By the second day I knew it wouldn't work. This was not the kind of parent I wanted to be." Rosie realized she had to find a job as an entertainer that would allow her to be a full-time parent. "I didn't have a mom growing up, so it's very important for me to be there for my son." Also, she became dissatisfied with the movie roles she was being offered.

So she began to explore her options. Comedy gigs didn't have such bad hours, but traveling the circuit with a baby was unappealing. From her earlier forays into television, Rosie already knew that TV shows offered more reasonable schedules for working mothers. But she also knew from painful personal experience that sitcoms were a big gamble, and she longed for more security. There were opportunities to do her own late-night talk show, but she turned those down because she didn't believe she had the right sensibility or hard edge for that audience. (Though the previous year she had been penciled in to do the *Tonight Show* during the weeks Jay Leno was away. However, no one had asked Leno's permission. He made it clear he wanted to work every week of the year.) Nor could she see herself as part of the daytime herd, chasing after ever more sensational theme shows—I married my daughter's boyfriend and she married mine. Her views on trash talk are clear: "All those shows give these people is a ticket to New York, and their shame is sold for that fee."

Rosie was a fan of the *Donahue* show when it first aired. "When Phil Donahue did it, it was like *60 Minutes,* a journalistic look at some alternative lifestyles or aspects of humanity you maybe hadn't contemplated before. He presented it with sensitivity and respect for the guests, and that's gone out the window. It's become a humiliation festival." (Though to her credit, she admits the truth about the premise for her show. "I didn't invent it—I really stole it.")

She knew exactly what kind of show she would feel comfortable doing—the kind she had skipped school to watch as a kid. The kind *her* child could watch when he was older. And Rosie had enough showbiz savvy to know she wanted to be the boss and own a hefty piece of the show. How Oprah earned her many millions wasn't lost on Rosie. Thus was born KidRo Productions.

As soon as her ICM agents got the word out that Rosie O'Donnell wanted to do a talk show, a bidding war ensued among the big Hollywood players, including Rysher Entertainment, King World, Columbia TriStar, and The Walt Disney Company. Revealing her business acumen, Rosie carefully considered each suitor's track record with similar shows. Although they weren't the highest bidder, Warner Brothers did impress Rosie with the way they handled Jenny Jones, revising her show during her second year and not giving up on her when her ratings were less than spectacular.

Rosie also paid close attention to the support Warner had given to its entertainment show, *Extra.* Jim Paratore, president of Telepictures Productions, the Warner Bros. division that produces Rosie's show, explained why he thinks she chose them. "It has to do with the kind of commitment she believes this company puts behind ideas we believe in." Warner had been seeking a host who could appeal to more of a middle-ground audience than the type Ricki Lake attracted. In that regard, "she's like a diamond that fell from the sky," said one Warner executive.

Warner Brothers quickly signed her to a syndication contract reportedly worth $4.5 million (plus those tantalizing profits as part owner of the show). Some analysts figure she could earn as much as $5 million the first year. Rosie began with as much security as you can get on TV—with a commitment for thirty-nine weeks.

To prepare for her new show she did stints filling in for Greg Kinnear on NBC's early-hours show, *Later*. Then she hung out with Regis while Kathie Lee was off tending her empire. While Regis and Kathie Lee have found success with their formula of friendly and not-so-friendly bickering, Rosie knew she wanted to do a show less riddled with conflict.

Art Moore, director of programming at WABC in New York, observed Rosie and said, "It's difficult for anyone to be in that seat next to Regis. To be comfortable and for him to be comfortable—it was almost as if she has been doing it forever. She was terrific."

WABC became the first station to give Rosie's fledgling show a nest. Within weeks, Paratore had most of the major markets on board just on the basis of Rosie's name and her proposed format. Eventually, *The Rosie O'Donnell Show* aired in 97 percent of the country. Warner then decided to debut the show in June instead of the fall, to give them a sort of television version of an off-Broadway run. First-run competition is low in the summer, as is viewership, and they figured they would have time to work out any kinks.

The Rosie O'Donnell Show dangled in the syndication world like a solid-gold carrot. "We are in the eye of a selling storm the likes of which I've never seen," exclaimed a Warner Bros. executive in January 1996, at NAPTE, the Las Vegas bazaar for TV-show buyers. "In a number of key markets there were several stations bidding against each other for the show. Phoenix had four stations that wanted the show." It didn't hurt that directly across the street from the convention hall, it was impossible to miss Rosie O'Donnell's name filling the marquee at Caesars Palace, where she was performing. Warner Bros. executives entertained 400 clients at one of her shows. It didn't take long for Warner Bros. to feel very good indeed about their newest star.

One TV station owner who passed on Rosie's show said, "I don't give her much chance for survival. No actor has made it as a talk show host." Another TV executive said, "It's harder than it looks. I give her three months."

Basing *The Rosie O'Donnell Show* in New York made everyone happy. It meant she could live near most of her family, especially sister Maureen and her youngsters. It also meant Parker could grow up in an extended family with several male role models nearby. "Most of my siblings are still in the New York area," Rosie said. "We're all pretty close and talk all the time."

And it meant the show could be broadcast live on the east coast.

Performing live was part of her careful plan to take control of her show and her life. "I was afraid if we taped it there would be executives backstage telling me to redo it." As she points out frequently after she has said something controversial, "It's live, it's my show, and I can do whatever I want."

For several weeks before the show started, the Warner Bros. publicity machine inundated every media outlet with press releases, sound bites, and interview opportunities. Since they were spending $20 million to launch the show, they wanted everyone in North America to know about it. Rosie eagerly took on the role of poster girl in the campaign to clean up daytime TV. She talked a lot about presenting an alternative to trash talk. About emulating Merv and Mike. About being *nicer.*

O'Donnell recalled hurrying home from school to watch Griffin with her grandmother and mother while they prepared dinner. "You never saw anybody on Merv Griffin appearing nervous," O'Donnell told the *Los Angeles Times.* "It appeared everyone was his friend and nobody felt in dangerous territory."

Rosie joked to *Allure* magazine that "come the first ratings period we'll have 'Midget mass murderers—today on Rosie!'"

Just two weeks before her show was broadcast, Rosie did a stand-up gig for Merv Griffin's Resorts casino in Atlantic City. When she sought his counsel regarding her new endeavor, he told her "The only advice I can give you is to listen and have fun."

"Those are the two rules I hope to follow," Rosie replied.

Several weeks before her show debuted, Rosie taped five practice shows as dress rehearsals. All of those shows had three guests each, and executive producer Daniel Kellison felt the pacing would be improved with four guests. That became the basic format, though exceptions would be made for megastar guests. In fact, as the months rolled by, Rosie said that she would be happier going back to three guests per show.

The staff managed to work out most of the technical problems before the debut, though a few crept into the first week of live shows. Rosie's diatribes at sound and cue-card people probably stung a bit more than she intended. What did Rosie think of her chances for success at the time? "You've just got to do it to it. Like the Lotto. You've got to be in it to win it," she said repeating the slogan of the New York State Lottery.

One rude awakening to the differences in film and television production came during a meeting between Rosie and Warner Bros. executives, who began discussing her weight and how to light the show. Rosie recalls that even though she was sitting right there, somebody said, "We're gonna have a problem with Rosie's chin—how are we gonna light her chin?" On a movie set, actors are usually protected from hearing things like that, things that might upset them and affect a performance.

By 10:00 A.M. on Monday, June 10, 1996, thirty-four-year-old Rosie was ready to rock and roll. All 180 seats in the former Phil Donahue studio in New York's Rockefeller Center were full. In fact, as Rosie would later learn from Dom Deluise, this was also the studio that her idol Johnny Carson had used when he did the *Tonight Show* from New York in the 1960s. That first day, the audience was in full summer-vacation mode and all pumped up, hoping something magical would happen, so they could say they'd been there at the beginning.

The Rosie O'Donnell Show broke with forty years of talk-show tradition in its first moments. Instead of a bombastic announcer belting out some variation of 'He-e-e-r-e-'s Rosie,' audience members (who are occasionally celebrities or Rosie pals) deliver the introduction with varying degrees of stage fright. Then John McDaniel strikes up the band for the bouncy theme song as the bright animated opening graphics set the tone for the lighthearted fun ahead. A fan of Fran Drescher's show, Rosie decided she liked the opening of *The Nanny* well enough to clone it. She hired the same artist to design her own retro look (though both shows' graphics owe a debt to *Bewitched*).

The cartoon sums up Rosie's career in twenty-two seconds. One twist is that each day Rosie does a customized voice-over verse about a featured guest. ("I'm such a big fan, of *Gilligan's* Mary Ann.") The irony of the animation is that Rosie is shown throughout wearing a dress—something she has done on her show only once. She was seen briefly in a long dress and tiara during a taped dance sequence, spoofing her own opening moves. Rosie is definitely a pantsuit-only kind of gal. "I hardly ever wear dresses, but it looked cute for the animation," she explained.

Bursting through her curtains, just like Johnny, and striding to the center of her colorful stage with a wry wink, Rosie acknowledged her debt to those who hosted talk shows before her: "This show is unique, original, and unlike anything you've ever seen on TV." Then she referred to her coexecutive producer as "Gelman," to her bandleader as "Branford Marsalis," and to her drummer as "Max Weinberg." Finally, she whipped a pencil through the fake window behind her to the sound effect of breaking glass. The audience got all her jokes and loved her for them. In the weeks that followed, Rosie did demonstrate that she and her staff were capable of creating some fresh, original bits.

Displaying only minor hints of first-show jitters, Rosie cruised through some patter with her musical director, John McDaniel, and some prepared jokes. By the time her first guest, actor George Clooney, entered bearing an armful of roses, she seemed to be in full control. When Clooney explained that he was only there "because Madonna couldn't make it," Rosie jokingly agreed, "That's right." Clooney then faked anger, grabbed his roses back, and stomped over to the band area, where he whacked the flowers onto the piano, scattering their petals. Rosie begged him back, then asked if he wasn't worried about being the third actor to play Batman— "You know, like being the second Darren on *Bewitched?*" Thus beginning an unending stream of pop culture references that endear her to her fans.

From that very first show it became apparent how Rosie would set herself apart from all her predecessors. She wasn't just the host of the show. She was also the fan sitting at home, seeking escape from a mundane reality or from a life too painful to face. "I have always felt more like an audience member than a performer," Rosie has said. "I don't know how or why, but it's my truth. And I think it's a blessing in many ways."

Bandleader McDaniel, who knows Rosie well, says this about her appeal: "It's her honesty people are responding to. She's totally real. It's heightened for TV, but not by much." He continued by saying she's not faking the enthusiasm she displays toward her guests. "She's really goo-goo ga-ga about these people. It's hilarious." Later in that first show, when soap star Susan Lucci of *All My Children* sat down, Rosie proved she could dish about goings on in Pine Valley dating back ten or twenty years.

Rosie has rarely had to fake interest in a guest. Her staff didn't have to tell her that George Clooney paid his dues in sitcoms. She could tell *them* that he played George Burnett, the Handyman on *Facts of Life,* and which episode might make a funny clip to show. Her knowledge of entertainment trivia from the last twenty-five years is encyclopedic, and she even amazes herself at times. She just seems to spew commercial jingles and lines from movies and songs right on cue, without even trying. "It is SICK that I know all these words!" she exclaimed on one early show. "Imagine what diseases I could cure if I could empty the useless crap from my brain! It's like a high-speed computer, but it only doodles."

At the end of the first show, George Clooney opened the champagne that he had brought, and all the guests joined in a toast to Rosie and her newest baby—*The Rosie O'Donnell Show*.

The next day, Rosie proved she wasn't afraid to mock one of the time-honored traditions of daytime TV—the cooking segment. Nor was she afraid to spoof *Good Morning America*'s Joan Lunden. Joan made the tactical error of trying to promote two things at once: her new passion for mountain climbing and a new cookbook. Rosie jumped on it with great zeal, and showed up for the segment in full climbing regalia, hoisting an ice ax, and then proceeded to assist Joan with her culinary demonstration.

Rosie soon got an opportunity to thank one of the godfathers of the daytime talk show when Mike Douglas appeared in July of her first season. She said in her introduction that if imitation was the sincerest form of flattery then he should feel really flattered, because "I set out to do a show *exactly* like his." She told Mike it was a little scary doing the show live. "You have no safety net." Mike replied that she seemed to like "living on the edge."

Though Rosie said she wanted it to be live "like your show," she was worried that while interviewing guests she was so in awe of that she would become speechless. Streisand, for one. Tony Bennett, for another. He had been on the previous week, and as she later told him, she had to have him on a second time because she was unable to speak coherently during his first appearance. "I remember my mother singing Tony Bennett songs in 1970 while making dinner, so it was a little overwhelming."

Rosie says she is only overwhelmed by her childhood heroes. Her peers, who became famous after she was an adult, do not intimidate her. "I just have respect and a kitschy appreciation of them."

Rosie actually knows who her guests are and why they are on her show—unlike other hosts who often seem mystified by their guests and their activities. At times, David Letterman, for example, doesn't even bother to hide his indifference. While some hosts barely make time to read the preshow interview notes, Rosie has already seen Tom Hanks's new movie before it is even released; she's already listened to Trisha Yearwood's new CD and all the ones before it; and she's even downloaded Teri Hatcher's latest photos from the Internet.

Rosie knows Cher's old song lyrics better than Cher does; she remembers Kate Mulgrew's *Ryan's Hope* storylines from twenty years ago; she saw Bette Midler on Broadway in 1973 and still has the ticket stubs. Rosie watched the season premiere of *ER* along with the rest of America— not just so she could discuss intimate details about nurse Hathaway with Julianna Margulies the next day on her own show but because Rosie is a regular viewer of the series. Like any fan would do, Rosie tried to get her to divulge future plot twists, and she campaigned for a reunion of Julianna's character with George Clooney's Dr. Doug.

Rosie validates the musical tastes of her viewers, though there seem to be very few singers that Rosie doesn't love. She features a musical performance on nearly every show, and she always claims to own all of that artist's output. Her tastes are eclectic, ranging from country sensation Shania Twain to Miami diva Gloria Estefan to soul sister Toni Braxton. As well as her icons: Bette, Liza, and Elton John, and the Captain and Tenille.

Rosie is also genuinely moved by gospel singers CeCe Winans and Tremaine Hawkins. After Tremaine sang her heart out, Rosie told her it was the third time she had been moved to tears on her show, first by Celine Dion, then by singer Jennifer Holliday. "You are so good, you just break me up." She paused to gain control. "You feel the spirit of oneness—God—whatever you want to call it—when somebody sings like you." She went on to explain that her emotionality is one reason it's difficult for her to attend concerts. "I start crying, then they write in the papers that I'm having a breakdown!"

Closest to her heart are Broadway show tunes. Rosie regularly presents musical numbers by cast members from shows currently playing in New York. Considering that Regis and Conan and Dave also broadcast from New York City, it has mostly been left to Rosie to showcase the theatrical talent. "When I was a kid on Long Island, I could come in and see a Broadway show, but somebody in the Midwest doesn't have that chance, so that's a phenomenal opportunity for me right there with my show."

The only music she doesn't understand is alternative rock. Even though she was a featured presenter at the 1996 MTV Video Music Awards, when she discussed it on her show the next day, Rosie confessed she didn't watch the rest of the program, but went home to bed. She said she felt out of touch with the kind of music MTV plays, as evidenced by her referring to the night's big winners, Smashing Pumpkins, as "those pumpkin people."

Rosie does have some hidden musical talent, which surfaced on an early show. After cast members from off-Broadway's *Stomp* performed a percussion number with tall wooden poles, Rosie joined them for an encore. She had either rehearsed the number or was a quick study. In either case, she demonstrated a genuine gift for beating out complex rhythms. On another show, featuring cast members from *Bring in Da Noise, Bring in Da Funk,* she joined in again, this time sitting on a crate, wailing away on an upturned plastic bucket with a pair of drumsticks. Rosie abandoned herself to the beat, displaying a talent for percussion instruments.

The real reason she performed so ably was revealed when actor Dan Ackroyd appeared on her show in September. After the chat portion they both moved to side-by-side trap sets—the complete sets of various drums and cymbals used in most bands. They immediately launched into a raucous extended performance that showed they both know their way around the tom-toms. At one point they traded fours, alternated four-measure solos. Inspired to play drums by seventies star Karen Carpenter, Rosie claimed: "I'm not that good....I did it while I was in high school."

A lifelong viewer of television, Rosie understands how her show fits into the evolution of the talk-variety show. Among the pioneers in the early years of television variety shows were Milton Berle, Ed Sullivan, Arthur Godfrey, and Dinah Shore. They developed formats and shtick that are still being used today in various permutations. The debut of the first incarnation of the *Tonight Show* with Steve Allen in 1954 added sit-down chat and interviews to the popular variety format. Audience tastes and hosts have changed over the years, but the basic design is essentially the same. In the 1960s and 1970s, talk-variety shows blossomed into daytime hours as well, with the feel-good shows that Rosie loved so much as a youngster: Merv, Mike, and Dinah.

It's quite fitting that Rosie should take over Phil Donahue's former studio, since his show's demise signaled the passing of the eighties era of issue-oriented talk. Oprah survives by evolving with the times. She still does some social issue shows but also plenty of glamorous showbiz lovefests. *The Oprah Winfrey Show* has never been a variety show, but it often presents theme-related shows. Rosie appeared on one that featured female comics. Sometimes she showcases the entire cast of a film or TV series. Oprah has also done her share of sleaze, but in recent years has cleaned up her topics—even though her ratings have slipped some as a result. But Oprah Winfrey is such a charismatic star in her own right that her personality drives the show as much as that of any of her guests.

Arsenio Hall's syndicated show (1989–94) broke some new ground, with his urban sensibility and the lets-stay-up-late-and-party atmosphere. Banishing the desk and the guest chair proved to be his best innovation. It liberated both guests and host to lounge on the furniture in whatever positions felt good at the moment, and that led to many uninhibited guest interactions. (Though Arsenio did sit in a large chair next to the couch, he was not behind a desk, and in fact he bounced around a lot from table to floor and over to the couch. Just like you might do in your own living room.) There was this hip party going on 'in the house' and you, the viewer, were magically on the guest list. It was a clever way to position his show, and he enjoyed a good five-year run.

One of Rosie's most memorable appearances on Arsenio's show was with Madonna, when they were promoting their film *A League of Their Own*. The loose mood of his show allowed the two new best pals to be relaxed and playful; they clearly overwhelmed their host, who just leaned back and let them riff.

Meanwhile, other contenders came and went: Pat Sajak limped along, stumbled, and fell; Chevy Chase quickly drowned in his own madness; Jay took over for Johnny; Dave defected to CBS in a huff; and NBC took a gamble on an unknown named Conan O'Brien.

Daytime talk shows took a decided turn for the worse in the 1990s. There seemed to be an unstated competition to see which show could offer the most salacious and arcane topic while simultaneously degrading their guests. Sally, Geraldo, Maury, and even Phil and Oprah joined in the fray. For a while, anyway, Americans appeared transfixed by these tawdry spectacles, much like passersby at a ten-car pileup.

The next hot new entry into the daytime mix, *The Ricki Lake Show*, appeared in 1993. An unlikely host, Ricki is the formerly rotund star of John Waters's cult films. She also performed as Holly the Donut Dolly on the TV series *China Beach*. With no experience as a host, Ricki brought her newly svelte twenty-something self to daytime like a cool breeze in August. She quickly captured the all-important Generation X market with a show that primarily explored relationships. Sleaze was still a factor, but it was sleaze with a hipper, younger spin.

Lake's quick success inspired a long line of Ricki-come-latelys: Charles Perez; former *Partridge Family* bad boy, Danny Bonaduce; *90210* alum, Gabrielle Carteris; Suzanne Somers; and many others. It became immediately clear that there were far more shows than viewers to support them. (Oprah attracts about nine million fans per show, whereas these clunker clones averaged about two million.) It soon became evident that Ricki Lake was a unique phenomenon—not a trend to be followed. Rosie made her position clear from the start: "I could never do a show like Ricki Lake or Jerry Springer. I'd say: 'You're an idiot. Why are you sleeping with your sister's husband?'"

Failed host Bonaduce confessed he never felt good about what he was doing. "I always felt strange asking people about their problems. It was like, Why am I asking this—and even stranger—why are you telling me?"

As the pendulum of American taste inevitably swung in the other direction, Geraldo Rivera repented and promised to dump the trash from his daytime show in favor of the weightier subjects, like the ones he discusses on his nighttime CNBC program, *Rivera Live*. In fact, Warner Bros. yanked their Ricki wannabe, Carnie Wilson, off the air to create a slot for Rosie. As TV executives evaluate Nielsen ratings and attempt to predict the next great trends in daytime TV, they will pay close attention to the kinder, gentler *Rosie O'Donnell Show*.

It's been tough on her writers, comedy veterans used to writing material with a harder edge. At *The Rosie O'Donnell Show, nice* is the four-letter word of choice. Rosie's long-standing rule: She won't joke about anything she wouldn't say to the person whom the joke is about. She certainly doesn't have to worry about having guests on that she doesn't like. That's another reason she wanted to be in charge. "I'm the executive producer, so there's nobody on the show I hate. And I'm only mean to people who have committed heinous acts or crimes against nature." (As fans of her stand-up act know, that means Woody Allen and O. J. Simpson.)

The jokes she does on her show however, often do have a modern edginess. "They're planning a sequel to *Independence Day*. A second group of spaceships come down to be near the mothership. It's gonna be called *Codependence Day*."

Rosie and her staff have managed to cook up a fresh batch of gimmicks, most notably the torque on Letterman's use of sound effects. Instead of relying on a guy backstage to insert the sound of glass breaking or viewer mail cards plunking into the Hudson River, Rosie herself takes control. Built into the command post of her desk is a digicard console with a multitude of programmable buttons, which she conducts with the flair of Leonard Bernstein. If she's especially pleased with how a joke went over with the audience, she congratulates herself by pushing a button, and Casey Kasem bleats out "Professional comedy" in an obvious radio-guy voice.

Conversely, if a joke bombs, Rosie can call on *Laugh-in*'s over-modulated announcer, Gary Owens, to chide, "Just not funny." Which, of course, brilliantly transforms any lame joke into a howl from the audience. Rosie undoubtedly learned all about how to save any comedy bit from disaster by watching Johnny Carson. No matter how the audience initially responded to a punchline, he had a myriad of ways to lure them into laughter, often at his own expense. Letterman deals with the situation in his own more acerbic manner by alternately threatening and bribing his audiences to cooperate: "Don't make me come out there" or "Canned hams for everyone."

Each show, Rosie loads up her console with sound bites of recordings from that day's musical guest—mostly as an excuse to sing along with snippets of her favorite songs. "I hit a button—sometimes I know what's on there, sometimes I don't," she said one day after failing to find the retort she wanted. It's definitely the best gadget on her set, which is a veritable theme park for her inner child. Against a backdrop of a roller coaster and an amusement park, Rosie clutters her desktop with an array of kitschy toys and dolls. She is indiscriminate and loves everything from McDonald's Happy Meals cheap giveaways to true collectors' items. When Shirley Jones came on the show, Rosie displayed the original *Partridge Family* lunch box that Shirley had sent her in a fancy wooden box with an engraved brass plate.

In addition, Rosie is always bringing onto the show objects from her own vast collection of toys and showbiz memorabilia. When Cher appeared, Rosie showed off the actual Cher doll she had played with as a child and serenaded it with her version of "I Got You Babe."

But the toy most closely identified with *The Rosie O'Donnell Show* has to be the Kooshball. From her first day on the air, Rosie has had an arsenal of them on her desk to launch at her producer or into the audience whenever the spirit moves her. In the beginning, she fired too many Kooshballs to compensate for first-week nerves. For the uninitiated,

Kooshballs are harmless fluffy balls that look like rubber sea urchins. They are propelled with a plastic launcher called a flingshot, which is similar to a slingshot.

Rosie featured her obsession on an early show with a Kooshing for Dollars segment. Each day for a week an audience member tried to shoot a Kooshball at the target: a hole in a life-size cutout of romance novel coverboy Fabio. (More evidence of Rosie's skewed sense of humor.) Day after day, the shooters failed, and in desperation the staff made the hole bigger and bigger. By Friday's show Rosie was reduced to shooting the Koosh herself through a seriously gutted Fabio, so she could award the prize of a cruise to a decidedly unathletic kid.

While Rosie has clearly opted not to imitate Leno's and Letterman's frequent videotaped forays outside their studios, she has featured one quirky taped segment: "Listen to Iman." Viewers either love it or hate it, but it clearly delights Rosie, who sometimes participates with her own Iman impression. Exotic supermodel Iman met Rosie when they were making the over-the-top film, *Exit to Eden*. In her distinctive global accent, Iman dispenses her unique brand of advice to stars, as well as everyday people, seeking help for silly questions. Katie Couric of the *Today Show* asked: "I'm so sick of being called cute and perky. What should I do?" The solution: "Katie, listen to Iman—kill a drifter."

In September when Iman finally appeared live on the show to promote a charity event for the Childrens Defense Fund in which she and Rosie were involved, Rosie introduced her with self-deprecating sarcasm. "Our next guest kicked my butt in the Oscar-snubbed *Exit to Eden*—please welcome the baddest, the toughest supermodel on the planet—Iman." They described how they bonded during the filming after Rosie nailed Iman's unusual accent in just a few days. Rosie even rolled a clip from that film's infamous fight scene between the two of them.

Iman is an example of the not-your-usual talkshow booking policy on *The Rosie O'Donnell Show*. Early on, Rosie demonstrated her far-ranging personal tastes and sense of humor in combining guests. Carol Channing was booked with *Politically Incorrect* correspondent Chris Rock; soap veteran Erica Slezak followed *Sesame Street*'s puppet Elmo; Tipper Gore gushed over Tom Cruise with Rosie, then TV cult figure Xena herself, Lucy Lawless, took the stage. It's a time-tested formula: Combine the recognizable with the skewed to produce humor.

It was soon obvious to all who were paying attention that Rosie O'Donnell was born to host her own TV show. Her youthful addiction to television, her years of networking on the comedy circuit, and her friendships made on movie sets helped to shape her into the penultimate talk show host.

Despite all her homage to Mike and Merv, in truth, they were modestly talented guys with middle-class tastes who made it big in daytime TV. They were often left behind by their guests—John Lennon and Yoko Ono cohosting with Mike Douglas in 1972, for example.

Rosie may do her share of fussing over celebrities, but at least it's genuine, so we forgive her for her excesses. (Down on her knees to greet Bette Midler with "I'm not worthy.") Fans also love that she seems to have a weak internal censor and usually says whatever thoughts come to mind. To guest Harvey Keitel (who appeared naked in the film *The Piano*) Rosie blurted: "I saw your pee-pee!" To Teri Hatcher of *Lois and Clark* she quipped: "You look good—if I looked like you, I'd probably be naked right now."

Clever and quick, spontaneous and sly, Rosie whips hip references by so fast that viewers have to stay alert to keep up with her. When the studio audience laughed so long at her jokes that they drowned out her punchlines, Rosie took charge and commanded them to "Stay with me people—fly—stay with me!"

✐ 16

Making It Big in the Big Time

Audiences nationwide were clearly ready for a change of daytime pace and immediately fell in love with *The Rosie O'Donnell Show*. The program averaged a 3.2 rating during the first two weeks (each rating point represents approximately 960,000 viewers), making it the best debut since *Oprah,* ten years earlier. Ranked number one in fourteen major television markets during its first week, the show suddenly had clout. Stations that had balked at giving an unproven show a plum time slot scrambled to juggle their schedules to make room for the new ratings bonanza. Rosie had some sharp words for such outlets, like Philadelphia's WPIV. "They put us on at two freakin' o'clock in the mornin'!" In fact, before long, there was a stampede in many markets to position her show in the prime afternoon spot leading into the local news, usually at four o'clock.

Warner Bros. executives were thrilled by the sensational reviews. New York's alternative newspaper, the *Village Voice* is not known for being easily won over by a television program. Still, their reviewer wrote an insightful article pointing out that Rosie is "delivering the realness that talk shows fake. O'Donnell is all gut, and viewers are responding to her authenticity." They went on to comment on her unique sensibility: "She is hip to queerness and the polyglot melt....she isn't beaming out white bread to the heartland but raisin-walnut pumpernickel."

The hip new interactive online magazine, *Salon,* gushed, "It's undeniable that this woman was born to steer a talk show desk into port. Rosie

O'Donnell succeeds mainly because her personality is so utterly unlike any other talk show host's, night or day. She's tart but not mean, warm but not gooey, silly but substantial." They went on to comment on how well she bonds with her audience: "You get a firm sense that—Hello!—there's a real person in there. She listens to her guests, makes them look good, and, in return, they allow her to get in some yuks at their expense."

Other online reviewers wrote in a similar vein. Said Mr. Showbiz: "O'Donnell is irreverent, she's gracious, she's frank, she's perky. She's brazenly hilarious without being trashy, she's...well...*nice.* Like Dinah Shore, only with chutzpah." According to the *Village Voice,* she is also "Joan Rivers without the self-loathing." Jeff Jarvis, writing in *TV Guide,* said, "Rosie has Johnny's ability to entertain her guests, her audience, and herself at the same time."

Many reviewers commented that she appears refreshingly open to new ideas, new voices, and definitely a new look for daytime TV. A look that is decidedly more diverse—more women guests, more minorities, many young performers. *People* magazine noted that Rosie has demonstrated she can be "sassy without being mean. In short: not Kathie Lee, not Dennis Miller." They called her a gifted interviewer who can put even the most reluctant guest at ease. "She delivers a refreshing dose of spunk, fire, and genuine fun" declared *Entertainment Weekly* magazine. They continued their comments with a comparison. "Simply by allowing Rosie to be Rosie, the show serves as a refreshing contrast...to *Live With Regis and Kathie Lee* (which will regain its composure only when Philbin starts swatting Gifford with a rolled up *New York Post* every time she starts to get weepy about some Kathiecentric slight)." The writer for *Newsday* enjoyed her enthusiasm and found her "captivating, even fetching," and said, "Rosie is like a twelve-year-old kid opening Christmas presents."

While some critics didn't understand her zealous love of most of her guests, the writer for the *New York Times,* did understand her intention. "There is, of course, a good-natured wink behind this Irish-style blather."

The ultimate accolade came just two weeks after the first show, when *Newsweek* crowned her "The Queen of Nice" in living color, on their front cover. Inside they enthused: "She mugs. She hugs. She plugs. *The Rosie O'Donnell Show* is a hit."

Later, Rosie spoke about how hard it was to live up to her new royal status. "It was nice to be on the cover, but I was a little startled.... I don't think of myself as nice. I just think when compared to other talk shows I'm pretty nice." She also said that at times it's become a detriment. If she says anything at all scathing, she is now called the Queen of Mean. On David Letterman's show she elaborated: "It's been a hindrance, this title, because when guests come on and they're a little rude or ornery, I can't say the things I'm thinkin', because I am—(dramatic pause)—the Queen of Nice."

Even though she must have been relieved by all the great press, Rosie is savvy enough to know this enthusiastic reception might not last. She was quoted a few years back in *Buzz* magazine saying, "I don't know what you have to do to the press to get them to hate you. I haven't had any problems with the press, but that won't last."

Like Newton's Law of Publicity, it is a natural cycle to build someone or something up, only to eventually tear them down. Rosie knows performers are especially vulnerable when their fortunes change. She recalled that after Roseanne had become a millionaire she was still doing jokes about buying a dress for $13.99. "I heard people go 'mmmmmmm' in the audience.... They only want the truth. Your act has to change as your life changes."

But for now, she's feeling confident enough to joke about being scheduled in the important Los Angeles market at 3:00 P.M., opposite Oprah, herself. She candidly told her own TV audience that in that situation she would watch Oprah. Then, laughing, she said, "No, I wouldn't," then whispering, "Yes I would." Then she said, "I'd tape me and watch me later." That spontaneous aside serves to underscore how often she'll choose being authentic over saying what might seem best for her career.

So who is out there watching Rosie at different hours of the daytime? Who are these fans who are giving her solid ratings? And why are they at home, anyway? The answer lies in the changing demographics of the American workforce. Sure, some of the viewers are the last known stay-at-home moms on earth, and some of the others are youngsters with stomachaches or who are good at faking them. But the core viewership is the new breed of American worker. Telecommuters and entrepreneurs taking really long coffee breaks; freelance artists, writers, and editors looking for a distraction, computer industry nerds who figured out how to work from home. Then factor in shift workers and workers who have been downsized, and suddenly, you have a sizable group of people uninterested in the standard fare of soaps and games. With Rosie, over four million people have found a cool way to spend an hour every day.

And advertisers have discovered this new group of daytime viewers and started to cater to their perceived tastes. Suddenly nearly every commercial break on *Rosie* includes a stomach remedy.

Salon magazine summed it up when it said that watching Rosie's show is "like playing hooky from life, one hour at a time. And you don't need a note from Mom."

At summer's end in 1996, the entertainment news show *Extra* conducted a viewer poll to select the hottest star of the season. The slate of contestants included Rosie; wild man Dennis Rodman; Olympian Michael Johnson; MTV vixen Jenny McCarthy; and Rosie's own favorite, Tom Cruise. When John McDaniel told her she had won, Rosie couldn't believe it, especially when she heard whom she had to beat. "Had I known about this poll, I would have voted for Tom Cruise."

By fall 1996, *The Rosie O'Donnell Show* proved such a hit that Warner Bros. guaranteed the run through the 1999–2000 season. The show has posted the highest ratings of any talk show debuting in the 1990s and consistently places in the Top 20 among all syndicated shows. When Rosie entertained Tom Cruise, 4.6 million viewers tuned in. When the numbers were added up for Rosie's first November Sweeps period, *The Rosie O'Donnell Show* came in second among daytime talk shows with a 5.1 rating. Oprah is still the queen, with a 9.6 rating. *Live With Regis and Kathie Lee* was down eleven percent from a year ago, and ratings for *Jenny Jones* were also down. During the start-up period for her show, Rosie often said that her program would not be "like *Jenny Jones*," which reportedly caused Jones to call Rosie and complain, in tears.

Her success means it's also going to cost more for local stations to buy the show. In Los Angeles, for example, KNBC-TV now pays $25,000 per week for the first two years; in 1998 it will start paying $160,000 per week. In a related move, Time-Warner, which produces the show, is forcing several major ABC-TV stations to air the low-rated *Lois and Clark* show for the next two years if they want *The Rosie O'Donnell Show*. This "leverage" deal, reporters believe, is being done without Rosie's knowledge.

Rosie is also being used to sell local newscasts. Warner Bros. ran trade ads in the fall of 1996, bragging that *The Rosie O'Donnell Show* doubles previous ratings for the early-fringe time periods leading into local news. Many stations who use Rosie as a lead-in to their news shows sent their anchors to New York to tape promo spots with Rosie on her set. The San Diego station that airs her show even put her on in prime time at 9 P.M.

Another sign she's hit the bigtime: In September 1996, the *New York Times* wrote that Rosie was now on the city's A-list of party faces. "You can tell they've arrived because they're now hot guests at splashy parties....Like money, their names are used as currency on invitations and in gossip columns."

One of the most flattering reactions to her show has been the response of fans using America Online, a computer online service and Internet provider. A seven-year veteran user of AOL herself, Rosie quickly realized the mutual benefits of having her very own section on AOL. All members have to do is type the keyword "Rosie" and they immediately arrive at her colorful animated site. Once there, they can bookmark it with a heart as a "favorite place," allowing for instant connection at anytime. The site itself is constantly expanding to accommodate viewer requests and suggestions. The features include a scrapbook with photos and sound bites to download and a "Hey Rosie" button that is a direct link to leave comments on the show and other E-mail for Rosie and her staff.

One colossal section is the message board area, where users create topics and post comments about every aspect of the show and Rosie's life and career. AOL users can post responses to any of the messages and also E-mail each other directly if they want to discuss fine points of Rosiana. She reads as many as she can, but the volume of messages becomes overwhelming. In August 1996 she told a live online audience during an AOL conference that she really appreciated all the people watching and posting messages. "See you in the Rosie Room. I will try to answer all my mail. Promise." She's going to need a lot of help, as the postings on her message boards number in the thousands.

In addition, Warner Bros. has created its own Rosie Web site at http:// www.rosieo.com. It is very similar to the AOL site and also includes a "Hey Rosie" option. In our increasingly fragmented society, it really isn't surprising that so many people will spend time online chatting about a TV show; we seem to crave common experiences and neighbors to share them with.

In October 1996 the first ever Online Icon Award was handed out.

During a month-long Internet poll conducted by *People* magazine, cyber surfers voted for their favorite online personalities. The choices included confessed "Nethead" Rosie, Teri Hatcher, Gillian Anderson, Meg Ryan, and Sandra Bullock. The award, presented at the Cool Site of the Year Awards, went to Rosie O'Donnell. She accepted via videotape: "This is the best award I've ever received," Rosie declared. "I am thrilled to death. . . . See ya online!"

Merv Griffin summed up the response: "Rosie was born to do a talk show. She has that Irish spontaneity, added with a touch of New York that'll knock you for a loop." Another thing Merv knows from personal experience, is that some day she'll be ready for a quality vacation from all the hubbub. His suggestion? A Mediterranean cruise on his personal floating resort. "Rosie's booked for the yacht any time she wants."

Certainly one of the nicer perks of fame.

One of the more unusual offshoots of her new popularity is "Really Rosie," a new shade of lipstick by L'Oreal. She modeled it one day on her show, acknowledging that she deserved such a tribute with L'Oreal's own tag line, "Because I'm worth it."

Other signs that she has "arrived" at the upper echelon of fame and power: Sarah Ferguson, the former Duchess of York, called her personally to accept an invitation to be on her show and to ask if they could have lunch first. Rosie eagerly agreed, while claiming her own version of Fergie's title. "She's the Duchess of York, and I'm the duchess of *New* York!"

One sign that Rosie is getting more comfortable with her own fame is how she handled that interview. Rosie was *somewhat* nervous, which she claims is why she lapsed into a noticeable New York accent: "How's Diana doing? I like the both of youze." (Rosie did say on the next show how horrified she was when she watched a tape of that interview. "It was like Stallone interviewing her. I'm sure I frightened the entire royal family.") Still, by the end of the interview, they were bonding over the problems of being famous. Rosie told her: "We think it's hard being a celebrity in America—it ain't nothin' compared to what you guys go through." In the final exchange, Rosie O'Donnell from Commack, New York, high-fived the duchess, telling her, "You do a lot for so many charities—rock on Sista Friend!"

Rosie had a funny brush with New York royalty at the premiere of *The First Wives Club*. As Rosie entered the theater, the paparazzi shouted to her to pose for a picture with the woman next to her. Since the woman looked vaguely familiar and was obviously also "someone," Rosie smiled for the cameras. While they were posing, the woman said "Oh, Rosie, we've asked to have you to dinner, but you've been so busy—I hope we can work it out." "Me, too," replied a clueless Rosie.

After the pictures were taken, she asked one of the photographers who the blonde was. Turns out it was Mrs. Giulianni, the wife of the mayor of New York City. Rosie told the story on herself the next day on the show. "What an idiot I am—it was Mrs. Mayor!"

Many of the famous guests on her show have offered their compliments and best wishes for her continued success. One of the more original accolades came from another of her childhood idols, Lily Tomlin. About the time Rosie was recovering from her mother's death, *Laugh-in* was pushing the comedy envelope farther out. Lily Tomlin had her first experience of fame on that show, as Ernestine, Ma Bell's best. In the course of interviewing Lily, Rosie brought up the subject of cheerleading. It seems Tomlin had been one in high school, though, she insisted, her squad was "soulful." To illustrate, she jumped up, began a dance step, and snapped out a syncopated beat with her fingers.

> "Rosie has a baby,
> she's a fabulous Mom.
> She can sing all the theme songs
> for every sitcom.
> Got two Chihuahuas,
> ever been to Okinawa?
> Got her own TV talk show,
> Oh, Ro—go, go, go!"

The look on Rosie's face as she watched this routine said it all: the reality of Lily Tomlin cheering for her was more than even she could have fantasized back in Commack, Long Island. *Lily Tomlin.* Cheering for *her.*

On a totally different note, ABC's Peter Jennings came on the show and begged Rosie to book Brad Pitt and invite Jennings back for that taping so he could score points with his teenage daughter. Rosie told him that his was the newscast she watches, and he returned a compliment, saying "You bring the past to life so much, which is why I think we all like it."

O'Donnell's stellar guest lists have sparked the rumor that Regis and Kathie Lee have started a booking war, refusing to schedule guests who appear first on Rosie's show. (It helps them that Regis and Kathie Lee air live at 9:00 A.M., an hour before Rosie.) It's possible to do both shows in the same morning, as Rosie pointed out one day when she heard singer Wynonna was appearing that day with Regis. Rosie did quite a long drawn out pout over the fact that buddy Wynonna wasn't dropping by to see her former opening act. She ticked off all the personal involvement she had had with her and her mother and seemed genuinely hurt to be snubbed. Ironically, a month later when Wynonna was scheduled to finally get back in Rosie's good graces, the show did not go on due to an electrical fire in the building.

Rosie is clearly enjoying all the rapturous attention she and her show are receiving. By the end of 1996 Rosie and her show were on virtually everyone's year-end best lists, and in late December, Rosie's glowing face sparkled from the covers of an armful of magazines. *Glamour* named her one of their Women of the Year. "It's a big thrill," Rosie said after learning of the honor. "I used to think the only way I'd make it into *Glamour* magazine was in the 'Don't' column." (She then imitated the infamous photos of fashion disasters by covering her eyes with her fingers.) Rosie was also chosen by Barbara Walters as one of the ten most fascinating people of 1996. In her chat with Walters, Rosie said, "When I sit back and look at it, I go— this has been a pretty incredible ride, so far."

US magazine put her on their cover and on their list of biggest stories for the year. Rosie also graced the February cover of the *Ladies' Home Journal* and was honored by them as one of the Most Fascinating Women of 1996, for "carving a nice niche amid the rubble of TV trash." Her fellow honorees included Hilary Clinton, Oprah Winfrey, and her girlhood idol, Bette Midler. The magazine also produced a television special about the women, and in her interview Rosie still sounded as humble as ever: "I don't think that I'll ever feel like a star. . . . I don't feel that I'm as big a star as the guests on this show, because no matter how successful I become, the people who inspired me will always be eons ahead of me."

Newsweek put her on their cover again and singled her out as the number-one newsmaker in the realm of television. They conducted a nationwide opinion poll to determine the top newsmakers in a number of categories, and Rosie won hers. They said she was a "life raft in trash talk's sea of sleaze," and that she had "put the show back in talk." Rosie also did well on a poll of younger readers taken by *Seventeen* magazine, who voted her their "ideal female president." *The Rosie O'Donnell Show* ranked at the top of *USA Today*'s list of the best TV shows of 1996. They referred to her show as "a tonic of high-octane cheer."

TV *Host* magazine put her show in the number-three spot on their Top Ten List of things worth watching. Agreeing, *TV Guide* also put Rosie in the third slot, for resurrecting the "up-tempo talk show." Rosie also made the cover of *People* and was the first star profiled inside as part of their "25 Most Intriguing People of the Year." They said she had "found her true calling as TV's hottest new gabber."

In October 1996, Rosie appeared for the first time, at number eighty-four on *Entertainment Weekly*'s list of the "101 Most Powerful People in Show Business." But the biggest year-end honor came from the same magazine, who featured her on their cover and crowned her "Entertainer of the Year for 1996." They said Rosie "made it *cool* to watch daytime TV again." Rosie is actually philosophical about all this hoopla and realizes that media darlings sooner or later often become media demons. As she told *EW,* she's prepared for the inevitable backlash. "I know it'll happen.... You'll write: 'Entertainer of the Year? Gimme a break—look at her rear!'"

What does seem inevitable is that sooner or later, Rosie will have to run out of childhood idols to enthuse over. At the rate she's gobbling up the Hollywood A-list of performers, she will have had them all on as guests in her first year. Sure, every season produces a batch of newcomers, and stars get recycled as guests every time they have a new project to pitch. But once Rosie has met everyone in Hollywood, the tone of her show will most likely calm down. Only the Nielsen families will decide if she can still act excited the fourth time she listens to Teri Garr shill her latest picture.

Given her ever-present need for a gig that allows her to put her son first, Rosie can probably keep her show high in the ratings as long as she puts her heart and mind and Kooshballs to it.

As Rosie acknowledged in her introduction of Mike Douglas, imitation can indeed be a form of flattery. Well, it didn't take long for show business geniuses to start looking for imitation Rosies. Contenders shopping around for shows include Bad Dog Donny Osmond, comics David Brenner and Sinbad, retired singer Naomi Judd, and the unforgettable in name only, Moon Unit Zappa. Most of those faux Rosies will take the same quick exit as all the Ricki Lake clones.

Mark Itkin, of the William Morris Agency, exposes the real problem.

"What happens is, people go after these giant names to host a show, and nobody bothers to ask, 'Can they even do it?'" He went on to say that "Rosie is successful because Rosie is a terrific personality. You could put Rosie in any format, and she'd be a success. But finding other celebrity names to repeat that success will be no easy trick."

"Just being famous isn't enough, and the industry is smart enough to recognize that," said one Hollywood agent. *Salon* magazine made the telling point, "She has revived a genre and doomed all who will follow her to failure just because they're not Rosie."

❧ 17

Protecting Parker

One important way Rosie is determined to be different is to keep her son, Parker, out of the public eye: "I'll do material about being a mom as opposed to things my child is doing. That's private." Rosie has said "I think it's a weird thing to show your kids on camera." Though she did joke about what she might do if the ratings needed a boost: "We'll have a Cody [Gifford] and Parker special." She even spoofed the issue by hiring a succession of child actors to portray her son at different ages. In a cute homage to another of her idols, she called her stand-in kid "Little Ricky." (In the early years of *I Love Lucy,* the Ricardos' son was also played by an actor, though on later versions of the show, Desi Arnaz Jr. did play himself as a teenager.)

When asked for some funny stories about her son during a live conference on America Online, Rosie typed: "Well, I worried that my boy would become Codyesque, so I try to stay away from his personal development details." She did add, though, "He is, however, adorable."

In an interview right before her show debuted, Rosie clarified where she draws the line regarding Parker. "There are stories that I hear about Cody pulling on his penis, and I think, Wow—that's going to be a tough thing for him to take when he's ten. You'll never see Parker coming out and sitting on the piano for the "I Got You Babe" segment like Chastity Bono did. I think that fame is a hard enough thing for an adult and nearly an impossible thing for a child."

On her own TV show, Rosie has occasionally felt a Parker story was so

158

amusing, she had to share it. One ongoing saga she has joked about concerns Parker's propensity for stuffing his Elmo doll and anything else he can get his hands on into the toilet. Rosie has done great comic riffs on the subject, updating her audience on each new attempt to thwart his compulsive behavior. Another long-running drama featured Parker's exploits climbing out of his crib at night. Rosie finally secured him in with a tentlike contraption but worried that he would become claustrophobic and need therapy as a result. ("Why do I always feel so trapped, doctor?") Rosie rejected one solution emphatically. "Not going to get a toddler bed yet. He's not exactly Mr. Oh-let-me-just-lay-down-in-my-toddler-bed and not explore every other nook and cranny of this room."

Even though he's still too young to realize it, Parker *is* having an extraordinary childhood. Yankee stars bring him autographed bats; Peter Jennings brings him a rare Russian hockey stick; Broadway star Betty Buckley brings him a bear dressed up as Norma Desmond; Tim Allen brings him a kiddie tool belt; Kevin Sorbo brings him a pint-sized Hercules outfit; Richard Simmons brings him a rhinestone-studded workout outfit; musician Kenny G brings him a starter sax, and Mr. Rogers drops by his personal neighborhood to play. (When at sixteen months of age, Parker first saw Fred Rogers in the flesh, he applauded. He already could recognize one of *his* idols.) Celebrity mothers who come to the show towing their kids pop them into Parker's play area.

Soap diva Deirdre Hall brought her two young sons with her and left them with Parker. Surprised to hear that, Rosie asked her, "He's cute isn't he?" When Hall replied that she hadn't seen Parker yet, Rosie teased her by saying, "You just put your sons in with a strange kid?" She paused for the laughter then added, "He's okay, my son, but he tackles babies—somebody check on the boys. I think it's because I tackle him when I play with him."

Parker's nursery is certainly the envy of all the other star toddlers who visit. Basically, his paraphernalia overtakes Rosie's office. In addition to Rosie's desk and computer, there is a multicolored hexagonal playpen right next to a large, comfortable armchair for mom. The office-nursery is a child's wonderland, overstuffed with Warner Bros. toys and all those fabulous gifts. Adjoining Rosie's spacious office is Parker's napping room. He even has his name on the door, spelled out in plaid clowns. A long and narrow room with one window, a lot is squeezed into it: his crib and changing table, an armchair, two strollers, and a high chair for those power lunches. The walls are decorated with cheery wallpaper, also courtesy of Warner Bros.

"It's a big luxury, bringing your child to work," Rosie says, fully aware of the day-care crisis in this country and how lucky she is. "They nicely gave me a nursery and office big enough to have all his stuff in it." Actually, as executive producer, "she" *is* "they" and could install a petting zoo if she wanted to.

As soon as she's done taping her show, Rosie hustles off down the hall to see her son. "Hello, zee Boo Boo!" she squeals in a perfect Yogi Bear impression. And her sturdy chubby-cheeked blond boy comes a-running for his mom's arms. Parenting has indeed transformed O'Donnell's life. "It changed my priorities in a moment," she told *People* magazine. "It was almost like you get to climb to another branch on the tree, and from your new perch you have a clearer perspective on the whole world."

During the workday, mother and son are often together, frolicking in his room or hers, whenever she can tear herself away from meetings and rehearsals. It didn't take long for her to be sure she had made a good decision. "You don't get those years back," Rosie said about those precious moments of first words and first steps. She wanted her son to have the stability of sleeping in his own bed every night. "So that's the reason I did the TV show. This was a lifestyle decision. This was not a career move."

With the great success she's having, it may also turn out to be a very smart career move.

In September 1996 when actor Michael J. Fox was a guest on the show, they got to discussing how having children prioritizes your life and why TV shows are better for parenting. Rosie commented that "you have balance, this whole other source of happiness that makes everything else sort of just icing."

Michael agreed, but made fun of their sentiment. "We're so sappy."

"Aren't we?" Rosie replied. "Well, that's all right, America likes sap."

America does like parents who aren't afraid to share their genuine feelings about children. "I don't want him to be a prop for my act," Rosie says repeatedly. She's also very clear about her priorities. One interview was abruptly cut short when Parker came crawling into her office. "Mama's taking too long here?" she asked the energetic young boy. "Sorry—gotta spend some time with him. He doesn't understand this celebrity stuff, you know? He just knows he needs me."

One day when she couldn't get her usual brand of diapers (Pampers Premium), she did a hilarious five-minute harangue on how she traipsed from one store in her neighborhood to another, "I ran—literally in this body—jogging," in search of this essential domestic item. At one point she was told her favorite diapers were being discontinued, "A chill ran through my body," so she gave a heartfelt testimonial for the product on the air and begged the company to reconsider. "Pampers people—I'm begging you...the diapers have never leaked for me....I think this is a rumor started by the Huggies people." Then she threatened to ransack all the stores in the New York tristate area and hoard a lifetime supply. Turns out they were just tinkering with the product, and before she could say "diaper rash," truckloads of free Pampers were delivered to their new unofficial spokesperson.

Rosie has learned that her every wish is some happy company's command.

Although she has a friend watch Parker while she is taping her show or in meetings, she doesn't employ nannies to relieve her of the endless mundane chores of motherhood. Rosie is ever-sensitive to the issue of parent absenteeism and tries hard to be the one who tucks Parker in each night. Even pop-music idols inviting her out to club hop get turned down. "TAFKAP," as Rosie likes to call the Artist Formerly Known as Prince, wanted to meet her for a drink one midnight. "I can't go out at midnight! I have a baby and a show to do," she lamented to her audience the following day.

Though she may not be an ordinary mom, she is the first modern career mom on daytime TV. Often tired, she has little time to go to the gym, and she's overloaded with errands. When asked about her life now that she's such a hit, she said it was "too busy, dull, and wonderful." She claims that all she has time for is the show, her son, watching some TV, and the occasional Scrabble game with friends. One of the things that connects her to her fans is that while she does get to jet to Los Angeles for the weekend to meet Tom Cruise, most evenings she is home, parked in front of the tube. And she's not ashamed of it: "I watch TV, I like TV, I never had a snobby attitude about TV." Fans love that she usually gives her critique of whatever shows she watched the night before.

Less visible and accessible movie stars live lives shrouded in mystique. Fans assume those stars live glamorous lives filled with Hollywood soirees, premieres, exotic vacations, and servants to fulfill their every whim. Not Rosie. She schleps down to the hardware store herself to buy a lock for her bathroom door so Parker can be stopped from flushing all his toys down the toilet. What should have been a simple installation of a hook-and-eye latch becomes an extended ordeal and a five-minute hoot on her show, as she explains how everything that could go wrong did. "How hard could it be? I nearly had a breakdown." She explained how it all went downhill after she discovered her cordless drill wasn't charged and decided to make the holes with a nail. "I kept going back to the hardware store...and now I have four big holes in the bright yellow door to my Looney Tunes bathroom."

More evidence of her love of children means booking such guests as Elmo, Big Bird, Kermit the Frog, and Miss Piggy. On one show, a larger than life H. R. Puffinstuff did the opening announcement. Genuinely thrilled, Rosie exclaimed, "When I was a kid, if you had told me that one day I'd have my own show and get to meet H. R. Puffinstuff, I'd have said, 'No way.' Proving dreams do come true."

As a first-time mom with her own talk show, Rosie has received more than her share of free advice. Much of the E-mail she gets is from other mothers sharing their tips:

"Dear Rosie, I was a single mom for years, and my best advice to you is to treasure every moment you have with him. When he tries to become his own person, let him think he is doing it by himself—but guide him lovingly and wisely so he doesn't catch on."

One afternoon while chatting live in the "Rosie Room" on AOL, Rosie logged off just like any other tightly scheduled mother, saying she had to go do laundry while her baby was asleep. Her online mail from other moms offers her a world of support:

"I read that you were the only one to get up in the night with your son—good for you! I have twin boys and could afford help but didn't take it. I promise it gets easier! Thank you for bringing the impossible to daytime TV: funny and decent!"

Another letter extolled the advantages of being a single mother: "Being a single parent means you have to have a support system of other loving adults to help with child care, so your kid grows up with adult friends to turn to when there are problems. Being a single parent has been the greatest. My kid's life won't be perfect, but it won't be any different than a kid with two parents. Go for it!"

Rosie also received this moving letter from a woman who was an adopted child: "My son's name is also Parker, and he is adopted—but I am the birth mom. I and other birth mothers are SO thankful for people like you. I love my son more than life itself, and I found someone who can take better care of him than I could. Good luck in all that you do; I am a big fan!"

Then there are the star mothers who offer their advice. To keep her ten-year-old daughter, Chloe, from growing up too fast, Candice Bergen joked that she "put a stone on her head."

Rosie asked her if she would "steer her daughter away from performing?"

Candice replied, "I've done my best."

"People say that about my son," Rosie added. "Do you hope he's a performer? I hope he's anything but.... it's a lot of rejection."

Rosie took the opportunity to play the adviser when Ricki Lake visited her show. Thirteen weeks pregnant with *her* first child, Ricki seemed delighted by Rosie's impromptu baby shower. Full of hard-earned advice, Rosie gave her a book of parenting tips, a baby carryall device that allows mom to have her hands free, a sound-and-light baby monitor ("This is good for sleeping"), and a mountain of diapers from her gargantuan stash.

At one point, Ricki said she was concerned how her beloved dog would adjust to the baby. "I've had my dog for seven years—he's like my son, but he needs to know that if he has a problem with the little one, he's gonna lose."

Rosie shared her experience with the same issue: "My little Pupper-Wupper and Valley Girl (her two long-haired Chihuahuas), they would go everywhere with me. Now they're starved for attention. They're just sitting home going, 'She's with that kid again.'"

Perhaps the best evidence of Rosie's natural gift for mothering is how she relates to the many children who appear on her show. Katie Schlossberg, the six-year-old actress who starred in *Multiplicity* with Michael Keaton and Andie MacDowell, came to plug her movie. This was her first-ever talk-show appearance and Rosie coached her through it, including how to set up her first clip—which she then delivered like a seasoned pro.

Rosie has an innate ability to talk to children at their own level. She doesn't talk down to them or treat them like trained seals. Because she's such a great mimic, Rosie is even able to speak in each child's voice, using the same pitch and inflections, creating the illusion of two kids having a chat. Katie mentioned that her father rarely got to visit the set because "he always had to WORK." When Rosie asked what her Dad did for WORK, Katie replied, "Let's see...he's an economist." Then Rosie asked what an economist does. "Uh, I don't exactly know." To which Rosie confessed, "You know what—neither do I." At the end of the interview, Rosie told her, "I hope you get to do more movies—if that's what you *want* to do."

Although Rosie isn't the one who selects them, many of the audience members chosen to do the live announcement at the top of the show are children. She's had triplets celebrating their birthday, the cast of a school play, and one especially overwhelmed little girl named, Andrea, who tripped over some particularly cumbersome names (CeCe Peniston and Heidi Van Belt). Halfway through she appeared ready to give up entirely, but somehow she pulled herself together and struggled through to the end. As soon as Rosie came onstage she gestured to the girl to join her. Andrea looked like she was expecting a reprimand. Instead, Rosie hugged her, high-fived her, and told her she did a good job. "You almost gave up there in the middle...but you put your head up and you kept going....Take a bow, Andrea." Much relieved, she went back to her seat, with a lesson about perseverence that she'll probably never forget.

And then there are the kids and mothers who send her things. She can't resist sharing some of them on her show. One nine-year-old girl wrote and recorded a song for her, and Rosie played some of it on the air. While the child was clearly no Carly Simon, Rosie reacted like she could be. Other times she just holds up funny photos of her youngest fans, some taken while the toddlers stare transfixed at Rosie's image on the tube.

To decorate her Christmas tree and studio in December 1996, Rosie invited kids to send her handmade ornaments with their pictures on them. Rosie adored the ornaments and all the "cutie patooties," as she lovingly referred to the kids in the photos, and she showed many of them on the air.

The Rosie O'Donnell Show has even been reviewed and recommended as a great place to take children to be in the studio audience. The reviewer for *Newsday* enthused: "This show loves kids....what other live show can you take your kids to where they'll see a good-natured, normal-looking celebrity? None." She also pointed out that to attend most shows you must be eighteen, whereas Rosie lets them visit starting at age five. Sure, sometimes a delighted squeal from a tiny audience member interrupts the proceedings, but Rosie seems determined to keep plenty of reality checks in her increasingly star-studded life.

Even in live performances as a stand-up, Rosie is alert to children in her audiences. Playing Caesars Palace in Las Vegas, she noticed some kids in the front row who looked too young for some of her R-rated material. When she discovered one of the girls was only ten, she explained, "I thought starting at 10 P.M. would deter prepubescents, but I was wrong." Ever the pro—and a conscientious parent—Rosie quickly revised her act. When she said the O.J. jokes would have to go, she told the disappointed audience, "You don't have the responsibility. Ten years from now you are going to watch *A Current Affair.* She is going to be on a tower with a rifle. They will say, 'Her name is Jessica. She keeps screaming "Rosie O'Donnell" and shooting people.'"

When asked to comment about her younger fans, Rosie said, "I love kids, always have. It means so much to me to brighten up a kid's day." Judging from the percentage of her online fan mail from children, many are having better days because of Rosie. There seems to be a whole crop of electronically adept latchkey kids who race home from school to watch her live or on tape, then go to their computers and dash off their views. Check out some of their messages:

"Rosie, I am a fourteen-year-old guy and I just wanted to say how much I love you and your show! Anyone who thinks you are fat or not beautiful needs mental help quick!"

"Hi Rosie! I know I am a little old (seventeen) to be posting in the kids' area, but I am a kid at heart. I wanted to tell you I really feel bad about what happened to your mother, because I lost my mother to breast cancer when I was fourteen. I look to celebrities to heal my wounds and to get me through some of the harder times so I could laugh a little. I am so happy you got your own show—you have no idea."

"Dear Rosie, I am eleven years old. I think you are great. It is nice to hear my mom laugh in the afternoon when she watches your show."

"Rosie, all three of us girls watch your show every day with our Mom. We are seven, ten, and thirteen. It is the only talk show we are allowed to watch. We think you are very pretty."

"Dear Rosie, I love your show and get up every morning to watch it. My mom watches it at work and she gets in trouble."

It seems sweetly ironic that a new generation of children hurries home to this Virtual Mom who dispenses warm fuzzies over the airwaves.

Home for Rosie and Parker is her New York City apartment on the Upper West Side of Manhattan.

It has a decidedly showbiz flair and features a colorful "Looney Tunes" bathroom. Dominating the living area, in addition to the piano, which Parker tends to bang into, are huge floor-to-ceiling shelves custom built to display Rosie's vast collection of toys and showbiz flotsam and jetsam. She is the first to make fun of her obsessive collecting of every scrap of show business detritus. "Have you picked up that I'm a little anal retentive with the memorabilia?" she asks, swooning over the latest addition.

When Marlo Thomas came on her show, Rosie showed her the old issue of *TV Guide* that featured her on the cover. "I have a *TV Guide* collection, because I'm a neurotic person with no life," Rosie told her. Marlo picked it up gingerly, then exclaimed, "It's amazing it hasn't turned to ash." Sheepishly, Rosie explained why. "I keep them in Ziploc bags."

Those magazines are Rosie's holy books—the records of shows loved, shows she's been on, shows she wanted to be on, shows friends were on. Those aging magazines chart her life.

She's no snob about her collections, either. She gets just as excited over a rare vintage doll worth $700 as she does over the latest McDonald's freebie Happy Meals toys. In a brilliant act of promotion, Disney and McDonald's honored Rosie on her 101st show with a boxed set of all 101 Dalmatian figurines. You would have thought she had been given 101 diamonds. "I'm one of the few people who has the whole set—ha, ha, ha, ha, ha! I'm so mature," she noted, without much remorse. And Rosie is having a custom-made shelf built to display them.

Of all the thrills and honors Rosie has received, oddly enough, becoming a Flintstones Happy Meal doll is certainly close to her heart. "The doll actually looks like me, and she's sort of chubby which is kinda cute," Betty Rubble said of her tiny likeness. "I think the doll captures my essence—it's got a thick waist, very long arms, and a sort of cavewomanesque demeanor, which is pretty much me."

Both Rosie as Betty Rubble—and her doll—wear a blue ribbon around their right ankles to disguise Rosie's tattoo.

One of her great pleasures is to meet the real people whose dolls she has collected over the years. Whenever one of them appears on her talk show, Rosie trots out the doll and usually does some bit with it, complete with her imitation of the actor in question. It must be a surreal experience for her at times, to see dolls she has had for years alongside their real-life inspirations. When Barbara Eden came on the show carrying a huge basket of new *I Dream of Jeannie* toys, it was Christmas in November. "Barbara, nothing makes me happier than toys and dolls." Some of the "living dolls" who have appeared on Rosie's show include

- Kate Mulgrew, *Star Trek* captain
- Cher, seventies version of herself
- Maureen McCormick, Marcia Brady
- Eve Plum, Jan Brady
- Christie Brinkley, swimsuit supermodel
- Lucy Lawless, *Xena, Warrior Princess* (who Rosie got to sing!)
- Susan Dey, Laurie Partridge
- David Cassidy, another Partridge, who brought his paper dolls
- Dolly Parton, "Backwoods Barbie"
- Cheryl Ladd and Kate Jackson, *Charlie's Angels*
- Sylvester Stallone, *Rocky*
- Barbara Eden, it's no dream, it's Jeannie
- Henry Winkler, the Fonz (complete with "Aaay!" sound effect)

Something else that makes it fun for children are Buster and Valentine, (also known as Pupper-Wupper and Valley Girl) Rosie's two long-haired Chihuahuas. She got Buster as a puppy on the advice of a psychic during the run of *Grease* and soon started carrying him around with her whenever she could, even onto the talk-show circuit. Portable and completely indoor dogs, they have wavy white-and-honey-colored fur and never need to be taken outside for walks, thanks to the invention of doggie "wee-wee pads." Some people are not as smitten with toy breeds, though don't dare cast aspersions on the breed in front of Rosie, as the acid-tongued actor Jay Thomas made the mistake of doing one day.

He began to tease her, saying the dogs have bug eyes and yap a lot. "You know how you always think your kids are cute, and other people's aren't? Well, your dogs are like other people's kids. I hate those little rat dogs."

Rosie, in a huff, responded, "They are not rat dogs. They're very calm, loving, beautiful animals."

Having said all that, she's not above joking about them in her stand-up act. "They're long-haired Chihuahuas. Actually, they were short-haired Chihuahuas, but I put a little Rogaine in their Alpo."

Nor is she above dressing them up in cute costumes and bringing them on her show to meet some famous dog guests. Photographer and author William Wegman brought two of his Weimaraner models, but once they spotted Rosie's tiny pups they acted like they had seen lunch, so Rosie hustled them away.

While her apartment provides a convenient city home, there is a much grander place she and her son will soon call home.

↶ 18

Her Pals Cher, Kate,
Dan, and Bette

It's one of the most difficult transitions for a performer to make when she decides to try hosting her own talk show. Once her opening monologue and comedy bits are over, a good host learns to recede a bit from the spotlight so that her guests can shine. It adds to the fun if the host gets some laughs of her own from time to time, but she has to walk a fine line not to steal the guest's thunder, especially if the guest is not a comedian or naturally witty. For the most part, Rosie has handled this well right from the start. (She *was* paying attention watching Carson all those years.) Of her idol Johnny Carson, Rosie says, "He always made sure if there was egg on anyone's face, it was his."

Sometimes her enthusiasm to share stories about her adoration of a guest can be a bit overwhelming for the star in question, but even that makes for entertaining television. Her obsessive-fan self is one of her most appealing qualities. It is clear that Rosie knows how to listen. "Johnny Carson was my hero growing up, and he was the best at that," she said. "He understood it wasn't his job to try and top everyone....You make people look good, and in the end you end up looking good."

Another challenge is to present the guest in the best possible way. She ragged on Jay Leno on her own show for his habit of dissing his guests just for a laugh (something David Letterman does a lot, as well). Leno called her up to complain, and Rosie dished it right back: "What a baby—with Jay, the big thing is, everybody's gotta like him or he gets upset. I just said I didn't like the way he makes fun of somebody instead of having a conversation. Johnny never woulda done that."

It's clear Rosie has a genuine gift for putting performers at ease, even those who often seem nervous on other talk shows. Singer Gloria Estefan and actress Christine Lahti both seemed less guarded and appeared more open while chatting with Rosie. Again, it probably has a lot to do with the simple fact that she really *knows* their work and can speak knowledgeably to them about it.

Her biggest problem comes when she interviews an idol from her childhood and gets tongue-tied with admiration. At those times she fails to toss her own clever asides into the conversational ring. She behaved that way while interviewing playwright Neil Simon. At the end of the segment she stumbled around trying to express her feelings toward him in some sensible manner, then finally gave up. She confessed, "I'm in awe of you, and I tried not to be, because Lily Tomlin told me if you have reverence for guests it makes a boring interview."

There have been very few guests that failed to come off well. (Actress Eve Plumb comes to mind. She apparently didn't enjoy Rosie's worship of her former role in *The Brady Bunch*.) A few duds are to be expected. Some people just don't do well at 10:00 A.M. on live TV, especially if they just got off a redeye from Los Angeles. When she interviewed her guru, Mike Douglas, on an early show, Rosie asked him how to handle difficult guests. He replied, "Always make guests look better than they are."

"With Cher you gotta be cool." Rosie knew it was pointless to try and hide her admiration for Cher, since she is one of the big role models of her childhood and beyond. Cher is a consummate performer—TV, variety, albums, music videos, and most impressive to Rosie—an Oscar–winning actress. And she seems to have done it all without compromising her uniqueness, something Rosie always strives to do herself. When July 8, 1996, arrived, Rosie claimed, "The whole night I couldn't sleep—I'm so excited that Cher is here."

Her bandleader, John McDaniel was equally excited: "She's my all-time favorite." He said that as a boy he had kept a Cher scrapbook and had cut

Coming out of the dugout to bat in *A League of Their Own* (1992). (Columbia Studios, courtesy Kobal, 1992)

Rosie attended the premiere of *A League of Their Own* in June 1992 with her sister Maureen. (Photo: Gerardo Somoza/Outline)

David Johansen and Rosie in *Car 54, Where Are You?* Based on the old TV show, this was her least successful movie. (Orion Studios, courtesy Kobal)

Talking it up at a prehistoric party with *Flintstones* costar Rick Moranis in 1994.
(Universal Studios, courtesy Kobal)

The "modern stone-age family" returns in the live-action comedy *The Flintstones*, with
Rosie (Betty), Rick Moranis (Barney), John Goodman (Fred), and Elizabeth Perkins
(Wilma). (Courtesy Kobal)

Hanging around with good friend Madonna in 1993. (Photo: Gerardo Somoza/ Outline)

Rosie in a scene with Meg Ryan in *Sleepless in Seattle* (1993). (TriStar, courtesy Kobal)

Becky, played by
Rosie, completely
understands her
friend's crazy obses-
sion with a man
she's never met in
Sleepless in Seattle.
(Courtesy Kobal)

Rosie attended the
June 1993 pre-
miere of *Sleepless in
Seattle* with Tom
Hanks and Nora
Ephron. (Photo:
Gerardo
Somoza/Outline)

Dan Aykroyd starred with Rosie in *Exit to Eden*, a story of two cops who go undercover at a fantasy sex resort. (Savoy Pictures, courtesy Kobal)

Rosie O'Donnell, producer Alexandra Rose, and costar Iman posing on the set of this combination comedy and love story. (Courtesy Kobal)

Rosie with Garry Marshall and Iman at the premiere of *Exit to Eden.*

Rosie in a classic dominatrix pose with Dan Aykroyd in a publicity shot for *Exit to Eden*.

Sonny's head out of all the pictures. He knew it was somewhere in his mother's attic in St. Louis, but she had been unable to find it. He had wanted to bring the scrapbook to show to Cher.

Rosie did bring in her very own childhood Cher doll, sporting a strange haircut, which Rosie had given the doll when she was twelve. Her digicard console was loaded up with all her favorite Cher songs, which Rosie brazenly sang bits of. Then the reality that Cher was backstage waiting came over her face and she flinched like a kid caught making fun of the principal. "I'm tryin' not to be nervous—but it's *Cher.*" Then she admonished herself, "I know—stop fawning over the guests!" She kept singing snatches of Cher's songs, complete with sucked-in cheeks and the trademark hair flick—Rosie was clearly over the edge.

When Cher finally made her entrance to a standing ovation, the first thing Rosie sought was her approval for her impression of her. "Was it close?"

Cher conceded, "I think it's, unfortunately, close."

Rosie was eager to show Cher her tattoo she said she was inspired by Cher. "First I got the cross at a church-slash-tattoo parlor, then I got the rest of it [an ankle bracelet of multicolored roses] to go around it." Rosie then proceeded to plant her right foot on her desk and hike up her pants to display her tattoo. "I don't know what I was thinking," she said, shaking her head. "It's hard not to keep getting them—once you get one, you want more."

Rosie had said in an interview that she got her tattoo on a lark with her sister a few years back, when Maureen was in a mood to do something different. They took her sisters' youngsters along and sat with them in their laps. "All these big biker men were flinching, but we just sat and talked as they tattooed our ankles." Cher confided that she was going to try and have all of hers removed because she was tired of them. "Once before I die, I'd like to look at my butt and just see *it.*"

Becoming more comfortable with each other, they went on to share more girl talk. Cher had just done David Letterman's show, and he had behaved in a very forward manner, even for him. (Dave doesn't bother to disguise his leers and peers down his guests' bodices quite openly. He also gives the longest, tightest "hello" hugs in television—to select female guests.) On the night in question, after Cher had finished singing, Dave came over to thank her. He put his arm around her and then to her great surprise, he put the moves on her. As Cher was retelling it, Rosie interrupted her to exclaim, "He grabbed your butt!"

"He sure did! And wait—" she shrieked, "he kissed me!"

Rosie asked what all of America wanted to know: "A real kiss—tongues and everything?"

Cher, visibly rattled recalling it, replied, "It was near—it was near."

They went on to discuss being a guest on his show and how he doesn't like to talk to anyone during the commercial breaks. Cher said, "He's very nervous—he's shy, kind of—or, he's a pain in the ass."

Then, as if they were at a sleepover, Cher advised Rosie on her hair. "You should get more streaks—you're cute." Sure enough, Rosie did as she was told, and soon sported dramatic new streaked highlights in her hair.

During a commercial break, workers swarmed over the set and transformed it into the Home Shopping Channel. It seems that Cher also has her own mail-order home furnishings business selling gothic gewgaws. Her catalog is called "Sanctuary" and contains some very exotic items that reflect Cher's unusual taste. Already a customer, Rosie proudly pointed out what she had bought. "I get my candles there—not the cross ones—I thought if my father [the devout Catholic] saw that, he'd have a coronary." She also purchased an incense holder and a thronelike chair for her office.

Looking at the cover of the catalog, which featured Cher in medieval dress and headgear, inspired Rosie to imitate her look. She then removed a chain-mail lampshade, forced it on her head, and posed like Cher: "This is nice if you want to joust someone when they come over." The audience went berserk as she continued to mug in it, and Cher nearly fell backward out of her chair, she was laughing so hard. Then in a clear example of upstaging her guest, she *continued* to wear it for several minutes while attempting to continue the interview and talk to Cher of other more serious things, like her relationship with Sonny and her daughter, Chastity. Rosie left no doubt what she thought of the congressman from California. "If it wasn't for you, he'd be pumping gas somewhere—who's he kiddin'." Finally, she took the lampshade off, to Cher's relief.

Rosie had walked a fine line between being playful and mocking Cher and her merchandise. Some would say she veered way over that line. There was, however, no arguing that Rosie was hysterically funny in the process.

After Cher's segments ended and she had left the stage, something happened that only happens on talk shows, especially where the host encourages spontaneity. *Two guests later,* Rosie welcomed actor Malcolm Gets from *Caroline in the City.* Also a huge Cher fan, he vamped in, sporting a Cher wig and a bared navel. Rosie quickly joined him in singing the Cher hit, "Gypsies, Tramps, and Thieves." It was clear, and again, no surprise, that Rosie knew all the lyrics.

Before long, the producer let Rosie know that Cher was still there and wanted to come back and meet Malcolm. Rosie naturally welcomed her back, but Malcolm appeared ready to collapse with delight. So as the crowd again went wild, Cher returned and Malcolm dropped to his knees and kissed her hand. "I heard you guys doing your really bad impressions of me," Cher scolded.

Malcolm shrank visibly and replied, "I feel like my mother just knocked on the bathroom door and said 'Are you okay in there?'"

Once again, the audience zoomed off the decibel meter with laughter. After discussing the finer points of Malcolm's Cher impression, they all joined in on a rendition of "Gypsies," and even Cher didn't know the lyrics as well as Rosie did. ("It's true," Rosie exclaimed later. "She was reading *my* lips!") They continued singing during the commercial break, and when the show resumed, Malcolm played the piano while Cher and Rosie sang "If I Could Turn Back Time."

It was a genuine showbiz moment. If Rosie could turn back time to 1971 when she first watched the *Sonny and Cher Comedy Hour* as a little starstruck nine year old and know that one day she would sing with Cher on *her* show, she would probably have had trouble believing it.

Unscripted performances like that are what talk-show fans live for. They watch faithfully every day, like birdwatchers eager to add to their Life Lists—hoping to be there when Drew Barrymore flashes her bare breasts at Dave or when Leno puts Hugh Grant in the hot seat and asks, "What were you *thinkin'?*"

On a show several days later, Rosie admitted that once when Cher had really short hair and had dyed it blond, the eagle-eyed fan that she is recognized her anyway and followed her all around a shopping mall. "I didn't tell her when she was on the show, 'cause I didn't want to scare her!"

Rosie has admitted stalking stars she admires: Cher, at a shopping mall; Billy Joel, at bars in Huntington, Long Island, when she was in high school;

Bette Midler, all over the country while she was on tour; Lucie Arnaz, at the Broadway theater where she was appearing; and Lauren Bacall, in the lobby of the Dakota, where many celebrities live.

"She's the reason I cut out of school many a day back before they invented VCRs." Rosie was speaking about actress Kate Mulgrew. "I don't know if I've ever been this excited before to have a guest on the show." Perhaps no other star could evoke such a girlish déjà vu for Rosie. As a youngster in Commack she had repeatedly skipped school to keep up with her all-time favorite soap opera, *Ryan's Hope,* all about an Irish Catholic family that had a teenage daughter named Mary Ryan, played by Mulgrew. Rosie was so invested in the storyline that when Mary Ryan received a marriage proposal on a Friday, she faked mono all the next week so as not to miss Mary's response, which didn't come until the following Friday. Rosie still remembers waiting in line for Mulgrew's autograph at the Smithhaven Mall in 1978 when she was sixteen years old. Of course she still has that treasured signed photo.

At the top of the show, Rosie was nearly overcome with emotion just thinking about Kate. "I don't know if I can adequately express the thrill it is to finally meet her."

Though Mulgrew went on to bigger roles (Mrs. Colombo and the first female *Star Trek* Captain), Rosie only had eyes for Mary Ryan. It was as though a part of her childhood had sprung back to life. Rosie even managed to find a clip to show of the young Kate. It was soon apparent, that yet again, Rosie knew more trivia about the guest's career than the star herself. At one point, Kate said that her character had been replaced on the show, and Rosie corrected her: "No, you died—"

Kate was amazed. "I died?"

Rosie was happy to fill her in. "On the show—then you came back as a ghost when your daughter got married, whose name was Ryan Fanelli, who was on our show, who's Yasmine Bleeth, who's now on *Baywatch*—and *then* they had another actress play Mary Ryan."

Meanwhile, Kate Mulgrew nearly fell out of her chair laughing at Rosie's rapid-fire recitation. Finally she turned to her young son in the audience. "Can you believe this?"

"I'm a stalker," Rosie jokingly warned Andrew. "If you see me outside your house, call 9-1-1."

Having been told what a huge fan Rosie was of the show, Mulgrew arranged for her best friend and former cast member of the same soap to also appear, as a surprise. When Nancy Addison, who played Gillian Coleridge on the show, came bounding out, Rosie shrieked and nearly lost control of herself as she enveloped Addison in a bear hug. "Oh my heart is beating so fast—you have no idea. I think I might be having a heart attack!" She couldn't wait to show Nancy her ear, which she had double-pierced when she was in the eighth grade in imitation of Nancy's character. Both actresses still look fantastic, remarkably similar to their younger selves, which may have created an illusionary time warp for Rosie, who wasn't able to calm down at all during their interview. As the segment ended, she summed it up with obvious sincerity. "Kate and Nancy—you have made my life complete."

In a strange way, perhaps they did. Perhaps coming face to face and hand to flesh with these very important adolescent fantasy figures did help Rosie put some of her teenage demons to rest, to accept once and for all that *her dreams have come true.* She no longer needs to live vicariously through Mary Ryan and her intact family. She has created her own family. She no longer needs to desire Mary's life. She has manifested a life even more exciting than her wildest teenage flights of fancy. Perhaps now she can leave Mary Ryan and her Hope to her past.

None of the guests is allowed to French-kiss the host on *The Rosie O'Donnell Show.* This new rule was imposed on August 8, 1996, after Richard Simmons and the singer known as Meatloaf both stuck their tongues where they weren't wanted. "I can't blame them," Rosie said, after laying down the new law. "Everyone wants to!"

The following day, there was nearly an attempt from another unlikely guest. Rosie was interviewing another star she had idolized since forever, Lucie Arnaz, and talking about seeing her over and over and over on Broadway in *They're Playing Our Song.* Before she could stop herself, Rosie rattled off the entire casting history of the show—"Then Tony Roberts took over the role after Robert Klein left....Hello, useless shit stuck in my brain, and—oops—did I just say—boy, we'll edit that, don't worry, oh, boy—*hello*—there we go, we just lost all of the South."

Lucie tried to make her feel better with, "That's all right. Wait'll I French-kiss you, then you'll lose the rest of 'em."

* * *

When her buddy Dan Ackroyd came on the show to plug his new TV venture, *The Psi Factor,* he started off with an amusing but genuine compliment, delivered in a New York accent similar to Rosie's: "I'm so proud a you—you got the desk here, you got a studio, you got a boy—you own New York—it's beautiful!"

They met while filming the movie they would both like to forget, *Exit to Eden.* At least they got to make the film in Hawaii, and as Dan recalled, "They said you and I were gonna be a team....They had great things planned for us, Rosie—"

"—And then the movie came out," she reminded him.

The good news, according to Dan was that "we salvaged a friendship out of it."

Turns out they have many mutual interests, including UFOs. Dan is intrigued by the paranormal and they discussed a number of famous cases of paranormal activity. Then Dan put Rosie on the spot: "I understand that you think you may have an implant scar?" Rosie proceeded to divulge a rather shocking thing: "I don't want people to think I'm wacko, but yes, I do." Then she had the camera zoom in for an extreme close-up of her left ear. Clearly visible just above her ear was a small round dent in her head. She said, "I'm pretty sure that aliens implanted something." She confessed she had even written letters to Whitley Strieber, author of *Communion,* a book about his alleged adventures with aliens. Rosie also admitted that her sister had begged her not to tell the story on television.

Dan's response to her tale was sweet and wonderful: "Well, if you were implanted, you were implanted with grace, intelligence, humor, and beauty—I must say that."

In describing Bette Midler, Rosie told her audience, "She's really the reason I'm in entertainment." Before Bette came out, Rosie went on to give the audience a rundown of her history with Bette. She told about stealing money out of her father's wallet, cutting school, and taking the train into New York to catch a Wednesday matinee of Bette when she appeared on Broadway in 1975 in *Clams on the Halfshell.* After seeing that performance, thirteen-year-old Rosie O'Donnell said to herself, "That's what I'd like to do."

Eight years later, when Rosie was crisscrossing the country on the comedy circuit, she obtained Midler's upcoming *DeTour* schedule from her fan club, then proceeded to book herself into comedy clubs in the same cities at the same times. Since Rosie was just the opening act, she could miss parts of the comedy show and even sometimes call in sick, then she would scurry over to wherever Bette was performing, buy a scalped ticket, and catch her act. "I must have seen the show like twenty-six times."

Then Rosie finally displayed one of her much-talked-about showbiz scrapbooks, containing all her Midler memorabilia. Rosie even admitted that she had signed the photo of Bette Midler herself. "Such a wacko am I." She also said she didn't want to show the book when Bette was present because "I don't want to scare her." Although they've become friends and have dinner together occasionally, Rosie still has to monitor herself. "I try not to go during dinner, 'Oh, my God—it's Bette Midler.'"

Realizing that time was dribbling out of her hour, Rosie said. "I'm not wasting my joke time when *she's* waiting back there."

When it finally came time for Rosie to bring Bette Midler out to the rose-bedecked set (roses for "the Rose"), she was visibly moved. "I've practiced this introduction in my bedroom since I was eight years old: As far as I'm concerned, our first guest is quite simply, the Queen of All Things. The one, the only, the Emmy–winning, the Grammy–winning, the Tony–winning, the Golden Globe–winning, the Oscar–nominated, Her Highness, royalty—Bette Midler."

And then Bette finally flounced out in sequined pants and told Rosie, "That was the best introduction I've ever had in my whole life." Rosie replied that she should have such an intro every day of her life. Feeling a bit sheepish for all her earlier gushing, Rosie asked her if she thought she was nuts.

"You're probably the most insane person I've ever met," Bette told her. "You know more about me than I know myself." Rosie began reciting classic Midler bits to her so often that she finally announced: "Bette Midler, This is your life." Then they told the story of how they met in a crowded limo on the way to the wedding of one of Bette's backup singers, affectionately known as The Harlettes. Rosie said she "sat as far away from you as I could so I wouldn't bother you." But then someone else decided they should all tell a Bette story. Rosie tried to pass, so she wouldn't scare her with tales of her Bette Midler obsession. Bette urged her to begin, but she couldn't get her to stop. "It was a fabulous wedding but the longest ride of my life," Bette reminded her.

Midler admitted that she hadn't seen Rosie's show until she sent her a tape. Just the same, she was thrilled for her success. Rosie gave her all the credit for inspiring her in the first place: "Look what you've done," she said gesturing all around her. "You've created me!"

Then Rosie begged Bette Midler to sing for them. The Divine Miss M finally said she would "If I'm joined by Rosie O'Donnell—oh, come on—I know you've been waiting since you were eight!" As everyone knows, Rosie does not need much encouragement to sing. After singing through the commercial break, Bette began shaking her head and exclaimed, "It's horrifying—to be standing here with somebody who knows all the parts to all my songs."

"And I change keys," Rosie admitted.

"That's all right," Midler consoled her. "Enthusiasm counts for a lot."

They belted out the rocket-paced song, "My Analyst Told Me." Secretly, Bette may have been testing Rosie with this very difficult-to-sing song. She was absolutely up to the challenge and seemed to stun Bette with her ability to keep up with the tongue-twisting lyrics. Afterward, Rosie gave the stage to Bette, who dedicated her song about a little girl and her favorite kisses to Rosie the Mom.

"After the Bette Midler show I cried," Rosie admitted. "Just because I looked up and saw my sister all filled with tears....Every time there is somebody from our childhood—Joni Mitchell, Linda Ronstadt, people we listened to twenty-four hours a day—my siblings are here."

On the next day's show, Rosie told John McDaniel that the show with Bette Midler was the best one they had ever done— "Such a dream come true for me."

ᘓ 19

Behind the Scenes

Even though Rosie freely admits to being a control freak, she cannot oversee all aspects of producing five hours of television every week. And though as executive producer her name is at the top of the staff food chain, there is actually another executive producer who manages the day-to-day operations. Choosing the right person for this job fell to Jim Paratore, president of Telepictures Productions, a division of Warner Bros. Because Warners decided to give the show a "summer tryout season" when the level of scrutiny would be lower, that meant a production staff had to be hired quickly. Rosie had a good idea who she wanted as her first lieutenant. New shows typically raid more established shows for staff who have had the experience. *The Rosie O'Donnell Show* stole from the best—David Letterman, who puts on his nightly program a few blocks down the street.

Rosie recommended Daniel Kellison, an eight-year veteran segment producer for Letterman. (Kellison claims it was he who persuaded Drew Barrymore to bare her breasts on television for Letterman's birthday celebration.) Rosie got to know him during her many appearances on Letterman's show. (He persuaded *her* to serenade Letterman with "Oklahoma!") Apparently they impressed each other with their abilities.

"Very few people can come on Letterman the first time and destroy the audience," Kellison explained. "Rosie did it." She quickly became a Letterman favorite. "We could call her two hours before the show and say, 'A guest just fell out. Can you help us?' She'd say, 'I have nothing to talk about.' Then forty-five minutes later, after telling you what happened at lunch that day, you're on the floor."

So, hoping to avoid the rumor mill at the *Late Show*, (and Letterman's wrath), Kellison flew to Los Angeles over a weekend to meet Paratore. So far so good. Then on the way back he was seated in first class next to one of Dave's frequent guests and special favorites, Teri Garr. She was suspicious, and quickly ferreted out his secret. However, she said nothing.

Once Kellison was hired, they took on another Letterman alumni, writer Randy Cohen. ("Seven years—950 shows," he says with exhaustion and pride.) Campaigning for the head writer position, Cohen had to prove he wouldn't be too hip for the room by writing a hundred mainstream ideas. Letterman's audience is dominated by young guys, the kind who like *Beavis and Butthead*. Rosie's target audience is women, twenty-five to fifty-four. So both Kellison and Cohen realized they would have to tone down their material for daytime. Letterman's set designer, Kathleen Ankers, was chosen to design something special for Rosie. Despite the raids on his staff, Letterman sent over enough "Good Luck" pizza to feed the entire staff on opening day.

Kellison, who claims to be thirty-one but looks much younger, sets the dress code with his blue jeans wardrobe. (Rosie contributed to the look by giving everyone on her staff an official denim jacket with the show's colorful logo on the back.) Kellison manages his crew from his office, which has a telescopic view down the long hallway leading to Studio 8G. Right away Rosie could tell her style would be an adjustment for Kellison. Early on, he interrupted an interview she was giving to let her know that Melanie Griffith was on the phone. Rosie explained later, "These kids, they get so excited—'Ooh, Melanie Griffith!' I'm friends with Melanie Griffith; if they're worried about whether she'll do the show, she'll do it. But Daniel's from Letterman—I don't think Dave palled around with celebrities."

The rest of the staff soon fell into place. The group is about eighty percent female, and all are under forty years of age. Actually, Rosie began the show with one token older person, forty-seven-year-old writer Kate Clinton (no relation to the president). Clinton, a popular openly lesbian comic, had been pals with Rosie for more than ten years and was known for her biting political humor. Clinton was enthusiastic at first, and even relocated to New York from Provincetown, Massachusetts.

"Rosie knows exactly what she wants, what works and what doesn't work," Clinton said. "My gay friends are all excited about the show. There's a way she's so funny, so camp, that we all appreciate." It was Kate's vision to "get some gay humor on the show." When asked how she felt about being the oldest person on the staff, she threatened to give Kellison "a big puberty ceremony."

Clinton remained for several months, but it was soon apparent that her style of humor wasn't suited to daytime television, and many of her jokes, while very funny, didn't make it onto the show. Kate Clinton left to resume her stand-up career and write screenplays. Rosie lamented how she hated turning down great jokes that she knew weren't appropriate at ten in the morning. Like the teacher she would have been in an alternate reality, Rosie marks the rejected jokes with an "XL," which means "No—but I love it. Because they're funny but mean, and I don't wanna do mean."

Here is an example of what she consderes mean. Halfway through a Dole joke on the June 28, 1996, show, Rosie backed off and refused to finish it. Here's how it didn't go: "Liddy Dole, like Hillary Clinton, also communicates regularly with the dead. Sometimes Bob responds, sometimes he doesn't."

All the writers had to learn by trial and error what works and what doesn't. Head writer, Cohen, knew right after the first practice show that he would need to put Rosie out in the audience doing comedy bits as often as possible. She can deliver jokes from her desk like the veteran stand-up comic that she is, but she shines best when she's interacting with people. "She's great with the audience," Cohen explained. "It wasn't like the desk pieces weren't funny, but we're not there to have our bright little words said. We're there to create an arena where Rosie will thrive."

"It's tough on the writers," Rosie says. "I do feel bad when I kill a joke." Cohen says her guilt passes very quickly. Rosie is used to writing all her own jokes and is very involved with the creation of the opening material. She takes a writing credit on the show, as do the other comedic talk-show hosts.

"The watchword around here from the start has been 'nice,'" Cohen said. "I mean, *determinedly* nice. And frankly, that worried me a bit, because by its nature comedy attacks."

It's easy to see why Cohen and Rosie ultimately clashed. "I don't think it's funny to be mean," Rosie explained. "I don't want to make a joke about somebody and then walk into a party and see them and feel embarrassed that I possibly hurt their feelings. I know the writers get frustrated by that sometimes."

Over time the writers have learned other ways to be humorous. They've all had to brush up on their pop culture, especially Cohen, who doesn't share Rosie's adoration of things seventies. "The stuff she loves are the things I think have contributed to the fall of Western civilization." Actually, all the producer really needs to do is turn the cameras on and let Rosie riff on her daily life. More and more, she does just that and cuts back on the prepared jokes as she runs out of time. Judging from her voluminous fan mail, her audiences prefer it when she ad-libs. Declared one fan: "Rosie, you are SO much funnier than what your writers give you."

The Rosie O'Donnell Show is Regis and Kathie Lee's opening segment without the angst and the home game. Viewers enjoy hearing how the other half lives—whether it's an earthy story about the tribulations of Rosie's life or the details of her close and personal encounter with Tom Cruise—her fans want to feel they really know what it's like to *be* her.

One thing Rosie learned from all those years of watching Carson was how to save a joke that dies. Johnny knew better than to pretend it didn't happen, and in making fun of himself in some way for the joke bombing, he turned it around completely. One of Rosie's tactics is to name which writer wrote the joke and share their preshow discussion about the offending joke, which then rights the wrong.

When head writer Cohen left the show, comic Judy Gold was hired as a writer. Janette Barber, who started out as a staff writer moved up to comedy producer. When there are "desk pieces" to do, her job is to stand near the cameras where she can gesture to Rosie and make sure she remembers to do the prepared bits. Letterman and Leno are big on these prepared bits, showing and playing selections from Dave's collection of obscure records. Letterman's Top Ten List and Leno's Headlines have become institutions and books. Rosie has yet to find a running gag like that, and in fact when she does try some canned comedy it's rarely as entertaining as just listening to her talk. Because of her tremendous sense of timing, her storytelling talents, and her perfect pitch as a mimic, Rosie is one of those people who could make you laugh just reading her grocery list.

Another key staffer is bandleader and musical director, John McDaniel, who conducted Rosie as Rizzo in *Grease*. He also conducted the cast album for the show that she recorded (and Brooke Shields's version, as well). He brings an impressive list of credits to *The Rosie O'Donnell Show,* including arranging and conducting for Patti LuPone, both live and for the record. Previously, the affable McDaniel had served for several seasons as resident conductor of the Long Beach Civic Light Opera and won the Los Angeles Drama Critics Circle Award for his music direction of *Chicago.* He has also conducted for a long list of stars, including Carol Burnett, Lucie Arnaz, Cab Calloway, Nell Carter, and Joel Grey. Though he arrives at the studio early enough to rehearse with the day's musical guest, John is pretty much done with his duties at Rosie's by 11:00 A.M., which allows him to conduct on Broadway as well. He is currently arranging and supervising a revival of *Applause* on Broadway.

John also composed the theme song for *The Rosie O'Donnell Show.* "We hope people will start singing it in their sleep," he said at the time. "It's an exciting time right now, having the chance to give birth to what the show is going to be." The theme song is sung by four cast members from *Grease.* As for Rosie's singing, John has to be on his musical toes every second during the taping of every show—he never knows when Rosie will spontaneously burst into song. To his great credit, he always manages to provide some basic melodic guidance. He can even switch keys just as fast as she can.

During the ad-libbed opening chat segment of the show, McDaniel also functions as Rosie's Ed McMahon. She usually asks what he did the previous night, and since he seems to see every play and movie in New York, they can dish about that. John's winning personality and sunny disposition on the show have earned him his own large following. He, too, goes on America Online (as The R0McD) and chats with fans and answers E-mail questions about the band. The other members of the McDLTs are Tracy Wormworth, Morris Goldberg, Rodney Jones, and Ray Marchica.

Another important early hire was the talent coordinator, Jeffry Culbreth, a veteran booker from the *Today* show and *Now With Tom Brokaw and Katie Couric.* It is his primary responsibility to line up all the guests for the show, which should be easier now that the show's a certified hit. Before the show debuted, however, both Daniel Kellison and even Rosie herself, also worked the phones trying to convince A-list stars that this would be a cool place to appear. Using giant wall calendars, Culbreth inks in the guests' names—blue ink for "unconfirmed" and black ink for "really going to show up." Before anyone knew what to expect from her show, Rosie had a hard time convincing some publicists that she wasn't out to lampoon or deride their clients. "I'm hoping celebrities will think this is a safe environment. I'm hoping to get them in and make them look good," she explained in May 1996. Once she got on the air, Rosie shamelessly begged for certain stars to appear, especially during the first weeks. A very special few even received their own "Suck-up Days": Elton John and Barbra Streisand.

For most Rosie fans their idea of heaven is a ticket to see a taping of the show. (It's broadcast live at 10:00 A.M. in New York and much of the East Coast, but taped for other markets.) While just *getting* a ticket is an achievement—there's at least a six-month wait—even that doesn't guarantee entrance. The show mails out more tickets than seats to account for no-shows. There is also a standby ticket line every day, but that's a long shot.

After a long wait standing in line in the lobby of Manhattan's Rockefeller Center, the lucky audience members are finally ushered upstairs to Studio 8G on the eighth floor. The first thing the audience notices when they enter the studio is the striking set. It took some tinkering before the show debuted to get the colors balanced just right— too many of the features of the first version were too blue for daytime TV: the host chair, the audience seats, the carpet, the floor tiles, the curtains. The effect on the home viewers would have been depressing.

So back to the drawing board for set designer Kathleen Ankers. She lightened up the floor, adding brightly colored random tiles in a mosaic effect. Then she changed the furniture to warm rust tones and jazzed up the curtains. Now it's a cheerful wonderland, reflecting the host's fun-loving nature. Visible right behind Rosie in most shots is a roller coaster in the twinkle-lighted faux amusement park set. It's all very appropriate, since she runs the show like a pitchman on a carnival midway.

She's even put a new spin on Groucho Marx's old tradition from his TV show, *You Bet Your Life,* in which prize money was awarded if a contestant said that day's secret word. On *The Rosie O'Donnell Show* the word is shown to the audience when Elmo descends from the rafters wearing it. Then when a guest uses the secret word, the studio audience receives presents.

Rosie has also rigged up various games of chance that she plays with her celebrity guests from time to time. In addition to her now famous Kooshball attacks, she has a new weapon happily provided by the Koosh people: a Whoosh, rather like a flat donut-shaped Frisbee. Rosie had short wooden dowels mounted on the cameras so she would have something to fling the Whooshes at—much like a ringtoss game. What made it more challenging, was that the cameramen kept moving their cameras around to up the ante. Rosie promised to give everyone in the studio audience a Disney video if she won the game. And being the great jockette that she is, she did it easily—and of course the crowd went wild.

In December 1996 the company that makes her trademark toy announced a special edition Rosie O'Donnell Kooshball, and all of her share of the profits will go to charity. As Rosie said, "Way to go Kooshballs!"

In yet another variation on the midway theme, Rosie challenged macho *Baywatch* lifeguard David Hasselhoff to heave Nerf footballs through paper targets off in the distance. Ladies first—she shoots, she scores! Many tries later, a humiliated Hasselhoff had to resort to running right up to the target to get his football through.

From time to time, Rosie adds items to the set. The bright red punching bag was a gift from fellow talk show host, Leeza Gibbons. The Queen of Nice can turn nasty when technical flubs occur. Once when some strange recorded music interrupted actress Phylicia Rashad's segment, Rosie became annoyed. As they went to commercial break, she could be heard shifting into annoyance mode and demanding "What the hell was that?" (She did explain on a later show that she thought her mike was off and made light of the event, saying, "The Queen of Nice ain't so nice, is she?") Another time, when the commercial ended, viewers saw Rosie and actress Barbara Eden sitting silently staring off into space. They had been told to be quiet while a clip was being shown—only there was no clip. Alerted to the problem, Rosie soon recovered, but she wasn't amused. "It's a live show—don't get me started. Every time we have a mistake I say I'm gonna fire people, but sort of as a joke. But then the crew gets mad at me, so normally when that happens I'd say 'Somebody's fired'—but I can't do that anymore, 'cause I get in trouble. But I'm *thinkin'* it!"

In truth, the error is funnier than the clip would have been anyway. That's the fun of live TV for the audience—they *hope* for screwups, because there aren't many entertainment forms that allow for such spontaneity.

But those flashes of Irish temper are seldom seen by the audience. Instead, as they make their way to their blue seats, audience members notice a pint of low-fat milk and a package of Drake's cakes on each chair. Comfort food to set the tone for the homey mood Rosie likes to establish, as well as a symbol of the ideal Mom who has cookies and milk waiting for you after school. (Though this is another idea she lifted from Fran Drescher's show.) It's certainly been great for Drake's—Rosie turns rapturous over their products on a regular basis, which has led to the Cult of Drake, with people in the Northeast mailing them to their deprived friends across the country.

Supermodel Cindy Crawford, among the uninitiated, was startled when Rosie handed her a Drake's Devil Dog. "I'm surprised you can show that on TV," she exclaimed rather salaciously, holding the cylindrical, creme-filled pastry daintily by one corner.

"It's a cake product!" Rosie admonished her. "Don't go there Cindy, it's a daytime show." Then shaking her head, she said, "I'm never going to be able to have a Devil Dog again—you've ruined them for me!" And then she gestured toward the always slinky Cindy and quipped, "You know the reason she looks like this—she never heard of Drake's cakes."

Once the audience is seated and pumped up on sugar, out comes the warm-up comic, Joey Kola. He and the band have the task of making sure these 180 people are wide awake and enthusiastic by the time Rosie emerges from behind the curtain. Kola tells jokes, dances with audience members, and gently delivers the rules: no shouting and no bodily noises. He also has the increasingly challenging job of picking the lucky audience member who will get to deliver the opening announcement on-camera. Sometimes celebrities are in the audience, like skater Kristi Yamaguchi, and are chosen in advance to do the honors... and plug their latest project. But most often it's a cute kid or someone's mom who gets picked.

One woman who brought her daughter to the show for her sixteenth birthday tried to bribe Kola—with ten one-hundred-dollar bills—to choose her daughter. The next day Rosie sat him down before the first guest came out to tell his story. Rosie found it a bit surprising that he claimed he wasn't tempted to take the bribe. "Joey, you are the warm-up guy-comic of my dreams."

The guest announcers rarely lack for show spirit, but sometimes they do get a bad case of nerves just when it's too late. One particularly frightened woman didn't realize how scared she was until she went to open her mouth and nothing came out. Then realizing that the camera was staring her down, she finally uttered, "Oh, my God." Backstage, Rosie could hear the woman panic as the stage manager counted down, "in 5, 4, 3..."

In the end, she came through, and Rosie, ever the gracious host, assured her it wasn't as easy as it looks to do live TV.

But before Rosie makes her entrance, she has to submit to a lot of fussing over by her wardrobe, makeup, and hair people. It is indeed a transformation. Offstage she favors very casual, practical, mother-of-a-toddler clothes. Her favorite trick is to wear a pair of shorts under her sweatpants, so that if Parker spits up on her or makes some other mess in her lap, she can whip off the sweatpants and still be presentable. She also says that "I never ever wear makeup unless I have to go to work." She has also said many times that she leaves all decisions concerning her hair to her hairdresser, David Evangelista. As for the mostly neutral-colored, custom-tailored pantsuits she wears every day on the show, most are designed and custom made for her by designer Dale Richards. About her clothes, her fans are divided. Some think she looks wonderful and others wish she would go for more pizzazz, some pattern and especially more color.

The pampering and primping Rosie receives also extends to her guests. When Olympic gymnast Keri Strug stopped by right after the games, she got her first taste of showbiz makeup. "Weird," she decided. Better, was the closet full of new clothes she got out of the deal. When Rosie's wardrobe people heard Keri was planning to wear a white suit on the show they took her over to Donna Karan, and before she could take any more flying leaps, boxes and boxes of Karan designs landed on her doorstep.

Rosie has also been very vocal in her support of women's athletics and has said how much she loves those Nike commercials that encourage little girls to Just Do It, too. During the summer of 1996 she featured many of the female Olympians on her talk show and made it very clear how much she revered their accomplishments. She's also a big fan of women's tennis and spoke on one show about having attended matches on the Virginia Slims Tour. Landing Keri's and Michael Johnson's first post-Olympic appearances was no small achievement among talk-show bookers. "There's a mini-Olympics going on backstage where everybody's trying to see who they can book," said Daniel Kellison at the time.

How did this brand-new show score so high? Segment producer Jeane Willis went to Atlanta and schmoozed with sports agents at the Nike and Speedo tents. Back in New York, she nailed down the bookings. It didn't hurt that as a longtime booker for *Good Morning America* she already knew Keri Strug's agent. But Willis gave most of the credit for her heavy-medal bookings to Rosie, saying that during the games many athletes sat around watching her show. "Rosie's is just the place everyone wants to be."

Backstage, Rosie welcomes her guests and makes sure they are comfortable before they head to the Green Room to await their entrance. The Green Room walls have quickly filled up with framed photos of stars who have appeared on her show.

Every single audience comes to *The Rosie O'Donnell Show* bearing gifts. But Rosie is a great gift giver herself, often planning well ahead for the stars who appear on her show. All the new and expectant moms receive a gift basket of her favorite baby gizmos; Walter Cronkite huffed and puffed over a blazing eightieth-birthday cake; and Bette Midler got bushels of roses. Rosie even asks guests on her show to help her with surprise gifts for future guests. When Peter Jennings was on he signed a photo of himself for Rosie to give a few weeks later to Clea Lewis, who plays Ellen Morgan's friend Audrey on *Ellen*. It turns out Clea has always had a crush on Jennings.

Other guests who are getting the royal treatment are accidental celebrities, such as Mort and Sylvia Drescher, Fran's parents. After Rosie and Fran became friends, whenever her parents visited Los Angeles they often spent time with Rosie, as well. "She's like a surrogate daughter to us," Sylvia says in the same Queens, New York, accent as her famous daughter. When Rosie was casting about for unusual comedy bits for her show, she remembered how hysterical the Dreschers became when discussing the early-bird dinner specials they routinely track down near their home in Florida. They found the prices at the places Fran took them astonishing. Rosie recalls that they "thought it was absurd—'In Florida we could get for the price of this appetizer the entire meal.'" Rosie quickly anointed them her official restaurant critics and sent them off with a camera crew to rate the local spots. Then in December 1996, they were promoted to movie critics and asked to review the holiday films.

Though penny-pinching seniors is not a new comic idea—(Seinfeld's been mining it for years)—the Dreschers' witty naturalness made them instant hits on Rosie's show. They *do* rehearse with each other what they're going to say, quibbling over who gets the funny lines. With their rating system of one to five knishes, they gleefully report on each restaurant and show photos of themselves dining, interrupting each other just like your Uncle Louie and Aunt Agnes, as they relate their experience.

One of the highlights of being in Rosie's studio audience is seeing what the home viewers do not see. During commercial breaks, a platoon of people dash out to fluff her hair, powder her nose, and snap photos of Rosie with her guest. This *is* live television, which is why she sometimes has that breathless, just-made-it-back-to-my-seat look after a commercial. It is also a time when producers confer with her about the next guest. On one memorable show, senior producer, Andy Lassiter, failed to scurry back out of camera range in time. Rosie simply worked it into the show as a spontaneous comedy bit as she told him, "Your butt was just on TV, I hope you know—tellin' me little Dean Cain notes before he runs away." She then reran the offending tape so he could see himself caught in the act.

The infamous Kooshballs also fly out into the audience during commercials, just to make sure the fans remain alert. One audacious woman even shot one back at Rosie, and when the break ended she was reprimanded in jest. "You will be escorted out and asked to watch *The Montel Williams Show*," Rosie threatened.

One of the most difficult challenges for Rosie as an interviewer is, surprisingly, interviewing her friends. When actor Peter Strauss came on the show they discussed hosting chores. Years ago, Peter had worked as an anchor on *Good Morning America* and said he found it "terrifying." Rosie said it was hard for her to appear natural when she asked her friends questions, "because I know all the answers." He very generously let her ramble on and usurp his precious plug time. When she was finished, she told him: "Thanks for lettin' me share. Those are the problems of my job, Peter."

Though she may have few peers as far as her job title goes, Rosie is just like the rest of us when her boss is involved. When Jane Fonda appeared on her show to push her new cookbook, she spoke eloquently about giving up her film career to challenge herself to have a really intimate relationship. She claims to have reached that goal with Ted Turner. At the mention of his name, Rosie chimed in, "Who is now my *boss*—I believe he just purchased all of television, didn't he?" Turner had, in fact, just merged his company with Time Warner, the corporation that ultimately does oversee *The Rosie O'Donnell Show*. Jane laughed and said, "He thinks you're great. I can't wait for you two to meet. You and Ted together—that's going to be great."

After the show is over, Rosie usually makes time to sign autographs for the kids, accept their gifts, and generally mingle with her fans. It's something she has done throughout her career, and one of the things people find most endearing about her. This is how one lucky young fan described the experience: "We chatted for close to ten minutes, then she signed an autograph for me and asked if my mom was gonna take a picture. Then she put her arm around me and we took the picture. She asked why my hands were shaking and I told her because I was so nervous meeting her! She said not to worry and gave me a big hug! I couldn't believe it—my life is now complete!"

By the fall of 1996, however, it became clear to Rosie that despite her show's success, there were improvements she could make to her staff. It became increasingly clear that Daniel Kellison wasn't the best person to captain the ship, and in early December Kellison was relieved of his duty by Jim Paratore, the president of Telepictures Productions. Rosie felt her show could do even better with the help of someone more experienced in daytime television. Replacing Kellison is longtime Telepictures development executive Hilary Estey-McLoughlin. She has a well-rounded background in development, marketing, and programming as well as an understanding of the daytime audience. Rosie continues as an executive producer.

While there have been rumors and rumblings in the press about backstage unrest, some turnover is inevitable on any TV show, especially a new one. Also, while Rosie is new to daytime TV, she does know exactly what kind of show she wants to do, and such conviction can lead to friction. And she does have an Irish temper that flares up now and then. Still, if she were a man taking charge of her situation, you can bet there would be less sniping at her. *Newsweek,* who had been so quick to crown Rosie The Queen of Nice, offered a very different opinion in their January 20, 1997, issue. In their weekly "Conventional Wisdom" feature, they gave her the "down arrow" and said she "Makes Leona Helmsley look like Mr. Rogers."

Much has been made of the numbers of staffers who have left the show. And since the original director left in July they have been making do with pinch hitters. As of January 1997 no new director had been hired. According to the *New York Observer,* one ex-staffer was happy to get out alive: "I've never seen anything so cutthroat."

Rosie doesn't often listen to others when she feels she knows what's best for her. "I stopped taking advice back when I was a veejay," she said late in 1996. "Everyone told me not to do the VH-1 show, and I did it anyway.

There's no map to success in this industry—you have to take a knife and hack your way through the jungle."

Although it was Kathie Lee Gifford's cushy, brief workday that enticed Rosie into the talk-show business in the first place, things haven't quite worked out that way for her. "I work a lot of hours," she admits. "I'd like to leave at 1:00 P.M., but it hasn't worked out that way yet." She does like to be home by 3:00 P.M. so she can put her son down for a nap, and sneak one in for herself.

☞ 20

Letterman to the Rescue

When her phone rang in the middle of the night on October 10, 1996, Rosie struggled from sleep to answer it, only to learn that the building where her studio was located was on fire. Though no one was seriously hurt, NBC programming originating in New York was interrupted, and so was Rosie's show, which uses their facilities. Luckily, nothing was actually burned in her studio, but there was smoke and water damage, and the entire electrical system was out. So reruns were broadcast on Thursday and Friday while Rosie and company scrambled to make other arrangements. Late Night talk host Conan O'Brien was also smoked out of his studio and solved the problem creatively by broadcasting from the skating rink at Rockefeller Center.

Rosie had a more comfortable substitute in mind. Executive producer Kellison used some of his pull with his former boss, David Letterman, to work out a plan to borrow Dave's place for a few days. Letterman's show would be on vacation the following week anyway. Besides, Rosie had bailed Dave out of some booking jams in the past and raced to do his show at the last minute when guests dropped out. So he owed her a favor.

Carting part of her set to the Ed Sullivan Theatre took some doing, but by Monday, October 14, Rosie was ready to settle in at Dave's place. The opening announcers were none other than two of the firemen from New York's Engine Co. 18, who helped put out the fire. One of them even baked peanut butter cookies for Rosie at the firehouse. She was very touched by their appearance and told them, "You risk your lives everyday—I think you're the real heroes."

Then she launched into a song. Rosie sang a specially written, clever parody of the telephone song from the classic musical *Bye Bye Birdie*.

> Hi David, it's Rosie—
> read the wire, we're on fire,
> do you think you could lend us a hand?
> Hey Rosie, it's David—
> do a great show, from the Late Show,
> need a place? Use my space.
> I'm so glad I could lend you a hand.

It was very heartfelt and well done and the huge crowd loved it. Dave's theater holds nearly four times as many people as can squeeze into Rosie's place. She clearly enjoyed playing to that many people and thanked Dave profusely, saying, "He's a classy guy."

Over at her desk, she held up a torn piece of paper that she had found "taped to her desk" the day after the fire. On it was a hastily scrawled note: "FDNY Engine Co. 18 says hello!"

Another feature she enjoyed in her temporary home was the balcony, which inspired her to shoot Kooshballs up into the rafters. Later, some intrepid stagehands mounted rods high up on the balcony for Rosie to whirl Koosh Whoosh discs at, thus "winning" prizes for the audience. "This is so much fun to be here—I feel like I have to do this," she said, seated at the desk, tossing a pencil over her shoulder and through the window to the sound effect of shattering glass, which, for those who don't stay up late, is Dave's signature stunt.

One especially upsetting thing about the fire for Rosie was that she had lots of great guests booked who couldn't reschedule anytime soon. So she decided to pretend they were there anyway and showed all the clips that she would have run had they been able to appear. "God forbid someone should miss their plug because of some measly fire," she explained. One of those booked was country star, Wynonna, and Rosie did her best to make it seem like she was there. Rosie showed pages from her scrapbook documenting her experience as an opening act for Wynonna in Vegas and played sound bites of her music. Wynonna actually let Rosie come onstage with her and sing backup. As Rosie showed the photos she pointed out that in retrospect she realized she had been improperly dressed for the occasion: "Here I am wearing jeans at Caesars Palace—what was I thinking?"

Rosie was especially peeved at missing out on Wynonna's appearance because she had already gone to Wynonna's hotel and rehearsed with her backup singers. "I'm going to therapy 'cause we missed her," Rosie pouted. "She came special—now she's on tour." Still, there was a great group of guests booked for the week.

While at Letterman's theater, both Rosie and her guests seemed to be in rare form, including actress Delta Burke (*Designing Women*). Delta spoke frankly about her struggles with her weight and the difficulty she had finding clothes she liked, which led her to design her own collection for "women of size." Delta astounded listeners when she launched into the subject of her hobby. It seems that she enjoys shellacking everything that isn't required to function again. She especially enjoys collecting dinner rolls from restaurants all over the country, taking them home, then preserving them for posterity with thick coats of varnish.

Rosie was hard pressed not to look dumbstruck by her explanation. "I like to keep things, and I noticed they didn't keep well unless you do something to them—and then I discovered shellac!"

Rosie shook her head, still trying to comprehend. "Is it like an addiction thing for you? Do you think you could shellac a Kooshball for me and send it back?" she asked, handing her one.

"I can shellac anything; I'll shellac this baby for you," Delta promised.

Actress Ann-Margret was another guest who wandered down some fascinating conversational paths. The two women seemed to bond over their ties to Elvis—Rosie used to do impressions of him in her act and Ann used to date him. Every minute or two Rosie asked Ann-Margret what gifts Elvis had given her. "Did he give you anything big? Am I prying? Do you want to tell us?" Ann never gave in to Rosie's pestering. They also discussed their mutual love of motorcycle riding. Ann told her she has a "1971 big black Harley-Davidson."

They also seemed fascinated with each other's accents and started imitating each other. Ann to Rosie: "Do you really talk like that?" Rosie to Ann: "What? You think I have an accent?" Rosie didn't seem able to get beyond the image of Ann from her sex-kitten days and kept looking at her as if she didn't believe she was real. Finally she told her, "You're funny and nice and very Ann-Margret. I love that!" Rosie also cajoled her into singing a duet with her at the end of her segment, "I've Got a Lot of Living to Do." Ann-Margret was clearly one of those stars Rosie never expected to meet.

Ever since her very first guest, George Clooney, brought her presents, Rosie has continued to amass an amazing collection of show business memorabilia presented by her stellar guests. Singer Chris Isaac showed up at Dave's with a remarkable marionette handmade in his likeness and dressed in a sequined suit. Rosie was delighted. "Look—he comes with his own guitar, and the best—he also comes with surfer-dude clothes." Actress Linda Lavin stopped by and offered up one of her classic aprons from her long-running TV show, *Alice,* which of course led to a duet of the theme song from the show. Linda, clearly a fan of Rosie, told her: "I love you—you are America's Sweetheart."

Here are just a few of the more exotic and noteworthy treasures Rosie has received:

- Delta Burke told Rosie she had samples of her clothing line backstage for Rosie, who replied, "You give me a nice swimsuit and I'll shellac it!"
- Gillian Anderson of *X-Files* fame brought props from her sci-fi show: rubber fluke worms. Rosie was a bit underwhelmed, but graciously piled them on a corner of her desk. Gillian also gave Rosie her own FBI photo ID card. Geez, you never know when that could come in handy.
- Singer Roberta Flack catered her appearance and served Rosie some downhome cookin'—spoon bread and catfish—interesting choice for a breakfast hour show! She also offered to give Parker one of the rare Shiba Inu puppies that she breeds.
- International heartthrob David Hasselhoff presented her with official *Baywatch* panties. "Size 6—perfect!" Rosie exclaimed with a scowl.
- Actress and seventies icon Marlo Thomas made a striking entrance flying her trademark pink kite from *That Girl*—only on closer inspection, it turned out to be a custom-made replica featuring Rosie's cartoon image instead of Marlo's.
- Soap star Susan Lucci stopped by to chat and brought Rosie a special scrapbook of her appearance on *All My Children.*
- Superstar Dolly Parton brought Rosie a Dolly doll, all dressed in red satin flounces, for her collection. Parton said of the doll, "She's pretty gaudy, but so is the other one."

The big attraction on the guest list at Dave's place was undoubtedly

Mary Tyler Moore. There were five women that Rosie idolized above all others as a child: Lucille Ball, Carol Burnett, Bette Midler, Barbra Streisand, and Mary. Rosie did meet Lucy very briefly before she died; Bette is now a pal and had already done her show; Carol she knew and was already booked and Barbra was begged—so that left Mary.

Rosie brought in her famous MTM notebook to show everyone, though she started to have second thoughts about exposing her obsessive side so blatantly. "I'm a little worried I might frighten her," Rosie confessed before Mary came out. "I frightened the staff when they saw this." She had the camera zoom in for an extreme close-up of her handwritten notebook about *The Mary Tyler Moore Show*. "Why did I feel the need to write this down?" she wondered, too many years later.

Rosie's heartfelt introduction did not go off exactly as planned, even though she had been rehearsing it for twenty-five years. "Our first guest is one of the most adored and beloved actresses in the history of the whole entire universe—" Mary is heard shouting something from backstage. "You be quiet!" Rosie told her. "It's my intro, and I've been waiting years to do it! Ellen DeGeneres, Paula Poundstone, and I, we all revere you. You're the reason we went into comedy."

After Mary was finally allowed to join her, Rosie wasted no time in presenting her with the sacred notebook for her inspection. It was as if she was transported back to the seventh grade, when she started the notebook, and Mary was the teacher Rosie so desperately wanted to impress. "Did you know there were people like me sitting around America taking notes?" Displaying her still-perfect timing, Mary replied, "I think you're the only one, Rosie."

Then they launched into an MTM trivia contest that Mary flunked and Rosie passed! Undaunted, Mary tried one last question: "What actor made his TV debut as Rhoda's boyfriend?" No contest for Rosie. She knew the answer was Henry Winkler, and she even knew his line. Mary declared, "You are amazing—you're a savant!"

Later, Rosie quizzed her about Elvis, since Mary has the distinction of being his last leading lady, in the film *Change of Habit*. Mary went on to divulge a startling fact. She said that Elvis admitted to having an affair with all of his leading ladies except one. "I don't want to bust anyone's cover," she said, "but I know who she is—I really know." Every so often, Rosie could be caught just gazing at Mary, taking it all in.

After Mary left, Rosie said, "That was probably one of the most thrilling moments of my life." A few weeks later Rosie welcomed actor Gavin McLeod to her show. Although he is best known as the captain of the *Love Boat,* he first claimed some fame as Murray on *The Mary Tyler Moore Show.* Rosie was still gushing over the experience of meeting Mary, and she told Gavin: "She signed my book and everything!"

For her fourth and last show from Letterman's studio, Rosie put on a production worthy of the Broadway address. The last joke of her monologue was an homage to Dave: A Top Ten List (from the Home Office in Commack, Long Island). To introduce it she sang a parody of "One Time Only." The subject: "Top Ten Ways I'm Going to Thank Dave for Letting Us Use His Theater.

10. Two words: Ring Dings.
 9. In the next K-Mart commercial, he can play the part of Penny.
 8. I will rig the *Late Show* water cooler to only dispense YooHoo.
 7. Send him 100 copies of my first film, *Misery.*
 6. Send him on a month-long vacation to the Caribbean with Nicole Kidman (punctuated with the Betty Rubble laugh).
 5. I've changed the sign on the Ed Sullivan Theatre to read: Dave, Now and Forever.
 4. Fill all the bathtubs in his house with Kooshballs.
 3. For Christmas I'm buying my entire staff his mom's cookbook.
 2. I'm giving up the Knicks. Now I'm now an Indiana Pacers fan.
 1. [*drumroll*] And the number one way I'm thanking Dave: My Donny doll."

On the last show Rosie did a very Dave-esque (and Carsonesque) thing—she endured a visit from an animal expert and her menagerie. The first animal, a baby cougar, elicited the usual "oohs" and "ahs" from the audience as Rosie fed it from a tiny bottle. She tried to be a good sport, but she looked about as thrilled to have a marmoset on her shoulder as Dave always did when Jack Hanna would bring some out-of-control raptor. Finally, Rosie told a full-grown lynx to "stay on that side of the desk." Then she asked the expert to come back, but to bring "animals that are cute and won't hurt me."

Rosie ended with a huge production number. She sang yet another parody, this time to the song "There Ain't Nothin' Like a Dame" from one of her favorite musicals, *South Pacific.*

There ain't no one like my Dave,
no one in the world.
About him I will rave,
he's my hero and he's my fave.

Confetti canons burst upon the audience while Rosie's entire staff marched out carrying homemade banners and signs spelling their thanks and adoration of Dave Letterman. It must have been a bit surreal for those staffers who actually used to work for Letterman. Meanwhile, Rosie strutted up and down the aisles, reprising the song and generally inciting barely controlled chaos.

When David returned from his vacation on Monday, he found two gifts from Rosie on his desk. Her Donny Osmond doll and a Yodel.

By Friday, things were mostly back to normal at *The Rosie O'Donnell Show*—with a few dramatic exceptions. In a total departure from the usual format, the show began with Rosie and John all alone on Dave's stage. They did a cute takeoff on *The Wizard of Oz,* complete with a stuffed Toto, then Rosie clicked her red tennis shoes three times, and uttered the magic line: "There's no place like home." After some intentionally cheesy tornado effects and a reversion to black and white, Rosie was shown at her desk in her own studio with her staff all around her, tending a bump on her head. She tried to convince her staff that she had been away for days, but they thought she was delusional. Distraught, she shouted: "Doesn't anyone believe me?"

Finally, like the Wizard himself, out popped Calvert DeForest, also known as Larry Bud Melman, David Letterman's longtime sidekick and prankster. "I believe you Rosie," he told her, and then proceeded to do the opening announcement. As the opening graphics rolled, full color was restored. It was a very clever bit and another act of revenge against the girl from Rosie's third grade class who got to play the coveted role of Dorothy.

The first joke of the monologue that day was, "Our office did pretty well in the fire, except all my Ring Dings are now s'mores."

❧ 21

Rosie Online: The Fans Talk Back

All show business stars have to learn to juggle their priorities. They are constantly distracted from their creative work by calls from agents, meetings with producers, rehearsals, meetings with business managers, auditions, interviews, photo ops, and so on. Along the way they must somehow sandwich in a personal life. The one aspect of her career that Rosie has learned to elevate to a high priority is her relationship to her fans. After all, a star with no fans is soon no star at all. Rosie has set a very high standard for herself—and met it. Her generosity with her time is legendary. And she is one of the most accessible stars around now.

There are four basic ways for a fan to have contact with her. First is the one-on-one public meeting that takes place by accident or by design. Rosie frequently talks about her plans ahead of time on her show: that she's going to the Neil Diamond concert at the Meadowlands next week, that she has seats for the World Series (a gift from Warner Bros.), that she's going to appear at a particular charity event. If you're in the New York City area, it's not hard to meet up with her. When she's doing a charity gig she likes to plug it ahead of time if that will help raise more money at the event. Such was the case with the Broadway Flea Market put on by Equity Fights AIDS. Though throngs of her fans boosted the take for the event, many of them showed up just to give her gifts. One woman even chased her down the street as she was driving away and stuffed a one-of-a-kind *Ryan's Hope* jacket in her car window. Rosie didn't get her name, but she thanked her on the next show.

She's also just out there in the real world, taking her son to the park, shopping at The Gap for Kids, buying dog food. And when fans intrude on her private time with her son, she does mind. She figures that behind any given bush is someone with a minicam hoping to catch her and Parker on tape—and sell it to *Hard Copy*. She has long had a rule about autographs: she only gives them to youngsters. With adults, she prefers to shake hands or exchange a few words, which she feels is more meaningful. Though late in 1996 Rosie decided to amend her policy. Adults who send a $5 check to Rosie made out to the Children's Defense Fund can receive a signed photo. The C.D.F., a favorite of both Rosie and Hillary Clinton, is a lobbying group for children's issues. On June 1, 1996 they held an event on the Washington D.C. Mall called "Stand Up for Children," which attracted twenty thousand supporters, Rosie O'Donnell among them.

Though this is happening less often now that she has a daily forum on television, Rosie has often been mistaken for actress Kathy Bates and for the "Snapple Woman," from the TV commercials featuring a funny, rather heavy woman. To set the record straight, Rosie invited Wendy Kaufman, the real actress in the Snapple spots, to appear on her show. Dressed alike, they did look like they could be sisters—"Separated at birth," Rosie joked.

The second way fans come in contact with her is by attending the taping of her TV show. Since the studio is small, there is a very long wait for tickets, but from the accounts of the lucky ones who have been there, it is worth the wait. From the beginning, Rosie has been committed to putting plenty of real people on her show. On an early show she featured an elderly woman whose hobby was making meticulous portraits of people entirely out of different-colored seeds. She presented Rosie with a charming likeness and with a second one of Tom Cruise. Like most of Rosie's fans, the woman had been paying attention.

At the end of the show, if there is a bit of time left, she often invites youngsters from the audience to sing or tell a joke or just chat. Or she will invite a group of children from the audience who have come to the show together to perform during the closing credits.

And the gifts they bring. Every day audience members show up bearing an amazing assortment of presents for Rosie and Parker. Many of these things Rosie quietly sends up to the pediatric AIDS ward of a local hospital.

The most original win a spot on the show. Food items are always a good bet, like a giant inscribed cookie or a really huge Hershey bar with her name on it. That last one sent her off on a rant against hotels that give their guests "ritzty-titzy-snooty truffles—I hate it. Why can't they just leave a Hershey bar with almonds—is that so wrong?"

Some gifts are clearly works of art and love. One woman from Portland, Oregon, sent a sculpted pewter music box she had made, featuring Rosie and Parker and their two dogs. Another woman must have begun her present the day the show first aired. Rosie was blown away when she opened the very large framed needlepoint depiction of all the lyrics to her theme song, illustrated with images from the show's opening graphics. And yet another person sculpted a jewelry box featuring her opening cartoon images. On another day, the opening announcement was performed by a woman who had long ago acted on Rosie's favorite soap opera. Even she came bearing more *Ryan's Hope* memorabilia for Rosie's collection.

Genuinely moved by the generosity of her fans, Rosie exclaimed, "It's like the greatest job to begin with, and then we get free stuff. It's too good to be true!"

The fans also respond when she's had a bad day at the office. On Tuesday, September 10, 1996, Rosie was interrupted during her opening segment by her producer telling her that she had a phone call from the mayor of Philadelphia, who wanted to speak to her on the air. This was clearly not a prearranged event, but since it had never happened before, Rosie trusted that her staff had checked the caller out properly before telling her about it on live TV. She may also have been thinking the call had something to do with the fact that her show first aired in Philadelphia at 2:00 A.M.—much to her fans' dismay. In any event, she took the call, and both voices were broadcast in all the markets that carry the show live.

Imagine Rosie's surprise when the caller turned out to be some jerk plugging Howard Stern's radio show, and in keeping with that show, called her a "fat pig" among other things. Turns out the caller was Stern's fan "Captain Janks," who somehow makes a living as an *un*professional annoyance. Rosie remained cool and managed to carry on without giving the stunt any more airtime. ABC filed a complaint with the police, who issued Janks a $147 ticket for public inconvenience and using obscene language.

Almost immediately, her cyber fans started filling up message folders with indignation and loving notes of support. By the following day, Rosie's office was flooded with faxes of consolation and numerous bouquets of flowers, showing her fans were proud of her handling of the unpleasant situation. Rosie related how later that night she had taken her family to dinner and received a free one. "The waiter said, 'I saw what that guy said, and the dinner's on me.'" And on the walk home a New York City sanitation truck screeched to a halt and the driver yelled at her: "Hey listen, Rosie, you're beautiful and I love you!" Rosie went on to thank many people by name who had written touching faxes, and looking genuinely moved she said, "It was an overwhelming show of kindness toward me, and it was really appreciated."

The third way to reach Rosie is to simply write to her. Maybe it's the control freak in her, but Rosie takes a very hands-on approach to her fan mail. For her fans who write her letters the old-fashioned way (using "snail mail," as E-mail enthusiasts like to call it), Rosie employs her "best friend since the age of two" and former Commack neighbor, Jackie Ellard, to review her mail. Jackie sorts it and answers it in a variety of ways, accommodating requests as best she can. She carefully sets aside letters of special interest for Rosie to reply to personally. There are actually companies that do nothing but process fan mail for stars too busy to respond to it themselves. By entrusting the job to her best friend, someone who is sure to know how to handle each special case, Rosie can feel certain that she's doing the best she can with the huge volume of mail she receives.

In fact, by October 1996 the volume had swollen to such proportions (over 2,000 E-mail letters a day!) that she began to change her policy and respond mainly to letters from young fans. She posted this apology on AOL: "I do answer the kids first...sorry. So much mail, so little time."

The fourth and most modern way to contact Rosie is online. E-mail can be sent to her through her home page at the Warner Bros. website or more directly through the computer online service America Online. Rosie has been a member for years and is thoroughly hooked on her computer and how it connects her directly and immediately to her fans. In the past she has gone online anonymously, using such screen names as "Lizard Lips" and "ROSIE OH O."

She would lie about her profession as a way of having a conversation with someone without the celebrity getting in the way. "When you're famous, it's hard to have a conversation on equal terms," she said in an interview on the subject. "People have a preconceived idea of who and what you are. You're robbed of your ability to relate to people. Online, no one knows who you are."

She also got off on making people laugh. How, you wonder, do you know someone is laughing, typing at their computer thousands of miles away? Easy. They type LOL (Laughing Out Loud) or even better ROFL (Rolling on the Floor Laughing) or the ultimate compliment ROFLMAO (Rolling on the Floor Laughing My Ass Off). It can be a fun way to pass time on movie sets, especially for a stand-up comic who misses her audience. Rosie admits she used to "live for those LOLs." She also said it was possible to "have sexual flirtations or computer sex."

In years past, she's even had her virtual wrists slapped by AOL for using very salty language to lash out at a racist pinhead she encountered online. "I got two violations for arguing with a bigot. I have behaved myself since."

One of her early cyber pen pals tells of finally meeting her at a comedy gig in Atlantic City. (He had E-mailed her for permission to come backstage after the show.) Rosie graciously welcomed him to her dressing room and offered him a beer. "We hung out for about thirty minutes. It seemed like we were old friends. She is as sincere and kind in person as she is on TV." This encounter took place two days before the debut of her talk show, yet she made time for a fan.

Some of her E-mail is very emotional, as fans express how Rosie helps them with their challenges: "Your show has literally saved my life. All through my surgery and recovery and chemotherapy for breast cancer, the one bright spot in my day is your show. This may sound corny, but it is really hard to find anything on TV that isn't depressing, scary, or just plain boring."

Rosie replied: "Thanks for your touching letter. You will be strong; I will be thinking of you."

Her AOL site is constantly evolving and expanding, adding new bells and whistles. There is a Show Notices bulletin board, where opportunities are announced for events like a kids' stand-up comedy contest or the Lookalike show. There's a list of every station in the country that airs her show and the time it is on. There are applications to become part of her volunteer online staff. You can find out how to get tickets to the show or read news flashes, like the story of the fire at 30 Rockefeller Plaza. There are Rosie trivia contests with prizes of free online time. You can download photos of Rosie with various guests or even hear a variety of sound bites. Like every good office, it even has a suggestion box for the show. Notes to the Queen of Nice are sent via the "Hey Rosie" button. Then there are links to Rosie's favorite Web sites (Bette, Barbra, and so on). Under Showtalk you can peruse the schedule of upcoming guests, comment on the day's show, or read comments about previous shows.

One of the most popular sections of the site is the Message Board area. Here fans post comments and questions and even comments on other fans' comments. It's rather like a time-lapse conversation that never ends. Messages are posted into folders on specific topics, such as discussions of each of Rosie's movies, comments on her wardrobe, a very hot topic, or "Rosie sightings," where fans tell about their close encounters. Fans ask questions about her career and sometimes Rosie answers them with a posting for all to read or she may elect to E-mail her reply directly to the questioner. Her bandleader, John McDaniel even has his own folder where he answers his mail.

A mother writes: "Everybody I know is talking about rearranging plans so they won't have to miss Rosie."

A wannabe mom writes: "You inspired me to start adoption proceedings! I have been waffling on becoming a single mom, and after hearing your experiences, have decided to go for it."

She has very young fans: "My eleven-month-old daughter doesn't normally watch TV, but she started dancing and clapping when you sang."

And she has some older ones, too: "You are the only one who gets my hormonally dysfunctional sixteen-year-old to laugh."

Another mother even offers herself: "I'm so sorry you lost your mom when you were so young. If you ever need a mom, I'm here for you, Rosie. I tape the show and watch it at night when I can savor it."

And some fans are just plain dedicated: "We planned our vacation around you. After breakfast we'd rush back to our hotel. You had us sitting on the edge of our beds in tears because we laughed so hard. The maid wanted in to make our beds, but we told her to come back later—we were BUSY!"

Periodically Rosie also does live conferences on AOL. Imagine hundreds of people all online at the same time, all typing questions to a moderator who then filters and passes them on to Rosie, who is typing her replies in real time. Thousands more are watching and reading the session as it scrolls down their screen. Here's an actual exchange from August 1996.

QUESTIONER: I am a surgeon who was on vacation last week and fell in love with your show. It is intelligent and hilarious. Do you have any suggestions on how to deal with "Rosie Withdrawal"?

ROSIE: Have a Yodel and call me in the morning.

Try being funny while typing fifty words a minute, your spelling and grammar skills on display for all the world, including your fifth grade English teacher, to see!

The most fun a Rosie fan can have online, however, is to be in one of her chat rooms when she shows up to hang out with her fans and answer their questions, one-on-one. Even though everyone believes that she still has AOL accounts in other names so she can still surf anonymously, when she enters her chat rooms she does so with her official screen name: TheR0SIE. Perfect typing counts for everything with screen names. Notice that hers is all one word and that the "O" in ROSIE is actually a "0" or zero. that's how you can tell the impostors from the real O'Donnell. Also, no one else on AOL can have a screen name that begins with TheR0 except Rosie and her staff. (John McDaniel is TheR0McD, for example.) Any other variation of that is a fraud. Occasionally Howard Stern's rude fans will go in one of the rooms just to try and make trouble. AOL has a great feature to deal with idiots like that: simply put them on "ignore" and their comments no longer show up on your screen.

When the show site was still new many people didn't believe it really was *her* online with them. "Nobody thinks it's me," she explained one day on her show. One guy even got belligerent and threatened to turn her in for a violation of AOL rules. Finally she asked someone who has two phone lines to type their phone number and she would call them. So she called Jimmy in Boston and he said, "Is it really you?" So she did the inimitable Betty Rubble laugh, and that convinced him. So Rosie told him "Now go back online and tell everyone it's me." Jimmy did, but the wacko guy didn't buy it. He insisted that Jimmy and the Impostor "are in cahoots." Eventually her appearances there became so frequent that most people can now believe it.

Rosie spends about an hour a day online with her MacIntosh Power-Book, tending to her mail and responding to about 150 people as she stops in her various chat rooms. One woman posted a desperate message wondering where she should go with her precious show tickets after Rosie was displaced from her studio by the fire. The very same day Rosie herself typed a detailed message to the woman explaining exactly where to go and when.

Sometimes in order to book a guest like Carol Burnett or Demi Moore and accommodate their full schedules, the show has to be taped and aired at a later date. Whenever this happens it is obvious to her fans (especially when Rosie goes on and on about "tomorrow being Halloween" and then it airs three days *before* Halloween). When that sort of thing happens, lots of fans want an explanation. Not wishing anyone to be upset with her, Rosie E-mails them back with an explanation and apology: "We messed up. There it is. Sorry."

Rabid fans have learned when she's most likely to pop in to talk, usually in the late evening after she has put Parker to bed, though she sometimes logs on in the afternoon. Thanks to another AOL feature called "Locate Member Online," it's possible to know whether she's on or not and even where she is. Once she has logged on, word spreads throughout the chat rooms and people start hanging around waiting for her to show up in their space. Each room holds only forty-eight people, and new rooms keep opening up as more people wander in. Sometimes when she is online as many as four rooms, or nearly 200 people, are patiently typing and scrolling, waiting for a chance to share a cyber moment with TheROSIE. It can get quite crazy as people race from room to room trying to be in the one she goes to first (and getting locked out as they fill up). It's rather like a feverish game of musical chairs.

First timers usually don't get all that much out of it, because following the conversations is next to impossible. She can't answer every question, so Rosie just picks one and starts typing, using the screen name of whoever asked it to signify she is answering that question. Then she picks out another one and answers that query. But by the time her answer is posted, there have been six or ten other questions posted, so it really isn't possible to follow it all in real time. It's much better to make a "log" of the session and print it out later. Then, using a colored pen, one can draw arrows to link her answers back to their questions. For fans who like puzzles and mazes, it can be a rush, but just reading it in a linear fashion makes no sense.

Need proof? Here's a portion of a genuine transcript of a R0SIE visit in October 1996:

MamaMya: Did WB get you World Series tix yet?

TheR0SIE: Kel, Delta was a riot

OGnkla: Hey Rosie...did you leave anything cute/funny/strange behind for Dave?

RO Chat2: Welcome Rosie [***NOTE that this screen name is NOT an official staff name; in fact, this person later disrupted the session.]

Bustardo39: Hi Rosie!

Sunbu95: Did you love the Ed Sullivan Theater or what?

SOXCELT: Rosie, did you ever go OUT when you were a kid, or did you just watch TV? You're amazing.

Lmiglia899: Rosie—you rock!

TheR0SIE: Yes Mam, they did [answers the question 8 lines ago about baseball tix]

BIG MAG1: Hi Rosie!!!

JC3456: I'm finally here with Rosie.

FranBraun: Rosie, are you walking at Jones Beach for breast cancer on Sunday?

WantBaby: cable is out...I have Rosie withdrawal

TammyAlex: We've been waiting forever for you

Kwilli2112: Rosie—Do you shop at Gymboree often?

Map Retrac: Rosie, please come to my Osmond party!

Char siegs: Thank you so much for my happy mornings, Rosie. Did you watch the debate tonight?

Dulless: Rosie, is that really you?

TheR0SIE: OG My Donny doll [answers question 16 postings ago about what she left for Dave]

It's not so bad for Rosie—she just picks out questions and types answers—she doesn't have to make sense of the talk as it rolls by. To her, it's akin to playing a video game, "Being an AOL old timer, I am kinda good at it," she says truthfully. Still, her willingness to do this day after day, when she could just as well be soaking in a hot bath or getting to bed an hour earlier or just about anything else, is astonishing. It's easy to see why she won the Icon Award for most popular online celebrity. It is doubtful that any other star is as loyal to her fans as TheR0SIE.

One other opportunity to express Rosie adoration is to join the Kooshball Club through AOL. This is her official fan club, complete with newsletter ("Rosie Oh!"), autographed photo, and so forth. The items are quite slick and very professional looking, with one glaring exception. In December 1996 someone had the idea to send her fan club members a special holiday greeting. What her fans received was a card reading: "A special holiday treat from Rosie!" and a color photo of Rosie, autographed on the back with the caption: "Rosie prepares for work."

The shocker is Rosie looks like she's preparing for work in a brothel. Though obviously intended as a joke, Rosie did pose for the photo, in wildly teased hair, too much makeup, and holding a glass of champagne. From her expression, she is already hungover. Considering that many of her fan club members are children, and that this was the *holiday greeting,* this seems to be in questionable taste, at best. Whoever dreamed up this greeting seems certain to hear about it. Rosie does, however, get redemptive points for her AOL cyber card that same month, urging fans to make donations to any of a very long list of children's charities.

Whatever the cause of that one slip in judgment, Rosie can be forgiven. In fact, her fans are very protective, especially other mothers who see in her a kindred spirit, someone who works so hard to juggle work and family. One fan wrote: "Rosie worries too much about everyone. She has to have time to be a real person and a mom. I couldn't imagine going to the park with my son and getting mobbed by people asking questions." Rosie's reply was revealing: "I guess I do worry too much. Whatever. Always a people pleaser. Hello therapy."

After four months of shows, some viewers groused they were getting bored with her format, to which she replied: "Johnny did the same thing every night—told some jokes, did the golf swing. I mean I am not reinventing the wheel, just doing a talk show. Sorry to those who think I am 'getting stale.' I'm doing my best. I swear."

✐ 22

Rosie's Obsession: Tom Cruise

Clearly, there have been some installments of *The Rosie O'Donnell Show* that displayed a level of creativity and preparation worthy of a weekly show. Her young staff obviously enjoys bringing together all the special effects and custom-made props for these special events. These extra-effort shows are a smart marketing tool, as the local affiliates get something unusual to plug and *The Rosie O'Donnell Show* inevitably gets special coverage in the entertainment press, which in turn keeps Warner Bros. and the affiliates high on Rosie.

Her fans didn't have to be told to come in costume to *The Rosie O'Donnell Show* on Halloween. There was no question that Rosie would throw a party on that holiday, sacred to children of all ages. Indeed, the set was specially decked out in spooky style, complete with a fog machine to set the mood. The curtains had to be parted extrawide for Rosie to make her entrance dressed as a "Jill-o'-lantern." Her pumpkin suit was huge and soft and looked to be sewn from orange foam rubber, and on her head she sported a pumpkin top with green sequined leaves. Looking out to the crowd, which was dressed in a wild array of outfits, she quipped, "I feel like Monte Hall with all you people in the audience." For those who never watched daytime television, Monte hosted the wacky game show, *Let's Make a Deal,* featuring contestants plucked from an audience of grown-ups in bizarre costumes. Soon the doorbell rang and Rosie welcomed a group of adorable costumed kids. For their trick, Rosie covered them with Silly

String, a colorful, messy substance shot from a spray can. For their treat, the Pumpkin Lady gave them candy and toys. Later, Rosie managed to sit down at her desk, but playing with her trademark toy was another matter: "It's very hard to shoot a Kooshball in a pumpkin suit."

Even the guests joined in the festivities. Actor-director Garry Marshall appeared dressed as a mailman, in which he plugged his new movie about the post office, *Dear God*. Actress Phylicia Rashad, best known as Claire Huxtable, swept onstage dressed as "Time" in a flowing gown representing the four seasons.

Many of Rosie's all-star guests have gone way out of their way to pay tribute to her. Here are some of the most notable ones:

- Wackmeister actor and former SNL cast member Mike Myers of *Wayne's World* appeared on an early show and made it very clear that his love of Rosie had gone to his head—literally. He had her show logo shaved and dyed into the back of his short hair.
- Veteran prankster Rip Taylor doesn't have the hair to copy Mike's stunt, so he did the next best thing. After prancing around the studio dispensing his trademark confetti, he sat down next to Rosie, doffed his toupee, and motioned the camera to zoom in on his bald head, which was painted with the show logo.
- Lauren Bacall also turned out to be a fan of Rosie's, much to her surprise. When the still-glamorous actress told her "It's such a blessing to have you on television now in the daytime," Rosie turned a lovely shade of rose and replied, "Oh, Miss Bacall!" Miss Bacall may have had second thoughts after Rosie went on to admit that she had lurked around the lobby of the apartment building where they once both lived, hoping for a chance encounter.
- Raquel Welch told Rosie on an early show: "Forget about Sandra Bullock—*you* are now America's Sweetheart."
- Bob Hope turned out to be a fan, and sent her a huge bouquet of white roses a month after her show debuted. The card read: "Congratulations on your new show. I would have sent them sooner, but I had to wait until dark so Dolores wouldn't see me picking them. Enjoying your show. My best, Bob." Rosie said she planned to frame the card.
- "You're made for this, you just *have* it," raved Sylvester Stallone.

- But the highest praise Rosie could receive came form one of her Top Five Idols, Carol Burnett. By the time she appeared on Rosie's show, they had already met. In fact, Rosie calls it the moment in her career when she really felt she had "arrived." In 1991, even before *A League of Their Own* came out, she had a meeting with Carol about possibly doing a sitcom together. That didn't work out, but Rosie was honored to be considered. When Carol stopped by Rosie's show the two chatted about their mutual adoration of the soap *All My Children*. Then when Rosie said she was taping old episodes of *The Carol Burnett Show*, airing on the Family Channel, Carol replied that she was taping Rosie's show.

The most unusual edition of *The Rosie O'Donnell Show* has to be the "Lookalike Day," held November 14, 1996. The idea for the show emanated from the fact that Rosie is like everywoman in her appearance, and many women have told her stories of resembling Rosie. The call for participants went out in October, asking people to send in photos of themselves looking like Rosie. After announcing the concept, Rosie expressed some doubt about it, "It's gonna be scary to look out and see two hundred of me." Audience members had to provide their own transportation to the show. Over 2,000 fans from all over the country vied for the 180 seats. Considering the wait for tickets exceeds six months, the lure of a guaranteed seat was huge.

The lucky ones chosen to be in this special audience were notified by letter and follow-up calls. They were all asked to dress alike, in black pants, black blazers and whites shirts and arrive at the NBC studio by 8:30 A.M. A handful of local participants also got to come in days ahead of time to tape promos for the event.

Once in line, the Rosies were entertained by the show's warm-up comic, Joey Kola, who also gave them last-minute instructions. A select group was ushered inside early to rehearse special features. Once inside Rosie's studio, they practiced doing the opening announcement in unison. The real Rosie came out before the show and thanked them for their special efforts and posed for photos with the whole group. It was, indeed, an odd sight and sound when 180 people proclaimed: "I'm Rosie O'Donnell, and this is *The Rosie O'Donnell Show*."

"This is kinda creepy," the real Rosie exclaimed while surveying her many selves. During the first segment Rosie ventured into the sea of imitators to interview some of the more unusual ones. One perky gal who really did resemble the Real Rosie turned out to be a nanny and took the opportunity to ask for a job. "It might freak my son out," Rosie decided. "He'd look at you and he'd look at me, and go 'Mommy? Mommy?'"

There was even a mom who brought her adorable one-year-old daughter, who indeed, looked like Rosie at that age. The most unusual lookalikes, however, were the few men in drag. One was a waiter from Washington, D. C., who Rosie told, "You have a little five o'clock shadow that I don't think I ever had."

After the first commercial break one of the clones sat at Rosie's desk and proceeded to introduce Burt Reynolds, until the real O'Donnell sent her back to her seat. "A girl can't run to the restroom during a commercial without having a lookalike take over her show," Rosie complained. Burt's first remark upon checking out the audience was, "Boy that line of clothing of yours really caught on."

Throughout the show, the twins participated by introducing guests and throwing to commercials. One guest who really went along with the gag was singer Mary Chapin Carpenter, who performed in a black pantsuit and Rosie wig over her long blond hair. Rosie told her, "When you first came out I thought 'Who is that?' It was you, participating!"

A surprise lookalike guest was the new *Sesame Street* puppet, "Rosie O'O." that will be used to teach the letter *O*. The puppet, who spoke with Rosie's Long Island accent, did a cute extended number telling Rosie about being mistaken for her.

At the end of the show, Rosie again joined the rows of Rosies to do their version of the "Hokey Pokey" while holding up all the free goodies they received in their Rosie tote bags. Afterward the whole group trooped over to the nearby Fashion Café for a lunch hosted by Rosie herself. "Trust me on this—we will not order the Kate Moss Plate," she told them, referring to the waiflike model. Rosie graciously posed for photos with her guests and seemed especially fond of her youngest lookalike, whom she held during all the interviews. She was, however, nearly mobbed by her adoring clones and glad that she had some bodyguards on hand.

The media swarmed all over the unusual photo op, and in reporting on the event, even *Hard Copy's* Jerry Penacoli donned the black and white outfit and Rosie wig. The reporter from *ET* tried the same gag and asked

Rosie if she understood such fan adoration, which of course, she did. "I'm the girl who stood outside the *Dream Girls* theater nine times just to *look* at Jennifer Holliday."

It's difficult to know what to say about Rosie O'Donnell and Tom Cruise. Rosie herself has spoken often about her "crush" on the megastar, some of it contradictory. Clearly, it is meant as a joke of epic proportions. And yet there are darker undercurrents that run through the numerous one-sided discussions Rosie has about "my Tommy." One needs to separate the reality from the fantasy from the public relations stunt. The reality seems to be that Rosie is genuinely a fan of Tom Cruise's body of work. She claims to have all his movies on laser disc and to have watched them numerous times. He has certainly been in some popular and even charming films. There is no denying his box office appeal, and he is blessed with a winning combination of boyish charisma, earnestness, and nonthreatening sexual allure. Women are smitten with him. And Rosie would have you believe she is, too. Rosie's "crush" is also a giant distraction she uses to sell her public image as a heterosexual.

Early on, Rosie clarified her adoration of Tom by saying, "This is not a sexual crush. I don't want him in the biblical sense. I just want him to come over to my house and mow my lawn in a pair of jeans." She seems to be saying she simply appreciates Tom as an ideal male specimen. He may not be every woman's first choice, but he is easy on the eyes. However, considering that Tom is happily married to another very public figure, actress Nicole Kidman, Rosie's increasingly intense obsession with him began to seem at times lacking in good taste.

In the early weeks of *The Rosie O'Donnell Show,* Rosie often made on-air appeals to stars she hoped would appear on her show. Tom was one of the first. She made it clear that she was a very big fan of his, but there was no real hint of the size of the obsession to come. Every few days she would mention him—and that she hadn't heard anything from *him.* Eventually, word did reach Cruise, who gallantly sent Rosie a megastar-sized bouquet of roses and a note saying he would be pleased to visit her show the following spring. The flowers were given a place of honor on a pedestal and displayed alongside a giant photo of Tom surrounded by a red 3-D heart. His response became her gold standard against which all other stars were measured.

After two months of on-air worship, Tom invited Rosie to Los Angeles to meet him—and emcee a tribute to him. No surprise, every tiny detail of the situation was dissected for her viewing audience. Rosie actually appeared to debate whether to attend. "I've lost sleep over this. He's gonna be there. He's flyin' in from wherever he is with his lovely wife Nicole—" (Rosie paused, sneered, and arched one expressive eyebrow to great laughter). "Maybe if I'm extra nice to him, he would come and do my show. But I don't wanna be suckin' up *that* much to people."

She wondered if it might not be more fun to wait and meet him on her own turf. Also, she is a working mom, and it would require a huge effort to rearrange her life to do the show for Tom. Her mostly female audience lived through it all vicariously and urged her to make the trip, though an online poll was vastly in favor of waiting. "I don't know if I *can* wait.... If Tom Crusie phoned *you,* you'd fly your butt out to L.A.!" she told her cheering audience.

So, it wasn't too surprising that Rosie decided Tom was worth the effort. And the visit wouldn't hurt the ratings during the first few weeks of the new fall season. The gig turned out to be a publicist's dream, and Rosie worked it to the maximum.

Ten days before she left for L.A. she began a Countdown to Tom, complete with photo flipchart. As the date neared Rosie did seem to be genuinely nervous—or maybe it was just part of the act. Nevertheless, emceeing an event in front of a room full of the Hollywood A-list could give anyone the jitters. With only two days to go, she appeared to be speechless. "It's becoming difficult to sleep at night.... I'm having mild heart palpitations.... I have no appetite, which is odd for me." She then told her audience she thought she needed a "Tom Cruise Moment," which entailed running the famous clip of him dancing up a sensual storm in *Risky Business.*

The next big drama concerned what she should wear to the event, a dilemma all women can understand. Ultimately she had her designer make up paper dolls of Rosie and Tom to help her decide. Tiny Tom was dressed in a nice tux, though Rosie mischievously flipped up his suit to reveal his underwear. To be fair, her doll also appeared in her underwear. "Notice how I made myself have a nice little curvy waist? It's my doll, I can do what I want," she said, dancing it around with the Tom doll.

She then proceeded to attach various outfits that she had considered wearing to the shindig. Jokingly, she showed the doll wearing her dominatrix gear from *Exit to Eden.* After an enthusiastic crowd response, she said, "That's a maybe." After other humorous suggestions, she finally showed the sleek black evening suit with a sequined collar that she ultimately chose. "I believe the meeting will go something like this," she teased, rushing the dolls toward each other to a climactic smooch.

The following day she brought out the dolls again and enacted a fantasy script:

TOM DOLL: "Rosie, you look so nice—I might leave Nicole for you."

ROSIE [*laughing*]: "Just a joke."

Then she had them kiss again.

On the day before she left for L.A., Rosie sang a parody of "Tomorrow" from *Annie:*

> I will meet Tom Cruise tomorrow,
> bet your bottom dollar that tomorrow he'll be mine...
> He's my Top Gun, my one and only...
> Tomorrow, tomorrow, I meet Tom tomorrow,
> Let's pray that Nicole is away.

And that time there was no giggle or other disclaimer that she was only joking.

All that remained was to pretape several shows to cover her absence of two days. Before she left for Los Angeles she warned her fans about the taped shows and admonished them not to be critical. "People get so mad when we run a taped show—as if I'm off sunning myself. But I have things to do, one of them being Tom Cruise." The audience jumped on the double meaning in her choice of words, which she quickly squelched. "I don't mean it *that* way!"

She went and she gushed. Shamelessly, Rosie shared her obsession with the crowd at the American Cinematheque tribute. She told them, "I was a tad bit worried about this obsession I have with Tom, so I saw a therapist and I asked him—'Am I obsessed? Honestly, tell me the truth.' And he said, 'You can't handle the truth.'" Which, of course, was Jack Nicholson's big line in the Cruise film, *A Few Good Men.* She then went on to display the extent of her obsession. "I feel Tom with me, close to me, every day as I do my show." She then lifted up the bottom of her jacket to show a photo of Tom in a red heart. "People say, 'That's sick.' I say 'No, you're wrong.' *This* is sick and obsessive." And with a grin and a flourish she pulled down her lapel to reveal TOM inked in large letters on her cleavage. It looked like she had finally made Tom Cruise blush, as he buried his face in his hands, laughing uncontrollably.

Afterward, Tom came onstage to thank the participants and pose for pictures. Suddenly shy, Rosie waited off to the side, afraid to even look his way. Then he was there, enveloping her in a giant bear hug. And kissing her. Over and over. On her cheek, on her hair. And she blushed like a thirteen year old meeting Elvis. "He wouldn't stop kissing me—the whole evening," she said later. The entertainment media played it up big, with all its titillating angles. And while they were all having a grand old time, $400,000 was raised for the organization, which promotes movies as an art form.

Later, Tom brought his family backstage to chat with Rosie in her dressing room. At one point Nicole announced she was off in search of a ladies room when Rosie said, "You can use my bathroom." To which Nicole shot back, "Thanks. And you can use my husband." As Rosie told the story, she vowed, "I got witnesses, Baby Love—you'd better watch your tongue."

The following week, Rosie gave a full report to her TV fans, complete with photos and juicy details. "He is everything I dreamed he would be.... he was such a gentleman. The whole night was phenomenal. We became friends—Nicole was a great sport—she totally was in on the whole thing; she did not feel threatened at all," Rosie groused, frowning. Her only regret was that she forgot to hold her head up during the photo sessions, and as a consequence her "forty-seven chins" were showing in all the photos.

Her dishing was interrupted by the delivery of another massive bouquet of roses from Tom, with a card reading: "It was a wonderful evening for me, and you made it truly incredible." Then before she could stop gushing over that, Mr. Cruise himself called the show live to thank her again: "You made the evening—you were funny and charming—you made the evening go right." Finally, delivery men arrived with two gigantic photo blowups of Rosie and Tom, framed by dozens of cutout hearts the size of five-pound valentine boxes. "I ordered a couple of photos for home use," Rosie joked. With those as her backdrop, Rosie leaped into a song parody of "Hey Big Spender."

> The minute he entered my life,
> I could tell he was a man of perfection—
> my big dreamboat—

good lookin', so refined,
wouldn't you like to know what's goin' on in my mind?

(Rosie paused dramatically and said: "I can't tell you, it's daytime TV.")

The moment he looked in my eyes,
Tom and I had such perfect chemistry—
me and Top Gun,
lived out my fantasy.

When she was done singing, she planted a kiss on Tom's likeness.

It wasn't long before Rosie started plugging Tom's upcoming movie, *Jerry Maguire* (someone wisely thought to insure that she was one of the first to see it). Soon all she could talk about was Tom coming on her show to plug the film, which was a coup. Cruise rarely appears on such shows anymore. Rosie even defied Warner Bros. executives and showed the entire trailer for the film on her show, saying, "I'm gonna be in so much trouble for that." In the weeks leading up to his appearance, there was another countdown flipchart, and she began to punctuate most of her shows with random references to him. She even loaded up her digicard with snippets from the musical *Tommy,* in particular: "Tommy can you hear me?"

Finally, the big day arrived. Her intro was flagrantly adoring: "My boyfriend is right around that corner. He's my one and only, I love him. Please welcome the most perfect man on the planet, my Tommy." And it was a very nervous Tom Cruise who waltzed onto *The Rosie O'Donnell Show* that December day. He was at his boyish best, hiding another monster bouquet of roses behind his back like a bashful suitor. (A very *rich* suitor—those bouquets contained at least four dozen mixed pastel roses and in Manhattan probably cost about $500 each.

They proceeded to hug and kiss—on the mouth—and hug and kiss, and hug. These were no Hollywood air kisses. These were genuine, prolonged, heat-emanating embraces. After the second one, Rosie mouthed heavenward, "Oh, my God." The audience, meanwhile, screamed their approval. Once he was seated, Tom immediately grabbed her hand, then he stood and leaned over and kissed her again.

Rosie then asked him if her crush scared him. He claimed it didn't. "Nicole's all right with it?" Rosie asked. "Oh, absolutely," he assured her. Rosie's continued adoration of him did cause Tom to hide his face in his hands quite a few times during the interview. Lots of giggling and hand holding ensued. At times it felt like a sitcom dream sequence. Tom got even by showing a clip from *Jerry Maguire* that he picked out just for her. It turned out to be a romantic scene, and while it was playing, Rosie and Tom could be heard chatting about it. And judging from the studio audience's reaction, Rosie made a face every time Tom kissed the girl.

Rosie then tormented him back by playing audio snippets from *Tommy*, which caused him to dissolve into embarrassed laughter. Finally, Rosie got serious for just a moment. "I know that you're just a guy who's an actor, and you have a wife and family. But somehow you make me really happy." The women in the studio audience concurred loudly. She went on to say: "It's been really great having you here, and a lot of people wouldn't have showed up, after all the stuff that I did....I'm just a moment away from being totally insane and living outside your house in a sleeping bag." Fortunately she cut to commercial, because Tom looked like he might be ready to believe her.

For the grand finale, Rosie and Tom got inside her official Photo Booth and posed together. "I just wanted to say, dreams come true on *The Rosie O'Donnell Show*, with my boyfriend, Tom Cruise, in a photo booth on prom weekend." And in fact, they had that same high-on-life, slightly drunk look of couples in most prom pictures. Rosie said she would show everyone the photo two days later, when *Mrs.* Cruise appeared on the show to promote her new movie, *Portrait of a Lady*.

But first, there was the intervening show to do, complete with more gushing and afterglow. Rosie set out a pillow on "his chair" which said, "My Tommy sat here." Then Rosie launched into her version of "The Morning After," which was *really* over-the-top, with references to her wanting a ring and wanting to elope and mary him. It didn't seem that funny.

Nicole Kidman quickly proved just how well she could take Rosie's epic joke at her expense. "I have a proposal," she told Rosie as soon as she sat down. "We could move to one of those countries where a man is allowed to have two wives, and he could marry you, and we could become best friends." Rosie responded by grimacing. "I can't share Tommy." She did, however, tease Nicole unmercifully and make her watch a clip of Tom kissing Rosie while a shot of Nicole was inset in the corner so everyone could see her reaction. It did seem like Rosie was overdoing it, coming from someone who doesn't believe comedy should be mean. Rosie clarified her feelings for Nicole's benefit. "It's not a sexual crush—I just want him to get me a diet Coke every so often....my love is pure."

Later, Rosie assured her that "I'll get over it; I'm going to therapy." Surprisingly, Nicole replied, "I don't think he wants you to get over it." Rosie was quick to respond: "Good to know," she said, hitting the digicard button for "Tommy can you hear me?" Finally, Rosie told Nicole that because she had been such a great sport, she wanted to give her a gift. Rosie then proceeded to hand over four photos of Tom with Rosie, each framed in red hearts. Nicole demonstrated that she is the epitome of grace under pressure.

Through it all, both Tom and Nicole have publicly appeared to take it in stride and to even encourage Rosie further. That causes speculation that they were consulted early on and gave their blessing. So the saga has been milked for over six months, and undoubtedly Rosie will continue to do so for as long as she can. Some of her fans began to grow tired of the gag to post messages on her AOL site begging her to end it. Many, in particular, found her treatment of Nicole to be in questionable taste. Only the three participants know the extent to which all of this has been scripted and sanctioned.

One thing is certain. It can't hurt to have the most successful star on the planet as your "boyfriend." Rosie can be very clever in promoting herself, her show, and her image.

❧ 23

The Talk Karaoke Show

One feature of *The Rosie O'Donnell Show* that is certainly no act is Rosie's love of music and the singers who sing it. She has featured a singing star on virtually every show since the first, when she welcomed pop sensation Toni Braxton. Part of the appeal can be attributed to her being very much a frustrated singer herself. As Rosie said on an early show, "You know in about a week, people are gonna be so sick of me— 'she's singin' again!'" Though she did live out her dream of singing in a Broadway musical, and even recorded a cast album, Rosie isn't likely to be remembered for her singing ability. Though she may well go down in television history as the nonsinger who sang the most songs on TV.

After only eleven weeks on the air, her TV show was being referred to as a talk-karaoke show by one reviewer. An apt reference to her habit of loading up her digicard with song bites from that day's singing guest and then singing along with great gusto. On a show early in September 1996 Rosie spoofed her love of singing by running a compilation clip of herself doing about twenty songs. "People say I sing too much on the show—" she began, but was interrupted by the audience shouting in unison: "No!" Then while she continued to rattle on about how she didn't think she had really sung all that many songs, a superimposed list scrolled by naming 147 "annoying songs Rosie has sung" on her show. Her taste is eclectic, to say the least, and ranges from old TV theme songs to show tunes to most pop tunes recorded in her lifetime.

The first star to appear on the show as a result of receiving his own suck-up day was pop superstar Elton John. During that special day of begging for Elton in July 1996, all the guests participated by singing an Elton song, including Meg Ryan and actor Richard Karnes, the droll sidekick from *Home Improvement.* But the most inspired stunt presented astronaut Buzz Aldrin giving a dramatic reading of Elton's "Rocket Man."

Flattery won Rosie the booking. The opening announcement was made by a Wisconsin teacher who earned the privilege because her students had deluged Rosie with letters from every single youngster in the school. They claimed she was the world's biggest Elton fan and begged Rosie to "Please let Mrs. Youra on your show or she will die." If there's one thing Rosie can relate to, it's another obsessed fan.

When it came time to introduce Elton, Rosie was genuinely choked up. "Please welcome a true musical genius...words I never thought I'd get to say: Mr. Elton John." After his first number, Rosie asked him if he had seen the suck-up show. "I got a tape of it," he told her, "and I thought, how can I refuse to do this lady's show?" They went on to discuss the other object of her adoration, Barbra Streisand, and Elton joked that he and Barbra had once considered having a child together. "With my luck, we'd have given birth to a ten-pound gay nose."

When Rosie began to discuss his past work, Elton mentioned an obscure soundtrack he wrote. "Oh, the pink cover," she said, whipping it out from a huge stack of her own Elton albums. Rosie then proceeded to fawn and gush a bit, though she really tried to rein it in. "Every time I see you in concert I cry." She explained that his song "Daniel" came out the year her mother died and she has a brother named Danny, and the poignant song made her whole family cry then. "Enough flattery," he told her, "my inner child can't cope."

At one point Rosie decided to really enjoy the experience of interviewing one of her musical idols. "I'm just gonna sit here with you for a second...just takin' it in. 'Cause sometimes I do my life, and I meet people, and then I think it didn't really happen. So I'm just gonna take a moment and savor—there, that was good for me."

Later, Rosie nearly choked on a mint and told Elton he almost had to Heimlich her. "People would've thought I did it on purpose." Elton was relieved not to be needed and told her: "We'd have been front page, Honey." Finally, Elton performed her "favorite song, ever," "Levon." After the commercial, Rosie turned to John McDaniel and said, "I gotta tell you—I *love* this job!"

On the following Monday, Rosie added to the Elton experience, "Can I just say what a great time I had that day. It was the best time I think I've had on this show." Over the weekend, Elton invited her and her entire family to a private concert he was giving in New York. He even sang "Levon" again and dedicated it to the whole O'Donnell family, which of course made her cry. "It was so surreal for me, for him to say that, because our whole family, we're Elton John freaks. So it was a great day for me....things like that happen and you think, 'This is a *really* good job.'" And then Rosie welled up one more time.

The creative minds behind *The Rosie O'Donnell Show* went all out to celebrate the 100th episode. The national touring company of *A Chorus Line* taped a special tribute version of their song "One" with lyrics just for Rosie, which was intercut with short video clips from previous shows. Then Rosie donned a top hat and welcomed them all to the live show as they came singing and prancing down the stairs from the back of the studio. The cast joined Rosie onstage to sing a rousing rendition of the original version of "One." It was another opportunity for Rosie to live the Broadway experience, and she clearly relished every moment of it.

Later, over at her desk, she mockingly said, "I don't understand why people are making such a big fuss over our 100th show." As she spoke a huge illuminated sign dropped down behind her, flashing "100." At that point, Rosie pushed a button and a ton of confetti rained down on the audience. Guest Jeff Bridges entered with champagne and two glasses on a silver tray, and they drank a toast to her success.

As a commercial break ended, the McDLTs were playing a Gloria Estefan tune, "The Words Get in the Way," and Rosie, as usual, was singing along with great gusto. When the music concluded, she realized she didn't even know *what* she'd been singing, and turned to John McDaniel to find out what song it was that she'd been belting out. Shaking her head, she said, "It's sick that I don't even know I know that song."

When asked once if she had some kind of photographic memory for song lyrics, Rosie replied: "Sadly, I do. I can't get the songs out of my head even when I try."

Although Rosie certainly was thrilled to have Elton John on her show, she was too in awe of him to suggest joining him in song. But when veteran crooner Barry Manilow showed up the following month, Rosie was ready to sing along to all her favorites. First, however, Barry serenaded her with "Everything Is Rosy Since I Met My Rosie," from one of her favorite musicals, *Bye Bye Birdie*. Then she pulled up a stool next to his piano while he played some of his hits. As Rosie continued to keep pace no matter which song he played, Barry seemed genuinely amazed that she knew all the words to all the songs. After the second commercial break ended they were still singing, until Rosie said, "I got to tell you—that was the best commercial break we ever had—oh, Barry—the whole audience was singing...so thrilling for me."

Manilow then attempted the impossible: to stump Rosie O'Donnell. He even resorted to playing obscure commercial jingles he had written decades ago. But she knew every last one of them. Barry just kept shaking his head. Clearly, he had never met a fan quite like Rosie. "Listen to you—you know all these things," he said, giving up.

"Isn't it scary?" Rosie asked him.

Barry concurred: "*Scary*—do you have a life?"

The duo then sang requests from the audience, finishing up with the fast-paced theme from *American Bandstand*. The studio audience, packed with his diehard fans, the "Maniloonies," went wild. After Barry had gone, the Queen of Nice acted like she had met her match: "He's as nice as I thought he'd be."

Not all the duets Rosie sings with her guests are rehearsed. In fact, some of the best ones aren't. When Dolly Parton came by to chat, they had a grand time reminiscing about the old days when Rosie opened for Dolly's concerts. When Parton got up to sing "Walkin' on Sunshine," she surprised Rosie by pointing out that she had set up an extra microphone for her over with her backup singers. Rosie didn't have to be asked twice. She bounded over to her spot and soon was aping the other backup singers' dance steps and choreographed gestures while also managing to chime in more or less on cue with some vocals. Toward the end of the number, Dolly motioned for Rosie to join her at her microphone and they finished the song together, pretty much in the same key. Rosie, who was breathless with excitement, told Dolly: "That's the most fun I ever had—no rehearsal!"

When Rosie invited singer Donny Osmond to be on her show, she never expected it would turn into a nightmare. Osmond had the nerve to tell Rosie he thought she was fat, though he lived to regret it. Donny was slated to do a rather dangerous stunt from a helicopter at an outdoor concert, and Rosie—who was indeed a fan of his as a kid—jokingly volunteered to take his place, to be his stunt person. Osmond replied that Rosie couldn't substitute for him because "the helicopter can't handle that much weight." Rosie's mouth dropped open and a collective gasp was heard coming from the audience. For days thereafter, Rosie ragged on him for his poor taste. As she told David Letterman on his show, she had to bite her tongue that day with Osmond. "I wanted to say, 'Listen you slimy "Puppy Love" piece of shit,' but I couldn't, because I *am* the Queen of Nice."

Finally she said she would forgive him if he came back on her show and apologized to her face. Which he did. His sister Marie was also on hand to razz her brother into submission. Then for his ultimate humiliation, he donned a brown flannel dog suit and sang to Rosie his teeny bopper hit, "Puppy Love." Later, Rosie was asked if he would ever return to the show. "I hope so," she replied. "He was a good sport."

Several months later Rosie reported that Donny had blown out his vocal chords. "Coulda been karma," she said, with her trademark arched brow. But it took Paul Anka (the original recording artist for "Puppy Love") to really make things right. Appearing on a later show, Paul told Rosie: "If anybody's going to sing you one of my songs, it's going to be me." He then proceeded to reach across her desk and take her chin in his hand, telling her, "I want you to know I've had a mad crush on you for a long time." An astonished Rosie replied, "Paul Anka!" He then took her hand and told her he had rewritten the song just for her.

"This is more than puppy love—he watches her movies and never misses her show...." He ended with a reference to the Osmond debacle: "...got himself into the doghouse, acting like a little Shitzu." To which Rosie absolutely shrieked in delight.

And then there are times when the vocal gods smile on Rosie and she even surprises herself. Such a time came in November 1996 when Chaka Kahn stopped by the show. As usual, before she brought out her guest, Rosie sang along to one of Kahn's recorded hits, "Through the Fire." Only this time she kept going—a cappella, no less—until the band jumped in to help her finish the verse. Rosie is a huge fan of Chaka's, but she had begun to worry because Chaka missed the 8:30 A.M. rehearsal with her band. She had been out late the night before, partying with singer Joni Mitchell. Rosie found that intriguing and said playfully: "Can you imagine Joni Mitchell turning to Chaka Kahn and saying, 'Let's do shooters!'"

As soon as Chaka finally sat down with her, Rosie said in her best streetwise inflection, "You can sa-nng, girl!" Which got a big laugh from Chaka, who told the audience, "She said it right! But you can sing, too." Rosie smiled but demurred, "I can't sing like this—" She then hit the digicard button and out came the first three lines to "Through the Fire," until Chaka motioned to her to turn it off and sing it for real. They proceeded to finish the verse in a heartfelt, soulful rendition, on key, even managing to harmonize at the end. Rosie was clearly thrilled with her own performance, as she threw her head back, looked up, held her hands in a prayerful, thank-you-God gesture, and even crossed herself. "You made my dream come true," she told Chaka.

Rosie then began her usual gush, then stopped. "Look at me, I'm fawning. I can't help it—I love everything about you," she said, inviting her back whenever she wants to come. Chaka then suggested that next time they have a battle of the drums, since they both play. Rosie immediately accepted the challenge: "I will paradiddle your head off, Chaka Kahn!" she said. (A paradiddle is one of the drumming rudiments, a specific set of movements played with sticks or bare hands.)

One outside gig Rosie couldn't say no to, was helping her friend Vanessa Williams by appearing on her Christmas special. Taped in November 1996 at New York's Shubert Theatre, it was yet another chance for Rosie to sing on Broadway. The special featured a huge cast of gifted singers who were introduced as they took solos in the carol "Do You Hear What I Hear?" Wearing a gorgeous plum velvet outfit, Rosie performed her part from an elegant box seat with that noted singing star Elmo, of *Sesame Street* fame. (The same Elmo who inspired that season's hottest must-have toy, Tickle Me Elmo.) As Rosie explained later, she had trouble chiming in on cue, and finally Vanessa had to gesture rather explicitly from the stage to get her to sing at the right moment.

For a later number, Vanessa introduced the duo again, saying she thought Elmo was Rosie's vocal coach. While Rosie tucked Elmo into bed for the night, they did a rather sophisticated version of "White Christmas" in which one sang the actual lyrics while the other sang a response. It was very sweet and clever and a big hit with the children in the front row. It will also be a wonderful tape to play for Parker when he's old enough to appreciate it. Afterward, Rosie spoke about the experience of being in the company of so many talented singers. "I had so much fun doing it, and all those people can sing, sing, sing—and me and Elmo are cute!" When it comes to singing, Rosie acknowledged she was no match for the rest of the cast.

For Barbra Streisand's official suck-up day, August 7, 1996, Rosie invited Richard Simmons to proclaim his undying devotion to Streisand, which is legendary. Rosie later declared the day "a bust" and said she "hoped Barbra missed it." Later on in October, when the time drew near for Streisand to appear on various programs to promote her new movie, *The Mirror Has Two Faces*, Rosie stepped up the pleading. She often looked into the camera and sang: "Barbra can you hear me? Come on my show." She parodied *Funny Girl* with "Don't tell me not to beg...." Her funniest plea was: "Barbra please—I just want to take one quick Polaroid with her, have it blown up, and made into wallpaper—is that so wrong?"

As Barbra was the sole remaining idol from her childhood she had yet to meet, enticing her to appear became an important crusade for Rosie. (Though she also had tremendous anxiety about how she would handle it if it ever did come to pass. She told Naomi Judd that if she did interview Barbra, "I'd have diarrhea.") Rosie's loyal fans even got in the act, barraging Streisand with letters begging her to do Rosie's show. Some fans even threatened to boycott the movie if she didn't show up.

Rosie did get to attend the premiere of the film in New York and told Barbra's people that if she didn't apear on her show, "my life will pretty much end." At the party afterward, afraid to approach her idol and content to worship from afar, Rosie tried to fade into the background as Streisand made her entrance. Suddenly Barbra spotted Rosie and came over to *her*, extended her hand and said in her unforgettable voice: "Thank you for being so kind to me on your show." Floored, Rosie nearly collapsed as Barbra turned and merged into her throng of admirers. The first thing Rosie did was call her sister on her car phone and tell her every single detail so she wouldn't forget it. Besides, no one knew better than Maureen what that simple sentence meant to Rosie.

As wonderful as that brief meeting was, Rosie still wanted to get Barbra on her show. Rosie did interview all the other stars of *The Mirror Has Two Faces*—Lauren Bacall, Jeff Bridges, and Brenda Vaccaro—and asked them all to put in a good word for her with their director, Barbra Streisand. She told Brenda, "I don't want to annoy her. I don't want to be like the weird stalker-fan person that I am." Jeff tried to make her feel better and brought her a portfolio of backstage photos he had taken during the filming. Rosie was overwhelmed by the gift and said, "Oh, my God! Can we go to commercial right now so I can look at it?"

As Barbra breezed in and out of New York on her press junket without stopping by Rosie's show, Rosie became noticeably depressed about it. (Barbra had spent a whole *hour* with Oprah.) "I don't know if the other talk-show hosts saw her movie three times. I don't know if the other talk-show hosts know the name of every character she has every played in every film she ever did." Finally, in desperation, Rosie warbled: "Barbra can you hear me? Try to understand me. You've done every other show in the free world, please do mine now!"

Alas, despite some hints that she might make a "surprise" appearance, Barbra Streisand did not find it within her heart or her schedule to appear on *The Rosie O'Donnell Show*. Perhaps because it's a live show, and Streisand is notoriously wracked by stage fright. Perhaps the degree of Rosie's adulation did frighten her. "The anxiety of thinking that she possibly *could* be a guest is giving me indigestion. If she ever *was* booked, I'd have to be on Valium for the three weeks prior to her appearance." Or perhaps Barbra hated all the weak imitations of her that Rosie has done since the show began. ("People, people who need Barbra, and they have their own talk show for you to do.") Whatever her reason, Streisand did miss out on one great publicity appearance for her film.

"Barbra Streisand was part of my childhood, part of the fantasy of what I wanted my life to become, some ideal I was striving for." Speaking of Streisand recently, Rosie said, "She had a tremendous impact on me as a kid, more than any human could ever live up to."

One thing is certain. Rosie doesn't plan to stop singing. "I've gotten a lot of complaints, people say I sing too much," Rosie told Dave Letterman recently.

"Well screw 'em!" Dave advised.

"Exactly!" Rosie agreed.

⌒ 24

What You See Is What You Get

On a very early show, Rosie explained that people come in all sizes, and this is the one she comes in at the moment. As someone who has struggled with her weight for much of her life and come to a healthy place of self-acceptance, Rosie has become the unofficial poster girl for the Size-Acceptance Movement, a heroine to larger women of substance everywhere. One self-proclaimed "Rosie-sized" fan wrote her: "I was really touched by your comment that 'some of us are just bigger.' Words aren't adequate to express how this made me feel."

Rosie understands all too well the many letters she gets on this subject. "I'm not the usual celebrity size. And I think that people who like to see images of themselves reflected back feel strongly connected to me." In our image-obsessed society it's virtually impossible to read a story about Rosie that doesn't include some comment about her size.

In 1996 her publicist advised against doing an interview in *Radiance,* a magazine for non-Twiggy types. Rosie disagreed, because, as she said, "that's my audience and that's me! I'm one of those people." When asked if she had had problems with her self-image growing up, she replied: "No, I wasn't really heavy until I was older. As I grew up emotionally, all of the issues surrounding weight that deal with emotions came to the forefront for me." She also said she didn't feel she had conquered the demons of self-doubt that intrude on her ability to experience self-acceptance. "I have to work hard to stand in front of the mirror and say... 'You're okay in this body, and you're a great, healthy, lovable, and loving person.'"

Back in 1992 she and costar Madonna appeared on Arsenio's show to plug *A League of Their Own.* During the show, Rosie did a dead-on impression of director Penny Marshall's directorial style. After the show Penny called her to give her even more direction. As it turned out, Rosie was being interviewed for *Entertainment Weekly* at that moment. After the call, she again mimicked Marshall to tell the reporter what she had said. "You were funny, but you looked so fat. You gotta lose weight before you do Nora's movie." Rosie laughed at the notion, and said, "You can print that."

Rosie is 5'7" and her weight has fluctuated most of her adult life from 140 to 180 pounds. Even during her stint hosting VH-1's *Stand-up Spotlight* her size varied quite a bit. There was a period in 1993 when they would occasionally do a marathon of the shows, Rosie recalls, laughing at the bizarre visual image. "Sometimes they'd show twenty-four hours of it, and you could watch me go from 140 to 170 in a matter of seconds." Reacting to herself with laughter was a hard-won victory. At about the same time she was quoted as saying, "I don't want to have a body like Madonna. I'm just trying to get to a place where self-loathing is no longer paramount."

Still, she's human, and not above a little good-natured envy. To Isabella Rosellini, Rosie said, "If I looked like you, I'd be naked right now."

Rosie doesn't remember being pressured about body size as a kid, but she thinks that that is mostly due to her mother's death. "When you have something like the death of a parent at the age of ten, everything else pales in comparison." She is, however, very concerned about the young girls who watch her show. "I don't want little kids who are overweight to think that looking like me is bad."

At the time her talk show first aired, she discussed her feelings. "Little girls have such struggles with their body image, and I don't want to add to it. I'm hoping that I can maintain a weight that I'm comfortable with. When I did *Grease* I was one hundred fifty pounds, and that was a comfortable weight for me. That's thirty pounds ago. But I'm going to try not to talk about it because it does so much damage to little girls' psyches, not to mention my own."

Few actresses are so candid about their weight. In December 1996 Rosie told *Entertainment Weekly* not to expect any Oprah-like transformation.

"I'm not the kind of person who'd get a cook and a trainer. If I do, call me up and remind me what I just said."

Speaking of her infamous scantily clad role in *Exit to Eden,* Rosie explained more about her personal weight issues. "One of the reasons I took that film was to try and face that part of myself, that sort of self-loathing about not being the appropriate size, and to realize that there is no one size. Not everybody can look like Cindy Crawford....I think that's why a lot of women identify with me or my characters, because I kinda look like them."

In 1994, in an interview for *Elle* magazine, Rosie offered this theory about her weight issues, and why she has such anxiety at the thought of being thin. "My mother got very thin before she died....I associated getting thin with getting sick and going away. So it also makes me frightened of my own mortality."

In a review of her new talk show, a writer for New York's foremost alternative paper, the *Village Voice,* had some wry observations on the subject. "The large women of daytime—Oprah, Carnie Wilson, and ex-fatty Ricki Lake—are humiliated by their bodies. O'Donnell calls herself fat and neither weeps nor apologizes for liking food. She isn't about to trade her authority for a seat at a twelve-step sisterhood."

Her fan mail on America Online proves she's been effective in her campaign.

A fourteen-year-old girl wrote: "I know what it's like to be called fat, since I am overweight. In that way, I really admire and respect you. People have called you all sorts of things, and you don't care. You are my role model now; I can look up to you. It doesn't matter what you look like on the outside; it is on the inside that counts, and I have realized that from you."

Another woman declared, "Rosie, I just love you the way you are. You are very pretty the way God made you, and I am proud to idolize you."

Among numerous messages on this subject was this one from a fellow mother: "Rosie is an attractive woman who doesn't fit the Barbie Doll size rules....She is a great role model for young girls, because she portrays a positive self-image and doesn't rely on others to provide her worth or value. She is truly priceless."

While she refuses to do fat jokes about other people, and rarely does them about herself, she is still capable of being hurt by someone's barbs, as Donny Osmond proved. On a 1996 *Saturday Night Live* show, cast member Norm MacDonald made a crack about Rosie being too large to be in a movie called *Beautiful Girls*. Rosie's reaction reflected her own rules about comedy. "Unless he'd say to my face, 'I find you tremendously unappealing,' I don't think he should say it on TV. Not that it wounded me so much, but unless you have the nerve to tell somebody to their face 'I think you're ugly,' you shouldn't do it on TV."

Rosie has done jokes about her compulsion to *buy* exercise equipment—not to *use* it! One day on her show she opened a gift from Maureen O'Donnell: the Chin Gym, which set her off on quite a rant. "This is my sister playing a joke. I buy every one of those stupid things that nobody ever uses. I buy the Health Rider—I have it. The AbRoller—I have it. AbRoller Plus—it's mine. Nordic Track ski machine—they're all in my house—all my clothes are on them. I NEVER use them!"

She went on to say how she keeps buying these contraptions hoping that the sight of them will incite her to action, but it never happens. "I look at it as I'm sittin' there eatin' my salt-and-vinegar potato chips—there's my AbRoller...looks good...I bet I could do that." She then demonstrated the Chin Gym, which is a bonafide exercise tool (complete with add-on weights) for people with two or more chins. "I want to thank my sister— I'm sure she'll be happy with the Thanksgiving gift I have for her: the Thighmaster." (Her sister is equally short for her weight.)

Another thing Rosie will joke about is food: "Eighty percent of people living in Haiti believe in voodoo. Eighty percent of people living in my house believe in YooHoo." Rosie revels in her enjoyment of food, in the sublime delight to be found on the way to the bottom of a pint of Baskin-Robbins mint chocolate chip. She acknowledges the folly that she and Madonna engage in. "We eat candy and drink diet soda. How absurd is that?" She does admit to being "an emotional eater." In 1994 she said that "eating is a great way not to have to deal with your feelings." Though she would prefer to be lighter, she is firm in her conviction that "my days of Weight Watchers and diet programs are over."

Although Rosie has had a cooking segment on her show every month or so, don't look for any macrobiotic recipes anytime soon. Rosie's idea of a really great cooking segment is booking the guy who invented her favorite sundae at Friendly's. Right at her desk, she demonstrated that she knew how to make the five-scoop Reese's Pieces ice-cream extravaganza. She deemed the concoction "a work of art" and called the man who invented it "a genius." And though she's demonstrated she can crack an egg into a bowl singlehanded, she says she's not much of a cook herself. "I'm good at defrosting things," she says proudly. She expects the cooking spots to be her biggest challenge on her show. "I live in New York City. I'm only good at ordering out."

She did have the Grand Dame of the kitchen, Julia Child, on her show, and is undoubtedly the first person to get Julia to discuss her favorite drive-through cuisine—McDonald's. The segment with Julia should go on a compilation tape as one of Rosie's funniest. Their goal was to make the complicated dessert, crème brûlée, which had them both donning dark glasses while Rosie wielded a blowtorch. Julia stood nearby, at the ready with a huge fire extinguisher should her pupil get carried away. After the mission was more or less accomplished, Rosie asked Julia an all-important question: "Are you into this fat-free stuff?"

Julia replied emphatically, "I hate it!"

Rosie may not be a gourmet cook, but she is, however, a connoisseur of junk food. She knows which outfit in New York City delivers the best goat cheese pizza (California Pizza Co.); she notices when KitKat bars change their packaging and lets them know they erred; she delights in a gift of a giant box of the new "designer colors" M&Ms and tucks them away for personal use; she does a free "commercial" for Almond Roca; and she is supremely pleased by a fan letter the size of her desk, created on poster board and featuring real candy bars glued onto it so that the names of the treats form words in the letter. Rather like an edible rebus. (The last line read: "I hope you get $100,000 every Payday.")

When she heard that a watchdog group had determined that eating onion rings was fattening, Rosie said in mock amazement, "Shocking! I had no idea. Thank God they published that report." Then as an afterthought she said, "I wish I coulda been in that study group."

She is also not shy about admitting her compulsions. One day she began her show by announcing, "I just want to tell everyone that I ate an entire box of sugar wafers last night. They should not be allowed to sell those. It's literally impossible to eat just one sugar wafer."

When fitness expert Jane Fonda appeared on her show, Rosie did make an exception and joked about her weight. After she told Jane that she looked great, Jane replied, "So do you." Then in her most sincere manner, Rosie explained: "Well I have to say, I bought all your tapes and I've watched them all, but I haven't lost a pound. I've seen *On Golden Pond* six times, and I'm still chubby."

Jane had a good laugh and seemed to genuinely enjoy her. Then Rosie got serious about the subject of exercise. "I do every so often really get into the whole thing, and it's really about your mind being in another place—to physically know that you're worth taking care of yourself—don't you think that's what it's about?"

Agreeing with her, Jane said, "That's right, it's respecting yourself, and it's feeling good about yourself—and clearly, *you* feel good about yourself, and that's what matters."

Jane was there to plug her new healthy cookbook, and in a clever demonstration she presented Rosie with a taste test to see if she could discern the nonfat dishes from the high-fat ones. Rosie shared this tip regarding fatty foods: "I prefer to call them *non-low-fat*—it makes me feel less guilty." As she ate the pizza and the enchiladas Rosie was amazed that she was twice fooled by the nonfat recipes. When she asked Jane if she wanted a taste and Jane declined, Rosie quipped, "That's the difference between you and me."

There was no stumping her though, when it came to the dessert. "Cheesecake, my favorite—this, I don't think you'll ever be able to fool me. I'm sorry Jane, I know it's your book, but I have a reputation to uphold." She did know faux cheesecake when she tasted it.

In addition to her candor about her fluctuating size, Rosie is remarkably un-self-conscious about things other women would pay a lot of money to disguise. Her seeming lack of vanity is unusual. You never get the sense that she is selling herself out just for a laugh, the way Joan Rivers so often does, or before her, Phyllis Diller. You won't catch Rosie saying "I'm so ugly" jokes. On one early show Rosie had the camera move in for an extreme close-up of something she had recently discovered growing on her body—a chin hair! (A little boy later sent her a smile mask to which he had attached a long piece of string to simulate the infamous hair. She showed that off, as well, and thought it was cute.)

Rosie always seems so natural—as though she's just sitting around chatting with a few friends—not at all aware that millions of people are examining her chin hair. On the following show she shared how all weekend people were coming up to her and asking her about the "hair on her chinny chin-chin" and trying to get a look at it. "So I yanked it out—I couldn't take the pressure." Then she added: "It'll grow back, and I'll show it again—something to look forward to."

On another show she flirted with the idea of getting liposuction on her chin. She had just seen a series of photos of herself smiling broadly with her double chin displayed prominently, and that got her to thinking about it. Once again, she played with the camera and had it zoom in for a close-up while she pushed the loose skin up with her fingers. Then she joked that she would use Scotch tape. "I could have like a little Bernadette Peters chin." Finally, she emphasized that she would never really do it and that the process grossed her out. "I saw it done on one of those *Dateline–20/20–60/60–Primetime Live–48-Hours* shows....they stick like a water pik in your skin and suck out all your fat."

One especially funny demonstration of her ability to laugh at herself occurred when actor Edward James Olmos stopped by to talk about his upcoming movie. To portray the father of murdered singer, Selena, he gained forty pounds. Rosie had been told about this in advance, but she was surprised that he still looked so fit. This inspired her to reach across the desk to feel his stomach for herself. "It's a firm kind of chubbiness," she declared. "Mine's much mushier," she decided, feeling her own, then guiding his hand toward her midsection to see for himself.

"I think it's the speed at which I gained the weight," Olmos explained. "Two months...a lot of tortillas."

"I think you beat my record," Rosie told him, giving him a high five.

Few subjects are off-limits for the Queen of Candor. One day she asked her bandleader, John McDaniel, if he noticed anything different about her. He couldn't come up with anything, so she sat up a little taller and divulged in a self-congratulatory voice that "I'm wearing a Wonderbra...and somehow I feel like I have superpowers. You sit up a little straighter, you feel just a little better about yourself in the Wonderbra." Then she shared her fantasy: "I'm hopin' I can be the new Wonderbra model." When Cher came to visit the show, Rosie hiked up her pantleg to show her tattoo—and in the process, her unshaven legs—and she just laughed about it.

In fact, Rosie seems almost detached from her body. Most actresses obsess over their looks, their hair, their makeup, their clothes. Not Rosie. When asked in August 1996 why she had cut her hair, she replied "Who knows? I have a hair guy, David. He makes all the decisions." Except, of course, for her beauty consultant, Cher, whose contribution was advising her to get her hair streaked.

When it comes to clothes, Rosie doesn't mind telling you that she's been on a worst-dressed list (Blackwell called her a "fashion strikeout"). "That's how I knew I was famous," she bragged, making it sound like an award. She went on to say that most women in show business wouldn't think of leaving home without full makeup, "But I always want to be myself. If I'm out and I look like this (in faded jeans and a sweatshirt) and the paparazzi are there, I say 'Go right ahead,' I don't run and hide. I'm just trying to be the same person I was in the beginning."

"Sweats are clothes," Rosie said, commenting on her usual offstage attire, a practical choice for a single mother who does her own errands. "Performers get into trouble when they allow other people to take care of everything. They lose touch with reality and with their audience. Comedy is about relating to people, and I think audiences relate to me because they know I go to the supermarket and the mall just like they do."

Rosie works hard at keeping fame at a distance. "You could go crazy with all this attention," she told the *Chicago Tribune*. "I think I was really fortunate to do my first film with probably the most famous woman in the world, Madonna. I've tried really hard to maintain my essence, which is what got me here in the first place." And Rosie enforces that same sense of authenticity with her talk-show audiences, too, warning them, "Don't clap unless you mean it—this isn't Sally Jesse Raphael."

Her laugh is loud, she's blunt, she blurts, and she's politically incorrect in all the right ways. Former costar Meg Ryan recalls: "When we were filming *Sleepless,* there were about eight of us gathered around a table for lunch. A big studio executive was telling us how he was going to release Woody Allen's *Husbands and Wives* early to capitalize on the public scandal that had engulfed Allen and Mia Farrow. Rosie told him she thought it was a really slimy thing to do. She was funny about it, but she didn't back off from telling him just how offensive she found it."

She has proved time and time again that she's a publicist's nightmare and a reporter's dream. A similar episode occurred a few years later in Aspen, Colorado, where Rosie appeared at the press conference to promote the U.S. Comedy Arts Festival. Also present was Ivan Reitman, a powerful producer and director (*Ghostbusters, Animal House,* etcetera), who was directing Howard Stern in the film adaptation of his autobiography, *Private*

Parts. He began to tell all assembled how funny Howard was, and that was just too much for Rosie to take. "Wait 'til he says he wants to fuck your daughter up the ass—then he's going to be really funny. Wait 'til he talks to a rape victim and makes fun of how she was raped, that's really funny, like he did to Fran Drescher."

Reitman paused, then continued with his accolades. Rosie shrugged off her effort, "And on that note, I'll never be in an Ivan Reitman film."

Her *Sleepless* director, Nora Ephron, wasn't offended by her directness. "Rosie feels like someone who you have known all your life—or wish you had. She is completely up-front. If she thinks something is baloney, she will say so, and she is genuinely interested in other people. She's not one of those celebrities who just wants to hear herself talk." Ephron goes on to say that Rosie "is the opposite of Roseanne." No matter what has happened to her or what her feelings are about it, it's never your fault or mine. She doesn't play the victim in any way."

A colleague from the comedy circuit, Lucien Hold, feels he understands Rosie's appeal. "She is very sure of herself, and that is an appealing thing—people that are really confident in themselves. They don't need you, they don't need your love—you like them or don't like them, it doesn't seem to phase them. Those people are always more desirable, and Rosie's full of confidence." He went on to say, "She doesn't take any bullshit and is very honest about what she believes in."

Rosie knows there is a downside to her smart mouth. "I'm very direct, and it gets me in trouble. I'd rather have people say it like it is. I think I'm tactful, but I'm not as gentle as I could be. I'm abrasive in some ways, and I'm often not conscious of it." And even if she knows that historically talk-show hosts have remained politically neutral, she doesn't give a damn. Ask her who she plans to vote for and she will tell you without hesitation: "Bill Clinton."

After she made that bias clear on her own show, she wondered if she'd get letters from Republicans. Then she realized, "What Republicans are watching daytime television? They're too busy tryin' to make more money than anybody else." On America Online she was even more blunt when asked who she would vote for: "Bill Clinton. Bob Dole is older than dirt." Her Democratic politics were also on public display during the 1992 election season, when Rosie had the time of her life playing drums for Melissa Etheridge at a campaign rally for Clinton.

Rosie did welcome U.S. Representative and Republican National Convention keynote speaker, Susan Molinari, to the program. Rosie didn't delve too deeply into the issues and managed to be polite to the New York congresswoman. Later, during an America Online conference, she was asked why she was so gentle with Molinari. Rosie replied "We are an entertainment show, not *Crossfire*. I had to be civil and not bombard her with pointed accusations about her party. It was tough."

The following week she got even by bringing on Tipper Gore, and the two of them obviously had a mutual admiration society going on. Rosie was her cozy self, and Mrs. Gore showed off photos from her new book. Best of all for Rosie, she got Tipper to dish with her about meeting Tom Crusie. They gushed over him like teenagers at a slumber party.

Rosie's highly visible and vocal support of the Clintons paid off in February 1997 when Rosie welcomed Hillary Rodham Clinton onto the show. It was clear the two were already well acquainted through their activities on behalf of charities that benefit children. Mrs. Clinton appeared relaxed and at ease, as if chatting with an old friend. They reminisced about the time the Clinton family enjoyed Rosie in a special performance of *Grease* at the National Theater in Washington D.C. Rosie laughed recalling how Chelsea brought all of her friends backstage afterward to meet her and then invited the whole cast to the White House for a sleep-over. Mrs. Clinton made several references to previous invitations she had extended to Rosie to come and stay at the White House, and they agreed that Rosie and Parker would finally visit them in the summer of 1997. Rosie said she would like to sleep in the Lincoln bedroom and wasn't spooked by tales of ghosts lurking about his room.

Clearly a fan of the show, Mrs. Clinton came prepared with boxes of official White House M&Ms and her own trivia questions for Rosie. She did manage to stump the Queen of Trivia just once (though it wasn't a fair question, since it involved a TV show that aired before Rosie was born). Mrs. Clinton, who stayed for three segments, discussed their mutual nostalgia for *The Mary Tyler Moore Show,* dished with Rosie about Tom Cruise and even warbled a song from *Bye Bye Birdie* with her. By the end of Mrs. Clinton's visit it was very clear that this kid from Commack had made some friends in the highest places.

Another way Rosie found to reveal her political leanings was to invite impressionist Rich Little to come on in various political guises. Using the gimmick of a doorbell, each time Rosie opened the door, Little stood or slouched there as a different politician. He was especially great as Richard Nixon: "I'm back—I got into heaven—I broke in!"

Of course she herself is not at all shy about making pointed fun of Dole and his cohorts. "It's part of the reason I think people like the show—because I'm not afraid to say my opinions," Rosie said in self-defense. In fact, her jokes were so one-sided that Warner Bros. urged her to launch a more balanced attack. Unwilling to skewer Clinton herself, she finally decided to let the writers come out and present the opposing point of view. Two examples from October 1996 illustrate the solution. Rosie: "Bob Dole has fallen behind in the polls, and he's been doing everything he can to get back on the voters' good side. In fact, today he announced that he's gonna show his butt on *NYPD Blue*."

Then she shook her head and said, "Sadly, it's time for the Republican response. Our writer John Hotchkiss will now do an anti-Democratic joke." John: "I can't believe how long President Clinton's speech was at the Democratic Convention—it was a startling sixty-six minutes. Not only did he stop twenty-two times for applause, he stopped three times to try and score Katie Couric's home number."

To which the crowd let loose with a chorus of "boos." Rosie had the last words though, as she scowled and repeatedly punched her digicard buttons with a vengeance. As she continued to make a sour face, Gary Owens's recorded voice boomed out: "Just not funny. Just not funny. Really bad. Wow, that was awful."

It was following one of those mandatory responses that Rosie welcomed Whoopi Goldberg to the show. Whoopi, also a Clinton supporter, asked her why she was doing that. "Well, I take slams at Dole," Rosie explained. "And some people have been writin'— 'Who do you think you are? You're not allowed to say your views. You only say Republican jokes'—which is *true,*" she admitted with her trademark Betty Rubble cackle.

Then Whoopi countered: "But I don't recall anybody being upset with Rush when he was slamming Democrats." She went on to point out that it was, after all, *The Rosie O'Donnell Show,* and she ought to be able to do whatever she wanted. The two women had appeared together at the ultimate Democratic event, the gala fiftieth birthday party for President Clinton. Whoopi, who served as emcee for the evening, didn't feel the need to censor Rosie when she yelled out "Dole sucks!"

They went on to discuss their common interests in various charities. Whoopi mentioned a benefit performance she had planned that would repeat her Broadway show. Rosie was familiar with it and told her she admired her because, "You always deal with social issues and put them in front of people in a way that they can relate to them—and you make people think."

Whoopi smiled and leaned back in her chair for a better look at Rosie. "You're just too deep, aren't you? I'm looking at you—and here's Rosie—and you got the number-one show on TV...and I know you!"

Rosie laughed and recalled how they had met doing Comic Relief on HBO and at a showing of the AIDS quilt. Rosie told Whoopi that she appreciated the way "you stand up for your charities." And Whoopi told her that her philosophy of life is, "There but for the grace of God go I."

They also chatted about the charity work they do for youngsters. "The kids love you, Whoopi." And Whoopi explained why: "'Cause they know that under this adult veneer lives an eight year old." Rosie got excited as she replied, "You know what, Whoop—I can relate. You want a Kooshball? Like a twelve year old, I have the toys." Their inner and outer children then Kooshed the audience together.

On another show, Rosie talked about a really powerful Nike commercial she had seen that featured multiracial golf whiz kid, Tiger Woods. She was so impressed by it that she asked the Nike people to send it on over, so she could show it for free. It arrived the next day. A controversial spot, it features still photos that trace Tiger's amazing career. There is no audio. The message is simply superimposed over the photos. All Woods's various championship titles and records are noted, and at the end, it puts these words in Tiger's mouth: "There are still courses in the U.S. I am not allowed to play because of the color of my skin. Hello, world. I've heard I'm not ready for you. Are you ready for me?" That was followed by the Nike swoosh and their slogan, "Just Do It."

Rosie was visibly moved and said afterward, "Gives you chills, doesn't it? I love the Nike people for doing it."

Rosie isn't shy about expressing her social values, either. On America Online she was asked: "If you could have three wishes, what would they be?" Her reply: "A cure for AIDS. That every kid in the country was safe. And that there was no more pollution."

AIDS charities are among those most important to her. Anyone who has been in show business as long as Rosie has lost many friends and colleagues to the disease. Over the years, Rosie has been a tireless fundraiser for many different AIDS groups, including AMFAR. (The American Fondation for AIDS research is a research charity founded in the 1980s by Elizabeth Taylor.) She cohosted the Miami AIDS walk with supermodel Cindy Crawford (whom Rosie volunteered to jog the course while she entertained the crowd). And she even auctioned off dinner with herself to generate money. When Estelle Getty appeared on her show, Rosie reminded her about the AIDS auction they both attended. Rosie was doing the auctioneering, but she couldn't get any takers for a dinner with Rosie. Then she spotted Estelle in the audience and called out to her, inviting her to be part of the dinner date. It worked— "and we got like $40,000 for dinner with the two of us."

At yet another AIDS auction, where she met actress Judith Light, a T-shirt auction wasn't going well. So Rosie said to the auctioneer, "Gimme the mike," and she took over. "I make people give money." Judith Light recalled the event when she visited the show. "I remember Luke Perry was there, and you got him to take off his shirt, and then you sold it for like $5,000."

In September 1996, Rosie and her staff members participated in the Broadway Flea Market, sponsored by Broadway Cares/Equity Fights AIDS. All the Broadway shows put up booths and sold memorabilia to raise money. Rosie signed autographs and sold T-shirts at *The Rosie O'Donnell Show* booth. Because she had announced on her show that she was going to be there, a mob of her local fans showed up to lend support to the cause—and to get up close and personal with her.

During October 1996, Rosie wore a pink ribbon every day to promote Breast Cancer Awareness Month. Proving that something so simple can affect people, Rosie received this letter from a doctor and his wife, who is struggling with breast cancer: "We go for experimental treatment every Wednesday, and it is emotionally and physically difficult. We watch your program religiously during treatment. It is the high point of the morning and provides us with the humor that we need to get through the therapy. Seeing that breast cancer awareness ribbon meant all the more to us."

Other causes she has supported include Pro-Choice and help for the homeless. In 1988 she said, "New York City has become a third world country. It wears at me when I step over homeless families to go into my high-rise condo. There's nothing funny about homelessness." For eight years she has participated in celebrity ski benefits for cystic fibrosis in Crested Butte, Colorado, where the kid from Long Island found herself surrounded by the beauty of the land. "I was sitting on top of a mountain and—this sounds so corny—I started to cry. I started singing John Denver songs!"

Now that she's a mother, charities that help women and children are foremost in her heart. One event she hosted and promoted on her show was a teddy bear auction for the Children's Safety Project at New York's Greenwich House, a shelter for battered women and their youngsters. Dan Aykroyd brought a "Blues Bear" on the show to donate to the auction. At the event, Rosie auctioned off the bears with actor Kevin Spacey. Rosie's own bear went for $5,800, more than twenty times what model Elle Macpherson's bear fetched.

Good friend and show regular Iman came on Rosie's show to publicize a celebrity plate auction for the Children's Defense Fund, a charity for which Rosie does a lot of work. It was a clever idea, wherein celebrities are given blank plates and the tools to decorate and sign them; the plates are then auctioned off at a fancy dinner. Rosie both designed a plate and purchased a plate. She was thrilled to acquire one painted by poet and novelist Maya Angelou.

One terrific project Rosie did for Nickelodeon, the kids cable channel, in the spring of 1996 was "Nick News Special Edition: The Body Trap." With her cohost, journalist Linda Ellerbee, Rosie helped youngsers question the messages they get about body image from the media. "You know the media perpetuates this image that the perfect woman is a size two or three," Rosie said, talking about the special. "That is in no way something to shoot for. It's an unrealistic weight that's not only impossible for most human beings, but also unhealthy."

About the same time she also participated in the Children's March on Washington to increase awareness of kids' issues. She has plans to "get a foundation going to help institute national standards for day care and to open nonprofit day-care centers across the country, like every other civilized country." She promises to put some of her money into the foundation.

As her life becomes more hectic, Rosie has to cut some corners to make sure there is time for really important activities. In November 1996 she was rushing around and didn't have time to change her clothes before attending a benefit for the Fresh Air Fund, an organization that sends city children to summer camp. Rosie didn't realize that this was a black-tie affair. "I looked like a hoodlum—the paparazzi were laughing at me—I felt like such a dweeb. But we raised a lot of money, and that's what matters."

As the holiday season neared and Rosie began to receive gifts from fans for herself and Parker, she made several on-air pleas for people to send donations to charities instead. She had an especially challenging time explaining about a program at post offices where adults can pick up letters to Santa to respond to. Fully aware that many young children watch her show, Rosie didn't want to disturb their ideas about how Santa does his work.

In December 1996, director Penny Marshall came on *The Rosie O'Donnell Show* promoting her new film, *The Preacher's Wife,* and also took that opportunity to show everyone a check she'd been given by K-Mart for $25,000. As part of their commercial deal with the retailer, Rosie and Penny got to pick a charity for their donation, and they chose the Pediatric AIDS Foundation.

Even without their commercials, Rosie can take credit for two huge toy crazes that year: Tickle Me Elmo, which Rosie introduced on her show, and, of course, the ever-present Kooshballs.

The demand for Elmos became so intense that Whoopi Goldberg was reduced to begging Rosie for two Elmos for her grandchildren. Whoopi came on the show right before Christmas to promote her new movie, *Ghosts of Mississippi,* and told how she had not wanted star treatment and had gone herself on a hunt for Elmo. She did manage to find only one— and also found herself in the middle of a wrestling match of shoppers trying to grab the last Elmo. Apparently many of the shoppers tried to work their way toward the doll by yanking on the Whoopi's long braids, to which she replied, "I'm *not* Tickle Me Whoopi!" As it turned out, Rosie had a stash of the dolls on hand for deserving kids and gave Whoopi two dolls. In gratitude for the dolls, Whoopi gave Rosie a check for $5,000 for the Children's Defense Fund.

Beginning in January 1997, a new television rating system took effect and Rosie's show earned a G rating for general audiences. Rosie decided to make use of this new fact and hustled companies to provide free presents for her studio audience that began with the letter G. Every day fans went home with gifts ranging from Givenchy perfume to Gumby dolls. But best of all, she also twisted the corporate arms of America into donating considerable quantities of their products (or money in some cases) to various charities. Rosie then graciously mentioned each company on air enough to ensure a win/win proposition, making her a one woman fundraiser of epic proportions. Rosie has certainly learned how to use her enormous vitality and media power for the greater good. Good going, girl!

Rosie said, "I think that to use my celebrity status to inspire or help or encourage children is really payback for all the celebrities who helped me so much through my childhood."

⌒ 25

At Home With Rosie

Another yearning we all have is for parental approval. While her mother was alive, young Roseann received plenty of approval and validation from her. But after her mother's death, Rosie's father simply abandoned her emotionally. With her mother, Rosie had closure, though she still misses her. Every Mother's Day is bittersweet, but she has moved on with her life.

There is a natural grieving process that people go through when a loved one dies, and the end result is usually some kind of acceptance of the new reality. But when a parent is still living yet is inaccessible to his child, this is a "death" without closure. It is nearly impossible to complete the grieving process because there always remains the tiny hope, no matter how slight, that magically things will change before one of them really does die.

When asked in 1996 if Edward O'Donnell had mellowed as a grand-father, Rosie replied, "He was never really available for his kids, and he's never seen Parker. He's not as connected to the family as he would like to be, perhaps. He retired, moved to North Carolina, got remarried. He's kinda separate from us now." She still makes excuses for him, still leaves the door to her life open a crack.

Nor has he been very supportive of her career. "I assume my father is proud of me. He really doesn't say very much. I've done stand-up comedy since I was sixteen, and I think he's been to three shows. It's not really a great track record." He does seem to have done a little better with her films. "He's seen the movies. He'll call me if somebody else thinks it's funny. He's not really into discussing his feelings. I really don't speak to him that much."

Her relationship with her father is thorny at best, and Rosie has spent "years in therapy since I was eighteen" to deal with all her family issues. "And I am by no means done with it," she said in 1996. "The father I have in the show is a lot nicer and a lot more approachable than the father I had in reality. My father in reality is not the affable Irish leprechaun."

One excuse she makes for him is his foreign birth. "My father was from a different world and different school. He's very Irish and very unwilling to change." Still, Rosie somehow manages to be philosophical about it. "That's too bad for him, perhaps. Not for me. Everything I've gone through in my life brought me to where I am, and I don't really have any regrets about it or about him. He has his own destiny and his own journey. He'll heal himself when he chooses to. Until then there's nothing I can do about it."

Rosie does confront her absent father through her humor. Sometimes she quickly retracts a bitter remark, sometimes not. But there's no mistaking the hurt she still feels when she speaks of him. On an early episode of her talk show, the opening announcement was done by a young boy from North Carolina. Rosie told him her father lived there and asked the boy if he knew him. "If you see him, run the other way." (Pause for laughter.) "I'm kidding." (Another pause.) "No, I'm not." On a later show, actress Goldie Hawn recounted a story about her early days as a go-go dancer and remembered one particularly lecherous customer. "It was probably my dad," Rosie quipped.

When Jane Pauley interviewed her for *Dateline* in 1996, Rosie offered this disclaimer about her portrayal of her father in her act: "My experiences, my frustrations, my inability to communicate with my father—I exaggerate and then put a comic spin on it."

Jane replied with a perceptive question: "So if you send a missile wrapped up in comedy at him, maybe one day you'll get a reaction?"

"Yeah," Rosie conceded. "I don't know—I've been tryin.'"

One problem may be that, unlike his daughter, Edward O'Donnell never sought the spotlight. He never asked to be famous, even by default. Parents of actors or singers are rarely forced into the glare of public examination, but parents of comics often take their children's punchlines on the chin.

Rosie's distant relatives do not seem to understand her either. "I have many relatives from Ireland and England who come over and come to the stand-up shows that I do, and they don't understand half of what I say," Rosie said in 1996. "They don't find me very amusing and let me know it at every opportunity."

Rosie is more protective when it comes to her siblings and their families. She has said they do not mind being included in her act, but they did have to get used to it. "It's definitely an intrusion having somebody famous using you as fodder for their act, but I've never done a bit I wouldn't do to their faces." Rosie does admit it can be hard for them. "I think fame is the weird part for them."

As much as Rosie did seek the spotlight, she has also been wary of it. She has always been mindful of the challenge to remain grounded in reality, to remain true to her own self-image. In 1993, when her success first started to really sweep over her, Rosie had this to say about it: "Fame is like being hit by a tidal wave, and all you can do is try and keep your head above water." One sign of her fame that does amuse her: Rosie has been immortalized in the lively black lines of the renowned caricaturist Al Hirschfeld, his trademark NINA visible splayed across her left thigh.

"Dealing with fame is hard for friends and relationships, and it's hard for love interests. But I have no regrets," Rosie has said. "There are a lot of good things about fame, too. You have access to everything—movies, theater, Wimbledon tickets." One good reality check for Rosie is having friends even more famous than she is, which is getting more difficult by the day. But for now, Madonna fills that role, and Rosie took a lot of mental notes during the early years of their friendship—rather like an apprenticeship in fame.

During a joint interview, Madonna asked Rosie if now that she's famous, she ever wished she was less famous. Rosie replied, "Fame is something you can never be prepared for, as much as you fantasize or crave it. Until you taste it, you don't know what it's like. And once you have it, you can't give it back—so it's a very strange thing."

Madonna then explained how she saw it. "Once you have it, it becomes its own animal. Sometimes it comes when you call it, and other times it just runs out of the room."

Rosie is still amazed at the way some people from her youth treat her, as though fame induces amnesia. "People from high school come up and say, 'Do you remember me?' and I'm like, 'Do you think I've been in a coma?

That I've forgotten the first twenty years of my life?'" Again, her friend understands. "The other day Madonna said to me that people talk about how fame changes you but never about how it changes people around you. I don't feel any different than before."

Maintaining her famous friendship certainly consumes plenty of her after-hours time. Rosie walks a fine line between their private friendship and her very public discussion of it. On an early edition of *The Rosie O'Donnell Show* Rosie let this quip fly. "Madonna and I are close friends, but we're very different. She sleeps with her trainer. I ignore mine." That, of course, is a reference to Madonna's live-in love and the father of her new daughter, Lourdes.

Before the greatly awaited birth, which seemed to become the media event of October 1996, the press pestered Rosie constantly, hoping for news of her friend. They even resorted to camping outside *her* apartment, figuring she would be one of the first to know. Rosie was unflappable to the end. When asked on October 14, 1996, by a reporter from *Entertainment Tonight* if Madonna's baby was due that week, Rosie dodged the question with, "I believe Madonna is due sometime soon," she said vaguely.

In fact, the Material Tot was born that very afternoon. On October 14, 1996, Rosie was spending part of her evening at her computer answering fan mail and chatting with fans on America Online when she suddenly signed off in mid-conversation, saying that Madonna was calling on the other line. Just hours earlier, Madonna had given birth to her first child, and she was phoning from Los Angeles to tell her pal all about it. (Rosie was rumored to be the godmother.)

The next day, Rosie went on the offensive: "I think it's very tough to have your first baby...never mind to have every camera crew on your front lawn waiting for your water to break. So I'm hopin' everybody will leave her alone until she announces the baby is here and healthy and fine."

Rosie also said she wasn't worried about Madonna. "She's a trouper, she runs eight miles a day—I'm sure she'll be able to get this baby out." The next day on her show, Rosie announced the birth and begged people to stop sending baby gifts to her. She told them to send them to a charity in the baby's name instead.

On *Dateline,* Rosie had plenty to say about Momma Madonna. "I think she's gonna be a great mother—she really wants this child and is invested in being a great parent. . . . She's wonderful with my son. Her persona is very different from her person—and who she is as a person is somebody with a tremendous ability to parent a kid."

Rosie's wish for relief from the media went unheeded, as Rosie told Dave Letterman soon after the birth. "The press has been following me around ever since the baby was born—like I'm the father!" Then she shared with him in a hilarious riff how she sees their future. "It'll be fun. Our kids will grow up together. I can imagine Parker coming home from playing with Lola [Lourdes's nickname]— 'Take off that bustier, I don't care what Aunt Madonna said. No, Mommy can't vogue—her back is out, sit down.'"

Madonna is grateful for Rosie's motherhood experience and has taken her advice about what baby paraphernalia to buy. "She's a nuts-and-bolts kind of girl. I like that," said the new mother. A month after Lourdes was born, Rosie found a way to put a stop to the press hounding her for the scoop on the baby. She placed a surprise call to Madonna during her live show, at 7:45 A.M. Pacific time. The groggy mother wasn't all that pleased to be awakened from a precious fragment of sleep.

But Rosie got her to tell everyone that they were both doing just fine. Then Rosie asked her, "Do you like being a mom?"

Madonna answered, "Yes I do, although I'm suffering major sleep deprivation—which brings me back to my question—why are you calling me?" After she hung up, Rosie defended Madonna's mood, and said she was "just another mommy looking for sleep."

Two months after Lourdes was born, Madonna was promoting her new movie, *Evita*. Everyone expected her to visit Rosie's show first, to serve up all the latest dish on motherhood. When she spent an hour with Oprah instead, the gossip mill fabricated a spat between them. Rosie quickly assured everyone that it wasn't true, that it was just a question of scheduling, and that Madonna would indeed appear on her show in January 1997.

Meanwhile, when Madonna appeared on Oprah's show, talk turned to Rosie and the supposed war between *them* over ratings and bookings. Oprah set the record straight: "I was really disturbed by those reports. I love Rosie. I watched Tom Cruise on Rosie myself the other day."

Madonna told Oprah about spending Thanksgiving with Rosie and Parker at Madonna's apparently yet-to-be-child-proofed home in Florida. "Rosie took my daughter away from me and wouldn't give her back. Parker was everywhere....tie down the furniture!" Later she said of Lourdes, "I named her after a village of miracles." To which Oprah replied, "And every time you look into her eyes you feel healed."

As promised, Madonna did grace *The Rosie O'Donnell Show* with her presence on January 9, 1997. Though she was clearly proud of her friend's success, Madonna made it clear she couldn't ever do Rosie's job, because she couldn't get up that early every day. Of course Topic A was baby Lourdes, and Madonna explained why, like Rosie, she didn't want her child photographed. "*I'm* in show business, not my daughter." Madonna also thanked her friend for all her maternal advice. "You taught me everything I know."

One of the highlights of the show was a duet parody of a song from Madonna's new movie, *Evita*. Rosie didn't seem too worried about singing with such a huge recording star, and said "I sing in the key of me." After so much discussion about their friendship in the press, it was great to finally see the two women together, clearly enjoying their lives as mothers and their current career highs.

The common bonds of motherhood seem capable of dissolving boundaries created by fame. Still, both Madonna and Rosie will be severely challenged to give their children any semblance of a normal childhood. Which is one of the things Rosie hates about fame. "You lose your anonymity, and when you do normal things like go to McDonald's or go to the mall, people are shocked. I think when you're famous, people forget you're a normal person."

Often, because she dresses so casually in public and wears no makeup, Rosie can enjoy some anonymity—if she keeps her mouth shut. "It's not until I talk that people go, 'You *are* her!'" And no matter how famous she gets, there will probably always be some other famous person who still impresses her. "I was on a flight and Burt Bacharach got on the plane. When he walked by I said to the lady next to me, "Oh, my God, that's Burt Bacharach.' And she looked at me and goes, 'Oh, my God, it's *you!*'"

Rosie admits some things are made simpler by fame. "If for example, you wanted to see the Knicks or a sold-out Broadway show, it's a lot easier to get tickets if you're famous. But there are some things that are harder, like trying to go food shopping or going out with my son to the park to play. People will be there with video cameras, and they will sell them to TV shows. That always feels weird when you just want to have a quiet time with your kid and people are around." Even before she acquired the megafame her talk show has brought, Rosie knew the truth of the situation. "Fame is like a tattoo. It doesn't come off. Once you have it on, it never really comes off."

Ultimately, as the demands of the public continue to encroach on a star's ability to lead any kind of normal life, they are forced to retreat behind high walls and security gates. Rosie, though, hasn't given up the fight for normalcy. "I hope fame doesn't change me, but people do treat you differently, so you begin to act like you are not a normal person. Even at the A&P [grocery store] they offer to help you. After a while some celebrities begin to feel they *are* different. Luckily for me, I have a lot of sweatpants, three brothers, and a sister, and they don't let me get away with it."

But fame also does strange things to families. Fame for one family member often trickles down onto other family members in unwelcome ways. Rosie is especially sensitive to this when it affects her sister and brothers and their families. "Whenever my siblings go out to dinner with me, they all say they don't know how I can perform like I do...but I'm beginning to realize the ramifications of fame. When my nieces were three and five, I was in the mall with them and holding one and feeding the other, when a fourteen-year-old kid comes over. My nieces get scared and say, 'Leave my aunt alone. She's my Aunt Rose. She is not on TV.'" Later, when Rosie's image as Betty Rubble seemed to be everywhere, it soon lost its appeal to her older niece. "My niece has a problem at school. The kids are saying, 'Betty Rubble's your aunt—hey, we're gonna call you Pebbles.' That may seem cute to me, but at age six, it's like a big tragedy." On yet another trip to the mall, when Rosie was approached for an autograph, her protective niece said: "My daddy works for the bank, and no one wants his autograph. This is just her job." Rosie agreed with her. "I thought, 'Exactly right, Katie. This is just my job.'"

Rosie is extremely close to her only sister, Maureen, or "Muffy," as she calls her, who is just fifteen months younger. A former banker, Maureen has worked for many years as Rosie's business manager. "I'm an active part of her life and her children's lives," Rosie said in 1994. "I'm more separate from my brothers. I think my career is harder for them. They find my lifestyle a little bit of an oddity. And they are forever being asked if they're related to me, which annoys them. One of my brothers said, 'Every time I open a magazine, there's your picture!' with sort of an undertone of discontent."

Her younger brother Timmy lives in Florida with his family, and is thus a bit more out of the family loop. By now, perhaps the perks that come with their sister's fame have offset the annoyances. Her brother Danny is also a big fan of Elton John and skipped work to attend that show. Then Rosie took her entire family to the private concert the next day.

Staying close—emotionally and physically— to her siblings is part of her plan to ensure that Parker has a large extended family and will always have people he knows around him. Whenever she has to travel without her son, Rosie leaves him with someone in her family. "I want him to know that sense of security, should anything happen, there are people to take care of him. I know when my mom died, that was a big burden—my mother was an only child, and my father's family wasn't particularly close to us before she died. So I think it's very comforting for my sister's children to know that their aunt knows what size clothes they wear and what they like—and I would like for Parker to have that same thing. That his aunts and uncles know how to take care of him, and he feels as nurtured and protected in their house as he is in his own."

As for Parker's second Christmas, in 1996, Rosie said, "I'm looking forward to spending it with my son, who now, I think, is big enough to understand what's going on. Everything is more fun as a mom. There's not one thing that hasn't been made better by the presence of my son."

Rosie was born to be a great mother. When Barbara Walters interviewed Rosie late in 1996, Walters said, "You must think a lot about your mother." Rosie answered, "There are moments that you feel the loss very strongly, and they usually involve your child."

Rosie nurtures her family ties in many ways and has been generous about sharing her wealth with her siblings. She has retained the values she acquired growing up in a modest suburb. Even though she can now afford just about anything she desires, she is still careful with her money. "I no longer buy used cars," she admits. She now drives a gray Volvo wagon, the ultimate safe-driving choice. Before Parker reordered her priorities, Rosie tooled around in a jazzy electric-blue Miata. She still shops at The Gap, and says she "can't pay $400 for shoes. I can't. I grew up without a lot of money, which helped create my character."

Besides, she wants to be sure her extended family is well cared for. "No one in my family lives a luxurious life, but we all live comfortably because of the success that I've had. We didn't have many luxuries when we were children."

Her brothers are doing well on their own. One is a lawyer, another is an advertising executive and the third is an accountant.

It's safe to say that Rosie is set for life financially. After several million-dollar movie paychecks, her lucrative nightclub contracts, her K-Mart residuals, and her hit TV show, she can laugh all the way to the bank. Her one big splurge since hitting the jackpot has been the wonderful home she bought in Nyack, New York, where she can raise her family with some measure of privacy and safety. In 1996 she paid $770,000 for the famous "Pretty Penny" estate formerly owned by Broadway legend Helen Hayes.

Nyack is a lovely upscale town in Rockland County, just twenty miles up the Hudson River from New York City, and an easy commute if Rosie so chooses. The twenty-two-room three-story mansion on the Hudson was built in 1881 and owned by Hayes and her husband, playwright Charles MacArthur, for sixty-two years, until her death in 1993. Ironically, Madonna looked at the house first but decided the brick wall around the property wasn't enough to guarantee *her* privacy. The home received its name when a friend of Hayes's remarked: "This place must have cost a pretty penny."

The hefty purchase price was only the beginning. Rosie embarked on an extensive restoration project to both preserve the Hayes legacy and make it suit her needs. "It's gonna be beautiful when it's done," Rosie says with great anticipation. She plans to retain the rose gardens that Hayes enjoyed, as well as a mural of Helen, her husband, and two children. One of whom happens to be actor James MacArthur, most often remembered for his stint on *Hawaii Five-0*. Rosie jokes that this makes her "related to Dano," his character's name on the show. She also says, "I'm probably gonna be sleepin' in Dano's old bedroom."

Another important feature of the home Rosie plans to preserve is "the huge comedy and tragedy mask that Hayes took off the Helen Hayes Theatre, which is still embedded into the entrance to the cellar." Rosie was a big fan of Helen Hayes and already knows anecdotes about her. "The night she met her future husband, he poured peanuts into her hands and said, 'I wish they were emeralds.' Years later, he poured emeralds into her hands and said, 'I wish they were peanuts.'"

Speaking of the house, Rosie said she is trying to return it to some of its original splendor. "It's a hundred-and-fifteen-year-old house, and it's difficult in that it's much more time and money to fix it than it is to buy it. But I'm lucky— when it's done, it'll be a place you can live in forever."

Given her predilection for Laura Ashley designs, one might expect the decor will be fittingly pastoral. And there will be plenty of red, Rosie's favorite color.

Now that he can walk and run, Parker (who turns two in May of 1997) can make good use of the space. He survived the tentlike contraption that Rosie had to install over his crib to keep him safe in bed at night, and he is into all the typical mischief of a child his age, including trying to eat mommy's Kooshballs! Rosie loves nothing more than spending time with him and vows not to do "any more movies until he starts school."

In addition to their new home, Rosie has had a condominium in Florida for several years, where she can escape for some rest and sun. "I love it there in Florida. I have a little place in Miami." She especially loves the funky South Beach scene and enjoys having a home away from home when the New York winters drag her down. From time to time she also performs there and has been active in local AIDS charity events. Besides, it's a great place to JetSki, one of her passions. During her Christmas vacation there in 1996, Rosie even became a hero, rescuing two teenaged girls from some rocks on her JetSki.

Though Rosie has demonstrated a few surprising culinary skills during the occasional cooking segments on her show—like cracking an egg into a bowl with one hand—it's also clear she barely knows which end of a spatula to pick up. She's honest about it. The motto around Rosie's place is, Eat out, take out, or order in.

To be fair, Rosie did not grow up with too many female role models. "I never learned those traditional girly, mother-taught-you-things," Rosie explains. "That's something I love about my sister's relationship with her children. Like, every Sunday she bakes with them. You know, you try to give your children what you didn't have."

Rosie does make an effort though, and she's very big on convenience items. Growing up, one of her surrogate moms was her best friend's mother, and Rosie keeps her posted on her domestic progress. "Every year I send a Christmas card to Bernice Ellard, Jackie's mom, and I tell her all the Ellardesque things I have in my house: an electric knife, Tupperware with the right kind of lids, and Ziploc bags. I'm so happy to have an Ellard kind of house for my son, because they provided me with safety and the feeling of being nurtured, things I didn't have in my own house."

Now that she's a mother, Rosie spends a lot more time at home. Now that she has to get up so early five days a week and go into an office just like most of America, she enjoys quiet evenings at home. She'll order in some Chinese food—shredded chicken with spinach—and watch TV or videos, play Nintendo, or surf on her computer.

When Sally Field stopped by the show in December 1996, they had a field day discussing their mutual obsession with the Nintendo game, the Legend of Zelda. Back when Rosie was a veejay on VH-1, out of desperation she asked on the air how to get past level six in the game. Sure enough, some kid sent her a forty-page map of how to do it.

Now when she has friends over, Rosie indulges in her latest craze: canasta. She just learned how to play it on her summer vacation in 1996, and already she's enjoying her victories. "I'm like an old lady down in Florida playing canasta on my days off." As she bragged on her show one day, "I totally beat my friends big-time. And not only that—I have my own TV show to gloat on! Ha, ha, ha."

And sometimes she just enjoys slowing to a halt. Unlike her more compulsive late-night counterparts Letterman and Leno, Rosie doesn't feel compelled to watch a tape of each day's show. In fact she says, "I never watch it." That frees up an hour a day right there. And after Parker finally settles down for the night there is sometimes an hour or two of pure calm in Rosie O'Donnell's hectic life. "I have alone time at night," she explains to a concerned friend.

Another way that she spends quality time with her child is on vacations. Besides Florida, she also loves Hawaii, and stayed there a week in the summer of 1996. When she's off duty, Rosie likes to play hard. Like riding her two motorcycles, a Suzuki she keeps in Florida and a Honda she keeps in New York. She also loves to take ski vacations and even has her favorite places. Aspen is not her first choice, because "it is sort of Hollywood removed. Telluride or Crested Butte is the place I like to go, because no one is usually there from Beverly Hills." She is even adventurous enough to try snowboarding. In warm weather and warm water, a JetSki is "imperative."

And she loves many classic sports, such as basketball and baseball. She watched the Yankees at the World Series in 1996, courtesy of Warner Bros. And earlier in the season, she even took batting practice with the world champs and showed them her stuff. And last, but far from least, Rosie has always loved to play tennis, and says yes to every opportunity to play in charity events. "I play, but not well; I play a lot of celebrity tournaments," she told some Olympic tennis stars visiting her show.

She also has an active social life. Though it has changed since adopting Parker, Rosie still finds time to honor the life passages of friends, such as attending Paula Abdul's recent wedding and Madonna's baby shower.

Rosie still makes time to stay current with the world of entertainment. Especially now that she has her talk show, she is constantly invited to movie premieres, Broadway openings, and concerts—all in the line of duty, so she can talk intelligently to her guests who star in all these shows. And sometimes she can give her nieces a thrill while gathering information. Rosie took her sister's young daughters to the premiere of *101 Dalmatians*, but Glenn Close was a bit too scary for all concerned, and they watched most of the movie from the lobby. And because it was a work night, and because she wanted to get home to Parker, Rosie didn't dance all night at the fancy party afterward. But making her nieces happy means a lot more to her, anyway.

Rosie, who turns thirty-five in 1997, has arrived at a time in her life when all of her years of hard work, paying her dues, schlepping from gig to gig are finally paying off. She can afford to catch her breath now. She has created a life for herself and her son that must exceed the fantasies of her youth. Rosie O'Donnell is now the star that *other* little girls dream about. Her picture is on *their* bedroom walls. "The truth is, I'm not shocked at my success—and that's not arrogance—it's sort of that I expected it to be like this. And I'm happy that it is."

Rosie has said a number of times that she doesn't plan to work all her life, that she would like to retire at some point and just raise her brood as a full-time mom. "I hope the show's a hit," she said, soon after it debuted, "because then, in five years, you won't see me anymore. I'll do it for five years and go 'Thanks for the money and good night.' Then I'm gonna work for child advocacy. When you have that much money, what the hell are you going to do with your life? If I was Oprah, you'd never see me again. Ever. I'd be off with Steadman somewhere or alone reading a book. Go to an island."

Some years ago, Rosie said her real fantasy is eventually to disappear. "My dream is to make money in show business then do a Greta Garbo, go to the Rocky Mountains—and people could wonder, *Whatever happened to that girl?*"

Epilogue

Taped to the Desk

"How do you know it's the last joke?"

With any hot new show comes speculation. When asked if she had any aspirations to move her show into the late-night arena, Rosie replied, "To go against Dave and the *Tonight Show* isn't something I'd want to do. I feel like they've cornered the market on people who are up at that time. The people who I relate to are people who are home during the day." There *has* been a rumor floating around that *The Rosie O'Donnell Show* might shift to a live afternoon show. What does seem certain is that whatever time of day she is on, Rosie O'Donnell will continue to enjoy a huge audience of fiercely devoted fans.

She is always being asked what other projects she has in mind. One is for Rosie to do the voice of Turk the monkey, sidekick to the king of the jungle, in a Disney-animated movie of *Tarzan*. Phil Collins has agreed to write the songs, and when he appeared on Rosie's show they discussed the project. Rather, Rosie *instructed* him on her expectations.

ROSIE [*gloating*]: "I'm gonna be singin' a Phil Collins song—"
PHIL [*hedging*]: "We *think*—"
ROSIE [*eyebrows up*]: "We'd *better be*." [*To audience*] "I told Phil he'd better write me a song, or I'm outta there."

While it's clear that she really means it when she says she won't do any starring roles or big projects until Parker is in school, Rosie loves acting too much to pass up the many cameo parts that are sure to come her way. She has already told Susan Lucci that she'd like to reprise her role on *All My Children*. Rosie is also booked for a guest spot on *Suddenly Susan,* the NBC sitcom starring Brooke Shields. And projects *for* children are always enticing to her. She also has an ongoing relationship with Nickelodeon and with *Sesame Street.* Thinking of scoring points with Parker, she joked, "I guess the ultimate cool career move would be a guest spot on *Barney.* Now that's superstardom."

Another project is a children's musical she's writing called *Double Wish,* which she would like to get produced. There's a role for her in it playing a magical nanny who makes children's wishes come true, which she may work on during a hiatus from *The Rosie O'Donnell Show* in 1997.

She has also vowed to honor her nightclub contracts and will appear very occasionally doing stand-up. However, it isn't likely that she'll make the time to create a new act, and those gigs are not mom-friendly, so don't expect to see Rosie too often on the comedy trail.

She has some unfinished business with scripts she has written and films she was set to direct. (Rosie had hoped to direct *Friends for Life,* with Nora Ephron producing.) Back in 1993 Rosie said, "I've written three movies, and I'm working on three more." While these films will have to take a backseat to *The Rosie O'Donnell Show,* she may not be able to retire until she has tried her hand at directing. "I think I'd be good at directing because of being a control freak and meticulous. There's no control as an actor, because all you are is a color of paint. The director gets to be the artist."

In the spring of 1996, Rosie signed a $3 million deal with Warner Books to write a book. It will be part wry memoir and include comic material. "I don't want to do a fluffy observational humor book," Rosie cautions. Though many stand-up comics have climbed the bestseller lists with similar books, Rosie had to be convinced she could write a memoir. "I have so much reverence for writers," she explained, saying she didn't want to just write some fluff. Finally, it was the lure of the money that seduced her. She plans to donate it to good causes. And when she looked at it that way, she had to say yes. "I felt not to do it was to give away that much money. It could do so much good." Her book was originally slated for release in the fall of 1997, but she has put it on hold for a while because she found it "too daunting."

Whoopi Goldberg tried to pass on to Rosie the baton of hosting the Oscars. She was willing, but the Oscar bigwigs reverted to veteran host Billy Crystal for 1997. Diehard Rosie fans have already started a write-in campaign for 1998. In fact, there is already a large internet website devoted to just that campaign, and a national organizing campaign to petition the Academy. Surely, a first! If anyone could breathe some fresh life into that behemoth, it would be Rosie.

The best news of all for Rosie fans is that her show has been renewed into the next century—through the year 2000, unprecedented for a new program. By then she will have met every living celebrity of her dreams. So don't be surprised if after several more years of entertaining us, one fine day Rosie packs Parker and the toys and heads off into a Rocky Mountain sunset to raise her family in peace and away from the spotlight. At least her fans will have a towering stack of VCR tapes to keep them laughing for a long time.

It only seems fair to let Rosie tell the last joke:

"Prince, or 'The Artist Formerly Known As Prince', now just wants to be called 'The Artist'. Myself, also known as The Queen of Nice, now want to be known as 'The.'"

Bibliography

Adato, Allison and Firooz Zahedi, "Love Ya (Kiss Kiss) Don't Change: Rosie O'Donnell Gets Ready for the Big Time on the Small Screen." *Life*, July 1996.

Baldwin, Kristen. "Ooh, What Merv!" *Entertainment Weekly*, 28 June 1996.

_____. "Picking Rosies." *Entertainment Weekly*, 2 August 1996.

Bellafante, Gina. "Rosie O'Donnell Show." *Time*, 24 June 1996.

Berryhill, Ken. *Funny Business*. Englewood Cliffs, N.J.: Prentice-Hall, 1985.

Burr, Ty. "The Flintstones." *Entertainment Weekly*, 28 October 1994.

Cunningham, Kim. "A Little Dabb'll Do Ya." *People Weekly*, 20 June 1994.

_____. "Mix Master." *People Weekly*, 17 July 1996.

De Vries, Hilary, "Everything's Coming Up Rosie." *Newsday*, 8 May 1994.

Denby, David, "Beautiful Girls." *New York*, 26 February 1996.

Entertainment Weekly "Coming Up Rosie." Staff article, 14 June 1996.

Entertainment Weekly. "Sound Bites." Staff article, 2 August 1996.

Entertainment Weekly. "Sound Bites." Staff quotation collection. 28 June 1996.

Everett, Todd. "Rosie O'Donnell Show." *Variety*, 17 June 1996.

Flaim, Denise, "Really Rosie's." *Newsday*, 5 May 1996, Sunday Home Section.

Flint, Joe. "Rosie-O Grabs Gab Spotlight." *Variety*, 27 November 1995.

Fretts, Bruce. "Now and Then." *Entertainment Weekly*, 3 November 1995.

Gallo, Hank. *Comedy Explosion*. New York: Thunder Mouth Press, 1991.

Garey, Julian. "Beautiful Girls." *Glamour*, February 1996.

_____. "Rosie the Riveting." *Entertainment Weekly*, 7 August 1992.

Gavin, Mary, Vincent Aquista, and Nicole Tsugranes, "Kidsday Talking With Rosie O'Donnell." *Newsday*, 24 July 1994.

Gilco, Jeff. "Playing in a League of Her Own." *Newsweek*, 16 August 1993.

Gleiberman, Owen. "A League of Their Own." *Entertainment Weekly*, July 1992.

_____. "Harriet the Spy." *Entertainment Weekly*, 19 July 1996.

_____. The Flintstones." *Entertainment Weekly*, 27 May 1994.

Glen, Kenny. "Exit to Eden." *Entertainment Weekly*, 24 March 1995.

Gliatto, Tom. "Comedian-Actress Rosie O'Donnell." *People Weekly*, 8 January 1996.

_____. "The Flintstones." *People Weekly*, 30 May 1994.

Griffin, Nancy. "That's the Way Love Goes." *Premiere*, July 1993.

Heldenfels, R. D. "Rosie O'Donnell May Succeed Where Gabrielle, Carnie, and Danny Failed." *Knight-Ridder News Service*, 5 June 1996.

Hiltbrand, David. "Stand By Your Man." *People Weekly*, 6 April 1992.

Hofler, Robert. "In My Own Words: Red Hot Rosie." *Buzz*, 27 August 1995.

Holmes, Anna. "Mother Love." *Entertainment Weekly*, 19 January 1996.

Jacobs, Alexandra. "Big Deal." *Entertainment Weekly*, 3 May 1996.

Johnson, Brian D. "A League of Their Own." *Maclean's*, 13 July 1992.

_____. "Beautiful Girls." *Maclean's*, 12 February 1996.

_____. "The Flintstones." *Maclean's*, 30 May 1994.

Kaufman, Joanne. "Sleepless in Seattle." *People Weekly*, 28 June 1993.

Klady, Leonard. "Exit to Eden." *Variety*, 17 October 1994.

Knight-Ridder News Service. "Tune In, Vegetate." Staff article, 21 November 1995.

Landman, Beth. "Really Rosie." *Entertainment Weekly*, 10 December 1993.

Lee, Luaine. "Conversations With Rosie O'Donnell and Bruce Willis." *Knight-Ridder News Service*, 10 October 1994.

Levy, Emanual. "Another Stakeout." *Variety*, 2 August 1993.

————. "Harriet the Spy." *Variety*, 15 July 1996.

Leydon, Joe. "Now and Then." *Variety*, 23 October 1994.

Marin, Rick. "Queen of Nice—Coming Up Rosies." *Newsweek*, 15 July 1996.

Martin, James. "The Rosie O'Donnell Show." *America*, 17 August 1996.

McCarthy, Todd. "Beautiful Girls." *Variety*, 5 February 1996.

Mediaweek. "The Backlot." Staff article, 22 July 1996.

Meyer, Marianne. "The Flintstones." *Video*, December 1994.

Mr. Showbiz (internet). "Star Bios—Rosie O'Donnell," 5 September 1996.

Murphy, Mary. "Rosie, Really." *TV Guide*, 15 June 1996.

Novak, Ralph. "A League of Their Own." *People Weekly*, 6 July 1992.

————. "Beautiful Girls." *People Weekly*, 25 February 1996.

————. "Exit to Eden." *People Weekly*, 31 October 1994.

O'Haire, Patricia. "Rosie O'Donnell Is Wisecracking Her Way Through Movies." *Knight-Ridder News Service*, 27 May 1994.

Pacheco, Patrick. "Wondrous Rosie O'Donnell." *Cosmopolitan*, June 1994 (72).

Papzis, Beau, Christie Kummers, and Jennifer Randazzo. "Talking With Rosie O'Donnell." *Newsday*, 14 July 1996.

Queenan, Joe. "Rosie O'Donnell Show." *People Weekly*, 15 July 1996.

Rosen, Marjorie, "On Base With a Hit." *People Weekly*, 20 July 1992.

Rozen, Leah. "Harriet the Spy." *People Weekly*, 15 July 1996.

————. "Another Stakeout." *People Weekly*, 2 August 1993.

Schickel, Richard. "Sleepless in Seattle." *Time*, 5 July 1993.

————. "The Flintstones." *Time*, 30 May 1994.

Schwarzbaum, Lisa. "Beautiful Girls." *Entertainment Weekly*, 16 February 1996.

————. "Exit to Eden." *Entertainment Weekly*, 28 October 1994.

Sharkey, Betsy. "Running With Rosie." *Mediaweek*, 10 June 1996.

Shaw, Jessica, "Everything's Coming Up Rosie." *Entertainment Weekly*, 10 June 1994.

Sheward, David. "Grease." *Backstage*, 27 May 1994.

Shister, Gail. "Motherhood, New Talk Show Take Rosie O'Donnell's Life on a Different Course." *Knight-Ridder News Service*, 31 May 1996.

Simolo, Steve. "Another Stakeout." *Entertainment Weekly*, 15 April 1994.

Thompson, Bob. "Part-Time Star, Full-Time Mom." *Toronto Sun*, 8 July 1996.

Tracy, Kathy and Jeff Rovin. *Ellen DeGeneres—Up Close*. New York: Pocket Books, 1994.

Travers, Peter. "Now and Then." *Rolling Stone*, 2 November 1995.

Tucker, Ken, "A League of Their Own." *Entertainment Weekly*, 26 July 1996.

————. "Rosie's Baby." *Entertainment Weekly*, 8 July 1996.

————. "Stand By Your Man." *Entertainment Weekly*, 10 April 1992.

————. "The Rosie O'Donnell Show." *Entertainment Weekly*, 28 June 1996.

Werts, Diane. "Glued to the Tube." *Newsday*, 2 July 1996.

————. "Retro Rosie? The Queen of Stand-Up Sits Down." *Newsday*, 9 June 1996.

Wickens, Barbara, "Harriet the Spy." *Maclean's*, 22 July 1996.

Williamson, Bruce. "Exit to Eden." *Playboy*, December 1994.

Wulf, Steve. "A League of Their Own." *Sports Illustrated*, 6 July 1992.

Sources

Comedy Club Owners and Managers

Lucien A. Hold, the Comic Strip, New York City; Billy Downs, the Comedy Connection, Boston; Paul Barkley; Karl Hosch, Forever Productions, Port Washington, New York; Frank Manzano; Jan Smith; Marty Nadler; Richard Eckhaus; Chick Perrin; Scott Day, the Comedy Store; Joey Balaska, Joey's Comedy Club, Livonia, Michigan; Norma Gubbheart, Tropicana Comedy Shop, Las Vegas, Nevada;

Comedy Club Staff Who Wish to Remain Unnamed

The Comedy Strip, New York City; Dangerfields, New York City; Stand Up New York, New York City; Comedy Connection, Langley Park, Maryland; Headliners, Wheaton, Maryland; Comedy Connection, Boston, Massachusetts; Doherty's Comedy Vault, Boston, Massachusetts; Giggle's Comedy Club, Saugus, Massachusetts; Comedy Connection, Chicopee, Massachusetts; One-Eyed Jake's, Iowa City, Iowa; Pepperoni's Comedy Club, South Bend, Indiana; Funny Face, Des Moines, Iowa; Stanford's Comedy House, Shawnee Mission, Kansas; Mainstreet Comedy Showcase, Ann Arbor, Michigan; Comedy Castle, Royal Oak, Michigan; Funny Bone Comedy Club, Springfield, Missouri; Tropicana Comedy Stop, Las Vegas, Nevada; Hilarities Comedy Club, Cleveland, Ohio;

People Interviewed in Commack, New York

Dolores Adams, Anthony Catarelli, Fred Brown, Lori La Rocco, P. Affe, Jan Fennick, Janice Schienbaum, Scott Ahrens, J. MacDonald, R. Alcana, Anthony Catanzaro, Frank Imburgio, Kelly Levine, Ralph Ferrara, Michael Shampanier, Robert Alcaide, John Carjon, Robert Imbnale, George Alexandrovich, David Witkover, Maryann Puglissi, Rick Vogel, G. N. Levine, Michael Alouisa, Jeff Biscardi, Harriet E. Ander, Ann Andrezzi, Denis Kosar, Gaetano Antenucci, Phil Antoci, Diane Lewis, P. Anwander, Maria Argiros, Jeanne Fitzgerd, Greg Linsday, Janine Russo, Richard Abbett, Stan Aberle, S. Alessi

Index